1984

REVISITED

Totalitarianism in Our Century

EDITED BY Irving Howe

PERENNIAL LIBRARY
Harper & Row, Publishers
New York, Cambridge, Philadelphia, San Francisco
London, Mexico City, São Paulo, Sydney

Excerpts from *Nineteen Eighty-Four* by George Orwell are reprinted by permission of Harcourt Brace Jovanovich, Inc.; copyright 1949 by Harcourt Brace Jovanovich, Inc., renewed 1977 by Sonia Brownell Orwell.

Grateful acknowledgment is made to the Estate of the late Sonia Brownell Orwell and Martin Secker & Warburg Ltd for permission to reprint excerpts from *Nineteen Eighty-Four* by George Orwell.

The following essays have appeared elsewhere as follows:
"1984: Enigmas of Power," by Irving Howe, has appeared in *The New Republic*. "Totalitarianism and the Virtue of the Lie," by Leszek Kolakowski, has appeared in *Commentary*. "On 'Failed Totalitarianism,'" by Michael Walzer, has appeared in *Dissent*. "Does Big Brother Really Exist?" by Robert C. Tucker, has appeared in *Psychoanalytic Inquiry*.

Designer: Sidney Feinberg

Library of Congress Cataloging in Publication Data
Main entry under title:

1984 revisited.

Includes index.
1. Orwell, George, 1903–1950. Nineteen eighty-four—Addresses, essays, lectures. 2. Totalitarianism—Addresses, essays, lectures. I. Howe, Irving.
PR6029.R8N5 1983   823'.912   82-48668
ISBN 0-06-015158-7
ISBN 0-06-080660-5 (pbk.)

83 84 85 86 87 10 9 8 7 6 5 4 3 2 1
83 84 85 86 87 10 9 8 7 6 5 4 3 2

dedicated to the memory of
Henry Pachter

Contents

Preface

Not so far now from the end of the twentieth century, we can look back upon our time and say unhesitatingly that its crucial sequence of events has been the rise of totalitarianism as brought to ghastly climax in the Holocaust and the Gulag. Almost every serious political thinker who has experienced, or lived through the time of, these events is driven to struggle with their meanings. What do they tell us about the nature of man? How do they reflect the breakdown of traditional values? Do they point to the collapse of liberal hopes? For a critical mind, it has been the rise of communism that presents the greatest analytical challenge, since in that movement the idealistic aspirations of millions of people have ended in a nightmare of repression and terror.

In the vast literature concerning totalitarianism, George Orwell's fictional *1984* occupies a central place. It is not a discursive or theoretical work, yet almost every analyst of totalitarianism writes with admiration, if at times also disagreement, about the theoretical grasp behind the book and the array of insights within it. *1984* has entered the common language increasingly, it seems, independent of Orwell's great work—a popular tribute which, as Mark Crispin Miller argues in the second essay here, has its complex and ambiguous aspects.

A number of contributors, as the year 1984 began to seem closer to us, decided it would be useful to look once again at Orwell's work and the political-intellectual problems surrounding it. A small foundation, the Foundation for the Study of

Independent Social Ideas—devoted to doing exactly what its name suggests—sponsored this collection, and we were fortunate to find in Harper & Row a publisher ready to make it available, as well as in Hugh van Dusen an editor at once sympathetic and critical.

The contributors span the gamut of serious opinion in the United States, for nothing could have been more in violation of Orwell's outlook than to bring out a collection hewing to a party line or monolithic ideology. And so we have, in one volume, writers as various as Milovan Djilas and Richard Lowenthal, Michael Walzer and Leszek Kolakowski, Robert Tucker and Robert Nisbet.

The book opens with several considerations of *1984* as literary and social text. A series of analytic essays follows, discussing both problems Orwell must have had in mind when he wrote his work and problems raised by the course of totalitarianism since his death. Last comes what I venture to say is an exceptionally important historical study by Richard Lowenthal, in which some of the propositions of earlier pieces are put to the historical test.

I. H.

PART I

THE BOOK

AND THE WRITER

1   1984: Enigmas of Power

I

It is a common experience to fear that the admirations of youth will wear thin, and precisely because *1984* had so enormous an impact when it originally came out more than thirty years ago, I hesitated for a long time before returning to it. I can still remember the turbulent feelings—the bottomless dismay, the sense of being undone—with which many people first read Orwell's book. My fear now was that it would seem a passing sensation of its moment or even, as some leftist critics have charged, a mere reflex of the cold war. But these fears were groundless. Having reread *1984*, I am convinced, more than ever, that it is a classic of our age.

Whether it is also a classic for the ages is another question. What people of the future will think about Orwell's book we cannot know, nor can we say what it might mean to those who will remember so little about the time of totalitarianism they will need an editor's gloss if they chance upon a copy. But for us, children of this century, the relation to *1984* must be intimate, troubled, nerve-wracking. In 1938 or 1939 the idea of a world divided among a few totalitarian superpowers, which Orwell made into the premise of his book, had not seemed at all far-fetched. I remember hushed conversations about the possible shape of a world dominated by Hitler and Stalin, with perhaps a shrinking enclave of democracy in North America. Such nightmare-visions seemed entirely real during the years just before the war, and with sufficient reason. When Orwell published his book a decade later, in 1949, one felt that, despite his obvious wish to unnerve us with an extreme version of the total state, he was presenting something all too familiar, even commonplace.

Also familiar, though in a somewhat different sense, was the body of detail about daily life in Oceania that Orwell built up. Many of the descriptive passages in *1984* were simply taken over, with a degree of stretching here and there, from Orwell's earlier books or from his life-long caustic observations of twentieth-century England. In a review for the *Times Literary Supplement,* Julian Symons keenly remarked that

> In some ways life [in the Oceania of *1984*] does not differ very much from the life we live now. The pannikin of pinkish-grey stew, the hunk of bread and cube of cheese, the mug of milkless Victory coffee with its saccharine tablet—that is the kind of meal we may very well remember; and the pleasures of recognition are roused, too, by the description of Victory gin (reserved for the privileged —the "proles" drink beer), which has "a sickly oily smell, as of Chinese rice-spirit," and gives to those who drink it "the sensation of being hit on the back of the head with a rubber club." We can generally view projections of the future with detachment because they seem to refer to people altogether unlike ourselves. By creating a world in which the "proles" still have their sentimental songs and their beer, and the privileged consume their Victory gin, Orwell involves us most skilfully and uncomfortably in his story. . . .

Symons might have added that in Orwell's earlier writing he had already focused almost obsessively on the gritty discomforts of urban life, the bad smells, the sour tastes, the grimy streets, the filthy rooms, the sweat-stained bodies. As it turned out, the unfuture of Oceania had some pretty keen resemblances to the immediate past of England.

Resemblances, also, to the years of Stalinist terror in Russia. The grilling of Winston Smith by the Oceania authorities, the alternation between physical beatings and sympathetic conversations, the final terrifying appearance of O'Brien, master of power—all these recall or parallel Arthur Koestler's account in *Darkness at Noon* of how the NKVD interrogated its victims. Koestler's description, in turn, anticipated closely what we have since learned about the methods of the Soviet secret police. It was to Orwell's credit that he understood how the imagination flourishes when it is grounded in common reality.

He knew, as well, that to make credible the part of his book which would spiral into the extraordinary, he had first to provide it with a strong foundation of the ordinary. Or to put it another way, he knew that his main problem was to make plausible—which, one might remember, is not the same as the probable—his vision of how certain destructive tendencies of modern society could drive insanely forward, unbraked by sentiments of humaneness or prudence.

Yet while rereading *1984*, I have come to recognize still another way in which it all seems decidedly familiar—but *this* familiarity causes shock.

The very idea of a totally controlled society in which a self-perpetuating elite rules through terror and ideology no longer strikes us as either a dim horror or a projection of the paranoid mind. In the few decades since Orwell wrote, we have gone a long way toward domesticating the idea of the total state, indeed, to the point where it now seems just one among a number of options concerning the way men live. The thought that totalitarianism is a constant, even commonplace possibility in the history of our time—this may prove to be as terrifying as the prospect that we might sooner or later be living under an Orwellian regime. No sensible person could have taken *1984* as an actual prediction; even those who read the book with malice or loathing knew it had to be taken as a warning, no doubt a fearful warning. That in its fundamental conception it should now seem so familiar, so ordinary, so plausible, is—when you come to think of it—a deeply unnerving fact about the time in which we live. But a fact it is.

II

To ask what kind of book *1984* is may seem a strange, even pedantic question. After all, you might say, millions of people have read the book and appreciated it well enough without troubling their heads about fine points of genre. Yet the question is neither strange nor pedantic, since in my experience there remains among Orwell's readers a good portion of uncertainty and confusion about what he was trying to do. People will often say, "Look, we're getting close to the year 1984 and we aren't living in the kind of society Orwell summoned; doesn't that mean he was exaggerating or perhaps that he was morbid?" To this kind of complaint there is a simple enough answer: It's in the very nature of anti-utopian fiction to project a degree of exaggeration, since without exaggeration the work would be no more than still another realistic portrait of totalitarian society.

Other complaints, being more sophisticated, take on a "literary" edge. Some of them, still often heard, are that the book contains no "real characters," or that there isn't enough of a credible social setting, or that the psychological vision of the story is somewhat rudimentary. Such complaints have really to do with genres or misunderstandings of genres; they reflect a failure to grasp the kind of fiction Orwell was writing and what could legitimately be expected from it. When a critic like Raymond Williams says that *1984* lacks "a substantial society and correspondingly substantial persons," he is (almost willfully, one suspects) missing the point. For the very premise of anti-utopian fiction is that it sketch an "inconceivable" world in such a way as to force us, provisionally, to credit its conceivability; that it project a world in which categories like "substantial society . . . substantial persons" have largely been suppressed or rendered obsolete. In actuality a society like that of Oceania may be impossible to realize, but that is not at issue here. A writer may, in the kind of fiction Orwell was composing, draw the shadows of "the impossible" as if they were real possibilities —if only in order to persuade us that finally they are not possible. As it happens, we have come close enough during the last half century to a society like Oceania for the prospect of its realization to be within reach of the imagination. And that is all a writer of fiction needs.

There are kinds of fictions that should not really be called novels at all: think of Voltaire's *Candide,* Swift's *Gulliver's Travels,* Peacock's *Crotchet Castle.* In *Anatomy of Criticism,* Northrop Frye, hoping (probably in vain) to check the modern tendency to lump all fictions as novels, describes a kind of fiction he calls Menippean satire, "allegedly invented by a Greek cynic named Menippus." This fiction "deals less with people as such than with mental attitudes . . . and differs from the novel in its characterization, which is stylized rather than naturalistic. . . ."

A quarter of a century ago, when first writing about *1984,* I thought this a satisfactory description of the kind of book Orwell had composed; but now I would like to modify that opinion. Almost everyone has recognized how brilliant Orwell was in finding symbolic vehicles and dramatic instances through which to render the "mental attitudes" about which Frye speaks. Think only of Newspeak and Big Brother, Hate Week and memory hole, all of which have entered our speech and consciousness as vivid figures. (A few years ago I visited a Canadian university where the wicked students had baptized a new campus building—vast, windowless, cement-ugly—as the Ministry of Love; and so, I am certain, it will be called for decades to come.) There remains, then, good reason to see *1984* as an instance of "Menippean satire"—but only in part.

For in going back to the book, I have learned to appreciate parts that now strike me as novelistic in the usual sense. Especially those parts in which Winston Smith and Julia try to find for themselves a patch, a corner where they can be alone and make love. Here bits of individuality begin to make themselves felt: Julia's boldness, for instance, in arranging their escapade to the country, where they can be free of the hated telescreen, or her charming indifference to all ideologies, as when she falls asleep during Winston's excited reading from the forbidden book, Emmanuel Goldstein's *Theory and Practice of Oligarchical Collectivism.*

I now think that *1984* ought to be read as a mixture of genres,

mostly Menippean satire and conventional novel, but also bits
of tract and a few touches of transposed romance. Such a description may be helpful, although not because anyone is foolish
enough to want exact categories; it may train us, at the least,
to avoid false expectations when we read.

III

An anti-utopian fiction must have a touch or two of excess.
There has to be a story which takes the familiar conventions of
the once-fashionable utopian novel and stands them on their
heads. Elsewhere I've described that touch of excess as "the
dramatic strategy and narrative psychology of 'one more step'
. . . one step beyond our known reality—not so much a picture
of modern totalitarianism as an extension, by just one and no
more than one step, of the essential pattern of the total state."
But this excess can of course consist of more than one step; it
might be two or three, yet not many more steps than two or
three, since then the link of credence between writer and reader
might be broken by a piling on of improbabilities.

What has especially struck me in rereading *1984* is that, yes,
it's true that in an anti-utopian fiction the writer can afford at
most a few steps beyond our known reality, but he is likely to
achieve his strongest effects precisely at the moment when the
balance teeters between minimal credence and plummeting dis-
belief. For at such a moment we ask ourselves: Can things *really*
go this far? And it is then that our deepest anxieties are aroused.
Is it conceivable that the total state could be so "total," could
break and transform human beings so far beyond what "human
nature" may be expected to endure? We think and hope not, but
we cannot be certain. We know that the total state has already
done things earlier generations would have supposed to be impossible.

One such moment occurs in *1984* when Orwell turns to
sexuality in Oceania. Members of the Outer Party—we remain
in the dark about the Inner Party—are shown to be trained

systematically to minimize and deny the sexual instinct, certainly to separate the act of intercourse from sensual pleasure or imaginative play. There can be no "free space" in the lives of the Outer Party faithful, nothing that remains beyond the command of the state. Sexual energy is to be transformed into political violence and personal hysteria. The proles are permitted to drift into promiscuity, their very sloth and sleaziness a seeming guarantee against rebellion, but members of the Outer Party caught in promiscuous relations with one another face the most stringent penalties.

About all this Orwell is very careful:

> The aim of the Party was not merely to prevent men and women from forming loyalties which it might not be able to control. Its real, undeclared purpose was to remove all pleasure from the sexual act. Not love so much as eroticism was the enemy, inside marriage as well as outside. . . . Sexual intercourse was to be looked upon as a slightly disgusting minor operation. . . . The Party was trying to kill the sex instinct or, if it could not be killed, then to distort and dirty it. . . .

It remains a fascinating question whether Orwell had captured here an essential part of the totalitarian outlook or had gone too far beyond "one more step." We know that in the years of Stalinism the Soviet Union favored, at least publicly, a prudish, sometimes a repressive anti-sexuality. But there is no evidence that during those years—and this is the period upon which Orwell drew for his book—Communist Party members were forced to suffer greater sexual repressiveness than the rest of the population. If the evidence is skimpy, Orwell was nonetheless touching on something very important here; he was taking an imaginative leap from totalitarian "first principles" concerning, not so much sex, certainly not sex in its own right but the threat of "free space," that margin of personal autonomy which even in the worst moments of Stalinism and Hitlerism some people still wanted to protect. And it was this margin that Orwell took to be the single great "flaw" of all previous

efforts to realize the totalitarian vision. Whether a complete or
"total" totalitarianism is possible, or possible for any length of
time, is not, I want to repeat, the question. All that matters, for
our purposes, is that it be plausible enough to allow a fictional
representation.

Winston Smith's journey from rebellion to breakdown is a
doomed effort to recover the idea, perhaps even more than the
experience, of a personal self; to regain the possibility of individual psychology and the memory of free introspection. And this
occurs in *1984*—I think it is one of Orwell's greatest strokes—
not so much through ratiocination as through an encounter
between two bodies. When Winston Smith and Julia make their
first escapade out of London, carefully finding a patch in the
woods where they can make love, they are not "in love," at least
not yet. What happens between them is only—only!—the meeting of two eager bodies, animal-like if you must, but wonder-
fully urgent, alive, and good. They are free from the grip of the
Party: this moment is theirs.

In this and a few other sections Orwell writes with a kind of
grieving, muted lyricism, a hoarse lyricism which is about as
much as, under the circumstances, he can allow himself. I have
found myself moved, far more than when I first read the book,
by these brief and unabashed celebrations of the body. A little
freer in our language than in 1949, we would now say that Julia
is a woman who likes to fuck, and it seems important to put it
exactly that way, since in the wretched precincts of Oceania just
about the best that anyone can do is fucking.

        IV

Bolder still than Orwell's strategy of "one more step" in treating sexuality is his treatment of power. He tends to see the lust
for power as a root experience, something that need not or
cannot be explained in terms other than itself, and here too, I
think, the passage of time has largely confirmed his intuitions.
Let me draw upon your patience for a minute as I recall certain

criticisms made by admiring critics of Orwell soon after *1984*
came out. Philip Rahv, in a fine essay-review of the book, said
that in one respect Orwell may have surpassed even Dostoevsky
in grasping "the dialectic of power." *The Brothers Karamazov*
shows the Grand Inquisitor as a tyrant ruling from benevolent
intent: he believes man to be a weak creature, who needs the
lash for his own good and can be happy only when the burden
of freedom is lifted from his back. During the interrogation
conducted by O'Brien, Winston Smith, hoping to please his
tormentor, repeats the Grand Inquisitor's rationale for the
holding of power:

> . . . that the Party did not seek power for its own ends, but only
> for the good of the majority. That it sought power because men in
> the mass were frail, cowardly creatures who could not endure
> liberty or face the truth. . . . That the choice for mankind lay
> between freedom and happiness, and that, for the great bulk of
> mankind, happiness was better. That the Party was the eternal
> guardian of the weak, a dedicated sect doing evil that good might
> come, sacrificing its own happiness to that of others.

All of this strikes O'Brien as mere cant; he scorns it as
"stupid." Turning up the dial of the machine that regulates
Winston Smith's pain, he chastises him in these memorable
words:

> The Party seeks power entirely for its own sake. We are not inter-
> ested in the good of others; we are interested solely in power.
> . . . One does not establish a dictatorship in order to safeguard a
> revolution; one makes the revolution in order to establish the dicta-
> torship. The object of persecution is persecution. The object of
> torture is torture. The object of power is power. . . .
> . . . Power is in inflicting pain and humiliation. Power is in
> tearing human minds to pieces and putting them together again in
> new shapes of your own choosing.

This exchange forms a key passage in *1984*, perhaps in the
entirety of modern political discourse. Commenting on it in

Partisan Review Philip Rahv offered a criticism in 1949 that seemed to me at the time both shrewd and valid:

> There is one aspect of the psychology of power in which Dosto-evsky's insight strikes me as being more viable than Orwell's strict realism. It seems to me that Orwell fails to distinguish, in the behavior of O'Brien, between psychological and objective truth. Undoubtedly it is O'Brien, rather than Dostoevsky's Grand Inquis-itor, who reveals the real nature of total power; yet that does not settle the question of O'Brien's personal psychology, that is, of his ability to live with this naked truth as his sole support; nor is it conceivable that the party elite to which he belongs could live with this truth for very long. Evil, far more than good, is in need of the pseudo-religious justifications so readily provided by the ideologies of world-salvation and compulsory happiness. . . . Power is its own end, to be sure, but even the Grand Inquisitors are compelled . . . to believe in the fiction that their power is a means to some other end, gratifyingly noble and supernal.

Several decades have passed since Rahv wrote these trench-ant lines and most of what has since happened gives one reason to doubt that he was entirely correct. Orwell was writing at a time when Stalin was alive and Hitler only recently dead: totalitarianism seemed an overpowering force, perhaps on the verge of taking Europe. The ideological fanaticism which a few years later would strike Hannah Arendt as one of the two underpinnings of the total state was still strong. For while it is true that Hitler and Stalin ruled through terror, it is also true that there were millions of people who took the Nazi and Communist ideologies, myths, and slogans with the utmost seriousness, yielding to them a devotion far more intense than traditional religions have been able to elicit in this century. Power may indeed be the beginning and the end of Party rule in Oceania, but at least in 1949 and for some years afterward it seemed hard to believe that an O'Brien would or could speak as openly as Orwell had him do, even to a victim he was soon to break.

Can we now be so certain that Orwell was wrong in giving O'Brien that speech about power? I think not. For we have lived to witness a remarkable development of the Communist state: its ideology has decayed, far fewer people give credence to its claims than in the past, yet its power remains virtually unchecked. True, there is a less open use of terror, but the power of the state—a sort of terror-in-reserve—remains a total power. As lethargy and sloth overtake the Communist societies, it begins to seem that ideology will become among them a kind of fossilized body of tiresome and half-forgotten slogans. Not many educated Russians, including those highly placed within the party, can be supposed still to "believe" they are building the Communist society first expounded by Marx and Lenin. But the party remains.

What then do the apparatchiks believe in? They believe in their apparatus. They believe in the party. They believe in the power these enable. That a high Soviet bureaucrat might now talk to an imprisoned dissident in the bluntly cynical style that O'Brien employs in talking to Winston Smith does not therefore seem inconceivable. It does not even seem far-fetched. The bureaucrat, especially if he is intelligent and has some pretensions to being sophisticated, might like to show his victim that he knows perfectly well that the totalitarian ethos has begun to decay, indeed, has entered a phase of transparency in which its cloak of the ideal has been stripped away. Now, this bureaucrat might not be as lucid as O'Brien, but he could easily speak to his victim as if to say, "Look here, my good fellow, I don't want to make a fool of myself with all that big talk about the 'classless society,' I simply want you to recognize, for your own good, who has the power and who intends to keep it."

I take it as a sign of Orwell's intuitive gifts that he should have foreseen this historical moment when belief in the total state is crumbling while its power survives. Whether such a condition signifies an explosive crisis or a period of low-keyed stability, we do not yet know. But there is now at least some ground for lending credence to Orwell's admittedly extreme

notion that the rulers of the total state no longer need trouble
to delude themselves, perhaps because they no longer can,
about their motives and claims. The grim possibility is that they
now have a realistic view of themselves as creatures holding
power simply for the sake of power, and that they find this quite
sufficient.

V

The most problematic, but also interesting, aspect of *1984* is
Orwell's treatment of the proles.

> They were governed by private loyalties which they did not ques-
> tion. What mattered were individual relationships, and a com-
> pletely helpless gesture, an embrace, a tear, a word spoken to a
> dying man, could have value in itself. The proles, it suddenly
> occurred to [Winston Smith] . . . were not loyal to a party or a
> country or an idea, they were loyal to one another.

With its echo of E. M. Forster, this is very touching, and it
becomes more than touching when Winston looks for some
agency or lever of rebellion that might threaten the power of the
Party. *"If there is hope,"* he writes in his notebook, *"it lies in
the proles . . ."* If . . . and then the paradox that even in the
half-forgotten era of capitalism used to bedevil Socialists:
*"Until they [the proles] become conscious they will never rebel,
and until after they have rebelled they cannot become conscious."* Orwell knew of course that traditionally Marxists had
offered a "dialectical" resolution of this dilemma: the imperatives of action stir people into consciousness, and the stimulants
of consciousness enable further action. A powerful formula,
and millions of people have repeated it; but like other left-wing
intellectuals of his day, he had come to feel dubious about its
accuracy or usefulness. In writing *1984,* however, Orwell was
wise enough to leave slightly open the question of whether the
proles could exert a decisive power in modern society.

Here, if anywhere, Orwell made his one major error. The

proles are allowed more privacy than Party members, the
telescreen does not bawl instructions at them, and the secret
police seldom troubles them, except occasionally to wipe out a
talented or independent prole. What this must mean is that
the Inner Party judges the proles to be completely crushed
and tamed, no threat to its power either now or in the future,
quite demoralized as individuals and helpless as a social
class.

But the evidence of history—which ought, after all, to be
crucial for a writer of an anti-utopian fiction—comes down
strongly against Orwell's vision of the future. Europe this past
half century has been convulsed by repeated, if unsuccessful,
rebellions in which the workers (or proles) have played a major
role, from East Berlin in 1956 to France in 1968, from the
Hungarian Revolution to the rise of Solidarity in Poland.

But let us agree, for the sake of the argument, to move past
the historical actuality or probability since, after all, it's always
possible to read the evidence in conflicting ways. Suppose, instead, we focus only on the criterion of imaginative plausibility
in forming a judgment about Orwell's treatment of the proles.
Even then, I think, our sense of credence must be strained
excessively. Let me take the liberty of quoting a few sentences
from *Decline of the New* that I wrote soon after *1984* came out,
because I think they are still pertinent:

> Orwell's treatment of the proles can be questioned on . . . funda-
> mental grounds. The totalitarian state can afford no luxury, allow
> no exception; it cannot tolerate the existence of any group beyond
> the perimeter of its control; it can never become so secure as to
> lapse into indifference. Scouring every corner of society for rebels
> it knows do not exist [yet they might, they could!], the totalitarian
> state cannot come to rest for any prolonged period of time. To do
> so would be to risk disintegration. It must always tend toward a
> condition of self-agitation, shaking and reshaking its members.
> . . . And since, as Winston Smith concludes, the proles remain one
> of the few possible sources of revolt, it can hardly seem plausible

that Oceania would permit them even the relative freedom Orwell describes.

If the "ruling circles" of Poland, Czechoslovakia, and Hungary could talk in private to O'Brien, they would tell him that, lucid as he may be on the subject of power, he may well be making a mistake in his view of the proles.

VI

An aura of gloom hangs over *1984:* the book ends with a broken Winston Smith drinking Victory Gin and blubbering his drunken love for Big Brother. He has made his "adjustment."

"If there is any hope, it lies in the proles," Winston Smith had said. But is there any hope? That is not a question Orwell is obliged to answer; he need only ask it, with sufficient honesty and the despair that shows him to be a man of his century. The gloom that hovers over the book has been "explained" by some critics as a symptom of the grave illness Orwell was suffering at the end of his life, at the very time he wrote *1984.* Perhaps there is a small measure of truth in this, but basically it seems to me a rather stupid idea. A merely sick or depressed man could not have written with the surging inventiveness that shapes *1984*—and, in any case, where have these critics kept themselves this past half century? Haven't they heard the bad news? No, the gloom of *1984* is real and justified; but it is an energizing and passionate gloom.

If the extremism of Orwell's vision derives from a close responsiveness to the idea of a world in which human life is shorn of dynamic possibilities, it also reflects his growing distaste for politics itself, at least a politics that leaves no margin for anything but itself. And this may also account for the streak of conservatism in Orwell's outlook—a conservatism less of politics than of sensibility: that is, an appreciation for the way people actually live, the strengths of received ties and feelings. One of the most affecting parts of *1984* is Winston Smith's recurrent effort to recall fragments of the past, the days before the Party took power. He tries to remember how his mother caressed him as a child, simply because he was her child; he tries to summon the appearance of a destroyed church; he tries to put together an old rhyme, trivial in itself but rich with associations:

> Oranges and lemons, say the bells of St. Clement's,
> You owe me three farthings, say the bells of St. Martin's,
> When will you pay me? say the bells of Old Bailey,
> When I grow rich, say the bells of Shoreditch.

This conservatism of feeling, already present in Orwell's earlier books, is taken by some readers to conflict with his democratic socialist convictions. That would be true only if socialism were seen—as indeed both authoritarian left and reactionary right see it—as a total expurgation of the past, an attempt by a bureaucratic elite to impose "utopia" through terror. Orwell understood, however, that democratic socialism is an effort to extend what is valid in the past, to enlarge our freedoms and deepen our culture. The conservative sentiments Orwell reveals in *1984* not only aren't in conflict with his socialist opinions, they can be seen as sustaining them. Or so, at least, one hopes.

While writing this essay I have been asked several times by an editor of an American magazine eager for a quick word: "If Orwell were still alive, would he have remained a socialist?" The question is absurd on the face of it, since no one can possibly know. But this much can be said: Within his generation of left-wing writers and intellectuals, some have turned to the right, some have tried to refine their socialist values toward a greater stress on democracy, and others have abandoned their interest in politics entirely. Which of these directions Orwell might have taken it would be foolish to say, except that it's hard to imagine him dropping his interest in politics entirely.

We do know that Orwell publicly repudiated efforts to use *1984* as a piece of anti-socialist propaganda. A letter he wrote to an American correspondent puts his opinion with characteristic bluntness and lucidity:

My recent novel [*1984*] is NOT intended as an attack on socialism
or on the British Labour Party (of which I am a supporter) but as
a show-up of the perversions to which a centralized economy is
liable and which have already been realized in Communism and
Fascism. I do not believe that the kind of society I describe *necessarily* will arrive, but I believe (allowing of course for the fact
that the book is a satire) that something resembling it *could*
arrive. . . .

This is simply Orwell's opinion, and we know that writers
often don't grasp the full implications of their work. It is quite
possible, therefore, for some readers to say that while Orwell
did not intend his book to be an attack on the socialist idea, it
can be read that way.

And so it can. The vision of things Orwell presents need not
necessarily lead to any one political conclusion, except a stress
upon the urgency of democratic norms. Liberals, conservatives,
and socialists can all argue from Orwell's text in behalf of their
views, though the more sophisticated among them will recognize that a political position must be justified in its own terms,
independently of any literary text.

Orwell understood that there is a profound tendency within
modern society toward economic collectivism; that this tendency can take on a wide range of political colorations, from
authoritarian to democratic; and that it can be deflected or
modulated but probably cannot simply be annulled. The inter-
penetration of state and society, government and economy is
simply a fact of modern life, quite as industrialization and
urbanization have been. In correspondence from 1940, Orwell
wrote, "There is [little] question of avoiding collectivism. The
only question is whether it is to be founded on willing cooperation or on the machine gun"—that is, whether it will be democratic or authoritarian. This puts the matter with admirable
precision. *1984* shows us what might happen if "the machine
gun" triumphs; but the other choice remains to us.

Mark Crispin Miller

2   The Fate of *1984*

When *1984* was new, and 1984 far in the future, the novel struck its most responsive readers as an unprecedented torment, an extreme and intolerable vision that stood out, not only from all of Orwell's previous writings but from all known visions of the horrible. "This is amongst the most terrifying books I have ever read," reported Fredric Warburg, who recommended that his firm publish this relentless "horror novel," although he himself had no intention of rereading it. "It is a great book," he concluded, "but I pray that I may be spared from reading another like it for years to come." Others were likewise affected. "I do not think that I have ever read a novel more frightening and depressing," wrote V. S. Pritchett in *The New Statesman and Nation;* "It is the most terrifying warning that a man has ever uttered," wrote Herbert Read in *World Review;* "Mr. Orwell has conceived the inconceivable," wrote Diana Trilling in *The Nation.* Even after this first pained reception, the novel continued, for a while, thus to stand out for its audience. "Some people dare not face this novel at all," wrote Laurence Brander in his *George Orwell*[1] (1954). "Many cannot read it a second time."

Such testimony reminds us that *1984* did, in its first decade, make a certain difference—a difference which, since then, has disappeared. As the year 1984 loses that sinister futurity which Orwell projected onto it, we find that the novel cannot stand out as it once did, that it can no longer be described in shocked superlatives. This, some might say, is proof that *1984* has sim-

ply not worn well, that its vision, once so compelling, has
turned out to be too far-fetched and/or crude to disturb the
reader still. And yet this easy argument would not explain the
novel's failure to stand out, because *1984* remains a "frightening and depressing," "most terrifying" book. Its evocation of
the life in Oceania is still oppressively convincing, its account
of Winston Smith's mute misery and final torture still appalling;
and such effects still grip us because the basic cultural state
which they connote is still a reality, still *our* reality, still legible
in 1984, in *1984,* to whoever might attempt to read it.

If Orwell's book, then, makes but a slight impression on our
culture nowadays, this fact reflects not on the book, which can
still horrify its readers, but on the culture, in which such horror
has no poignancy or status. Despite (or because of) its initial
impact, the book has slipped into that cultural morass in which
all books, *all* works, *all* utterances seem trivial and "dated"
almost instantly, regardless of their strength or truth. In other
words, *1984* has been undone, not by neglect, but by complete
inclusion. It has become a standard text in colleges and high
schools, it is invoked and quoted endlessly in other books, in
movies and on television, its eerie coinages have long since been
entirely integrated into the common speech of journalism; and
yet this very currency has actually obscured the book's significance. Although *1984* retains its power to horrify, this horror
seems no longer worth remarking, because the book has been
around for years, whereas the cultural morass continually yields
brand-new atrocities for us to shudder at, and then forget.

In such a context, it has become all but impossible to tell
what's lasting from what's evanescent, impossible, indeed, to
recall what "lasting" means. No work, it seems, can now sustain for long a formidable aura, as, say, *King Lear* once daunted
a wide audience for many decades. *1984,* however, differs in a
crucial way from all other spuriously antiquated works. Orwell's book, in fact, is not simply undiminished by its disappearance into the morass, but has become *more* valuable for the
obsolescence forced upon it. Far from proving that the novel's
vision is far-fetched, the fate of *1984* is proof of that vision's

profound accuracy; for *1984* evokes, through its excruciating metaphor, the very forces that have finally vaporized it.

Thus there is an elusive and significant relationship between the novel and its history, between its history and ours; and in order to grasp this relationship, we must begin by reading *1984* according to our instincts, and not in terms of some all-too-simple political or biographical assumption. That is, we should not read *1984* as a bitter allegory on the evils of Stalinism, nor as the terminal effusion of a dying man, nor as the ultimate map of Eric Blair's unconscious. Subjected to these commonplace interpretations, *1984* itself is "lifted clean out from the stream of history," deprived of all connection with ourselves, reduced either to an anti-Communist polemic, or to mere symptom, illuminating nothing but the peculiar illnesses of one George Orwell. For all their reference to some larger context—Soviet history, Orwell's life, the works of Freud—such readings are ultimately no less ahistorical than the most hermetic formalist analysis, the kind that would look down on *1984* as an aesthetic object, "flawed" but "powerful."

Rather than thus deny the book's connections with, fulfillment in the present, its revealing place within the long continuum from Orwell's last year up through this one, we ought to reconsider our neglected horror, the horror that those first reviewers felt compelled to mention, the horror that compelled Orwell to write *1984*. And once we recall this necessary feeling from the margins of our critical experience, we must account for its endurance, for such a feeling could not continue to arise from anything so dull and dated as an anti-Stalinist fable, or the psychic record of a man long dead. Rather, the horror of *1984* derives not from any such specific, fixed signification but, on the contrary, from its *total* ambiguity—its atmosphere of impending, unintelligible menace, the radical uncertainty of time and place and all identity, the dangerous transparency of thought. *1984,* in other words, is neither mere political satire nor an unconscious psychic testimony, but a work carefully partaking of both forms, a work that perceives the nightfall of an evil history through the mind of its last subject, who struggles to regain his consciousness, his memory of day; a work, in short, that deliberately evokes the state of perfect nightmare. *1984* is Orwell's conscious dream of history, a dream in history, and meant to be interpreted, as well as recognized, by those inhabiting that history.

Orwell clearly considered it a challenge thus to create the sense of nightmare through the medium of words, because he thought this medium basically inadequate for such a task. "How do you describe a dream?" he wrote, around 1940, in an unpublished essay entitled "New Words." "Clearly you *never* describe it, because no words that convey the atmosphere of dreams exist in our language." You can recount a dream's "major facts," and even explicate its symbols, but "the *real* quality of a dream," he concludes, "is outside the world of words." And yet, through these same refractory materials, Orwell succeeded in establishing the nightmare of Oceania, a dream world that seems both unreal and inescapable, a creation based on what we know, yet not quite recognizable.

> It was a bright cold day in April, and the clocks were striking thirteen.

Where are we? When is this? We are suddenly dropped into territory that seems only half-familiar. At first, it looks somehow like home. The opening reference to "April" places us within one of the oldest of English poetical traditions, whose appeal derives from and depends upon two sequences still older and more basic—the cycle of the seasons, the historical continuum of England. Thus the sentence implicitly alludes to a long-standing national past; and the rhythm reconfirms this implication, for the sentence (nearly) breaks apart into a neat pair of old-fashioned trimeter phrases, as in some well-known British ballad, which would also start out with a plain and unspecific reference back to "Once upon a time":

> It was a bright cold day in April,
> And the clocks were striking thirteen.

And yet Orwell obviously shatters these conventions, which ought to orient and therefore comfort us, so that the sentence actually cuts us off from all sense of the familiar, leaving us bewildered, dispossessed, like Winston Smith, denied the reassurance of tradition. Although evidently synchronized, "the clocks" are utterly disorienting, "striking thirteen" as if they had always done so; and this violation of experience finds expression in the violated rhythm, for "thirteen" terminally jars the sentence from its regular balladic beat, which calls for "twelve" or "two" or some other monosyllable.

For that matter, "a bright cold day in April" is itself a violation of the very topos which it seems to represent; for that literary April always calls to mind a month not "bright" and "cold," but rainy, warm and cool by turns, half-overcast, a month ambiguous and mild after a hard white winter: "Aprille with his shoures soote," "The uncertain glory of an April day," and even our eerie modern April, "the cruelest month," with its fecundating "spring rain." This "bright cold day" suggests that the Oceanic "April" bears no relation either to the April which the poets sang nor to the April through which we carry raincoats. In Oceania, where the Party has overruled the sway of time and nature, "April" can have no temporal or natural referent, but, like "1984," and nearly every other Oceanic term, means only what the Party says it means.

Thus the opening presents us with a world that only half-resembles ours, a closed realm that adopts the terms and features of our experience only to incorporate and alter them, as the sleeping mind transfigures the phenomena of daily life. This is Oceania, where life is but a dream; and it therefore seems that Orwell chose that infamous place name quite carefully, for he was struck by the image of the ever-dreaming mind as an all-consuming ocean. "The disordered, un-verbal world belonging to dreams is never quite absent from our minds," he writes in "New Words."

> Certainly the dream-thoughts . . . influence the verbal thoughts, and it is largely they that make our inner life valuable. Examine

your thought at any casual moment. The main movement in it will
be a stream of nameless things—so nameless that one hardly knows
whether to call them thoughts, images or feelings. In the first place,
there are the objects you see and the sounds you hear, which are
in themselves describable in words, but which as soon as they enter
your mind become something quite different and totally indescrib-
able.[2]

And then, significantly, Orwell re-expresses this conception in
a footnote, by quoting part of Marvell's famous metaphor from
"The Garden":

> The mind, that ocean where each kind
> Doth [sic] straight its own resemblance find,
> Yet it creates, transcending these,
> Far other worlds and other seas, etc.

Because Orwell wants to argue that the mind contains an
inexpressible diversity of "thoughts, images or feelings," he
deletes from Marvell's metaphor its final couplet; for those last
lines, in fact, subvert the notion of an endless and ineffable
variety within the mind, suggesting that those "other worlds
and other seas" are actually no different from the mind which
has appropriated them:

> The mind, that ocean where each kind
> Does straight its own resemblance find,
> Yet it creates, transcending these,
> Far other worlds, and other seas,
> Annihilating all that's made
> To a green thought in a green shade.

Although it contradicts the argument in Orwell's speculative
essay, Marvell's full metaphor could easily serve as the epigraph
to *1984,* if an epigraph were appropriate: Oceania takes its
name from this annihilating ocean, "the mind," at once closed
off, wide-ranging, and omnivorous. Oceania, however, is not
simply like the mind in general, but like a mind overwhelmed

by its underlying "dream-thoughts," a mind locked in night-mare, and actively prolonging, feeding, validating that bad dream. Like some monstrous psyche, collective and external-ized, Oceania ingests and transforms everything and everyone into its own dark element.

Winston Smith resists this transformation, keeps trying to wake up, to break out of this sick sleep, by self-administering a kind of inverse therapy, not trying to recall his dreams from the standpoint of reality but trying to recall reality from the dubious standpoint of a dream; and this attempt, of course, must fail. Because the dream is perfect in its self-enclosure, sustained by millions synchronized in pure delusion, like "the clocks" that strike in uniform deviance, there is no "outer world," no daybreak that can interrupt it, nor any way to live outside of it. Even in his opposition to the Party, Winston Smith plays his part in its dream, leading a life that is itself unremit-tingly dreamlike.

Although justly praised for its verisimilitude, *1984,* however credible its physical details, recounts a story whose component episodes are far too strange to be considered naturalistic. First of all, the narrative is primarily internal, since Winston Smith seems, as it were, to spend more time inside his skull than he spends in the streets and cubicles of London. Beset by Oceania's "bright cold day," he retreats into "the disordered, un-verbal world" within himself, there to dwell in reminiscence, memory, dream, fantasy, workings of the mind that charge the story with an ambiguous, ever-shifting subjectivity. This subjective mood, however, is not exclusively a feature of the inner landscape. Despite its squalor and monotony, the hero's outer world seems no less magical or insubstantial than that morbid world within the hero's mind, as if the barriers between both worlds had simply vanished.

As in a dream, events in Oceania sometimes occur as if willed, wished for, along the lines of what Freud calls "the principle of the 'omnipotence of thoughts' ";[3] as when Winston, hoping to talk to Julia during lunch, fears that "the little man"

ahead of him in line will sit nearby and spoil the conversation,
whereupon there is suddenly "a tremendous crash," as the man
unaccountably, and conveniently, goes "sprawling on all
fours," as if Winston's *mind* has knocked him down. Or, again
as in a dream, thought frequently seems not omnipotent but
transparent, as clear and open as if shouted out, as when Syme,
and then O'Brien, speak directly to Winston's objections, although Winston has not uttered them, as if these men have seen
right through his solid face. Because events occur with super-
natural fortuity, and because thoughts appear to leap from head
to head, there are instances of seemingly gratuitous coinci-
dence, as random phenomena suddenly and inexplicably appear
to work together, to confirm each other. For instance, as Syme
and Winston sit at lunch discussing Newspeak, Winston over-
hears someone at his left

> talking rapidly and continuously, a harsh gabble almost like the
> quacking of a duck. . . .
>
> Syme had fallen silent for a moment, and with the handle of his
> spoon was tracing patterns in the puddle of stew. The voice from
> the other table quacked rapidly on, easily audible in spite of the
> surrounding din.
>
> "There is a word in Newspeak," said Syme. "I don't know
> whether you know it: *duckspeak,* to quack like a duck. It is one of
> those interesting words that have two contradictory meanings.
> Applied to an opponent, it is abuse; applied to someone you agree
> with, it is praise."
>
> Unquestionably Syme will be vaporized, Winston thought again.

Contrived of such peculiar passages, the novel is consistently
nightmarish. And what, precisely, is the meaning of this ugly
dream? If we were to subject the nightmare to a strict psychoanalytic reading, we would actually deny the dream's significance: for such a reading would create a lucid two-level
structure, contriving a clear difference between the nightmare's
"manifest" and "latent" contents, which in turn derives from
a further clear distinction, the division between the unconscious
mind and its mediating faculties, and so on. Similarly, readings

that confidently see the nightmare as an anti-Stalinist allegory
also deny the nightmare itself, by assuming a broad and obvious
difference between two entities, the "free world," where the
book was written, and the Soviet dictatorship, which the book
condemns. To criticize such readings is not to quarrel with their
assumptions, but rather to suggest that those assumptions of
clear difference cannot comprehend the nightmare of *1984,*
whose very horror and significance arise from its relentless
evocation of a world in which there is, will always be, *no
difference.*

Throughout the novel, there recurs repeatedly a definitive
locution, seemingly casual, yet in fact implying an essential
realization. Early on, Winston sits before his diary: "Whether
he wrote DOWN WITH BIG BROTHER, or whether he refrained
from writing it, made no difference. Whether he went on with
the diary, or whether he did not go on with it, made no difference." Later, lying at Julia's side, Winston contemplates the
same futility, concluding with the same expression: "When
once you were in the grip of the Party, what you felt or did not
feel, what you did or refrained from doing, made literally no
difference."

This repeated axiom of fatalism is reasserted time and time
again, each time no different from the last or next. Hoping for
release through writing, Winston describes his encounter with
the aged prostitute, an act that made no difference, just as this
act makes no difference: "He had written it down at last, but
it made no difference. The therapy had not worked." Later,
Winston tells Julia how he had once almost tried to kill his
hated wife, admits regretting that he had failed to do it, and
then adds, " 'Actually, it would have made no difference.' "
And after having gone through weeks or months of agony
inside the Ministry of Love, Winston thus considers his tormentor: "O'Brien had tortured him to the edge of lunacy, and in
a little while, it was certain, he would send him to his death.
It made no difference."

For all its colloquial terseness, this repeated statement is
crucially ambiguous. It would be inaccurate to say that, in

Oceania, "nothing makes a difference," or that "something
does not make a difference." These expressions tell us that some
action or some force has failed to make a certain change within,
to stand outside from, the status quo, in other words, to make
some difference; whereas to say "it made no difference" is to say
that "it" has not failed, but *succeeded* at *un*making such a
change, that "it," deliberately and actively, has annihilated
some distinction, some divergence, "making," where there once
was difference, no difference.

This is what the Party wants to do, what it has all but
accomplished—to *make no difference,* to eternalize its own
rigid hierarchy by wiping out all dissidence, eccentricity, variety, comparison. (That such destruction can be termed a kind
of "making" is a contradiction perfectly attuned to the illogic
of both doublethink and Newspeak.) The Party plans to make
no difference whatsoever; and each time Winston Smith employs the phrase, each time he thus reveals that he cannot
conceive some difference, he thereby wins a little victory for the
Party, fulfilling, in his fatalism, the Party's program of complete erasure. Nor can he do otherwise, locked as he is inside
the dream, so that even in his opposition he maintains those
same convictions of deep helplessness and insignificance that
help to keep the Party strong.

According to *the book,* that alleged manifesto of the Brotherhood (if any), the Party seeks to wipe out difference on two
fronts. "The two aims of the Party," Emmanuel Goldstein
writes, "are to conquer the whole surface of the earth and to
extinguish once and for all the possibility of independent
thought." However, this description of the Party's strategy,
while basically correct, preserves a neat division that is basically
misleading; for, in working to annihilate all difference, the
Party cannot use a strategy that actually *preserves* a major
difference, i.e., between "the earth" out there and the world
within the mind. Rather than attempt to wipe out difference in
each of those two regions, the Party works to erase all difference
utterly from both at once by dissolving the basic difference

between them, working from the ruinous premise that "both," in fact, are one. "But I tell you, Winston, that reality is not external," says O'Brien. "Reality exists in the human mind, and nowhere else."

Once that basic difference disappears, all other differences become impossible—impossible to talk about, perceive, or even to imagine. Doublethink, for instance, makes difference absolutely inconceivable, by subsuming every contradiction, every possible exception or disproof, into its own incontrovertible illogic. Because it neutralizes any thought of difference, any different thought, doublethink is actually not a form of thought, nor could it be, in Oceania, since "thought" is something different from the other actions of the mind, and often makes some difference, moving from one different point to another; whereas doublethink is all that happens inside the Oceanic mind, a travesty of dialectic thought, automatic, non-progressive and self-canceling.

Newspeak too obliterates all difference, and thus is (as it must be) basically no different from doublethink. Lacking words for difference, different words, Newspeak renders difference absolutely inexpressible. As a radical abridgment of English (Oldspeak), Newspeak represents not only a device that makes impossible all future reference to, description of, debate about any kind of difference, but a deliberate rejection of the English past, the memory of whose differences resides within those differences that constitute the English language. "The greatest quality of English," Orwell wrote in "The English People" (1944), "is its enormous range not only of meaning but of tone." Of course, all language, as Saussure tells us, arises out of intricate and subtle differences; and in fact Newspeak is not a form of language but a medium for communicating numbers, and for making frequent noises of assent. "In the end," Syme tells Winston excitedly, "the whole notion of goodness and badness will be covered by only six words—in reality, only one word. Don't you see the beauty of that, Winston?"

While thus rendering the Oceanic mind incapable of conceiv-

ing or expressing difference, the Party also diligently censors all
experience in order to prevent the uncontrolled reemergence or
appearance of some different thing. This enormous effort would
appear to be unnecessary, since doublethink and Newspeak
would completely mitigate the impact of any such intrusion. In
fact, the Party's actions are not practical, but express the naked
will to power, which must stamp out all signs and vestiges of
difference, however slight or ineffective. Therefore the Ministry
of Truth rubs out all wayward photographs and phrases, therefore the Thought Police keep watching for the tell-tale facial tic,
therefore the citizens of Oceania are allowed "no contact with
foreigners," are "forbidden the knowledge of foreign lan-
guages," and so on. "Cut off from contact with the outer world,
and with the past," states *the book,* "the citizen of Oceania is
like a man in interstellar space, who has no way of knowing
which direction is up and which is down."

Although disoriented and alone within this monolithic system, Winston Smith finds common ground with Julia. It is
significant that Winston first discovers Julia's sexuality out in
the distant countryside, among the bluebells and the hazel
bushes: for the country, like the body, is a realm of pleasurable
difference, different from the city, different in itself. The body
and the country both are various, both go through change, each
with its April and its other months. Both give us life, are
crucially unlike the deadening city; and so each functions as a
sensuous basis, a center that allows us to perceive the stark
encroachments of the superstate. The body *feels* that the state
of Oceania is something rotten, through "the mute protest in
your own bones"; and the country sprawls beyond the city as
both a respite and reminder, an ancient, careless counterargu-
ment.

Orwell had long cherished this all-but-forgotten contrast.
"But quite soon the train drew away into open country," he
recalls in *The Road to Wigan Pier,* "and that seemed strange,
almost unnatural, as though the open country had been a kind
of park; for in the industrial area one always feels that the

smoke and filth must go on for ever and that no part of the
earth's surface can escape them."⁴ Watching the winter countryside roll by, Orwell feels himself restored, discerning, in that
different landscape, images of sexual difference. The snow "lay
so deep that only the tops of the stone boundary-walls were
showing, winding over the hills like black paths," a sight which
Orwell likens to "a white dress with black piping running across
it." And then, "I saw rooks treading. . . . The female stood with
her beak open and the male walked round her and appeared to
be feeding her." Soon he has forgotten "the monstrous scenery"
of the city, but then other such surroundings begin "to close in
upon us," as the train approaches "another industrial town."

In Oceania, the citizens take trips into the country, not to
rediscover their desire, but to walk it off. They cannot perceive,
much less appreciate, the difference between London and its
countryside, the differences within that countryside, which, as
far as they can see, is just another sector of the Party's grounds.
Blind to natural difference, they are equally indifferent to each
other's bodies, which, in any case, are all indistinct within the
Party uniform. Winston's wife Katharine, "very straight," with
"not a thought in her head that was not a slogan," is such a
nonentity, an emanation of the Party. "On a community hike
somewhere in Kent," she and Winston become separated from
the other hikers, and then Winston notices below him, growing
from a cliffside, a "tuft . . . of two colors, magenta and brick
red, apparently growing on the same root," and calls to Katharine to come look at them: " 'Do you see they're two different
colors?' " Thinking only about catching up with her comrades,
she complies "fretfully," her response to this natural difference
as tepid and reserved as her sexual response; and at that moment Winston thinks of killing her (although it would have
made no difference).

With Julia, this experience is repeated, but redeemed, as a
natural difference leads its two beholders into bliss, beyond,
outside the nightmare of the Party. When the lovers are finally
alone out in the country, a thrush settles on a nearby bough and

its sudden song enchants them, drawing them together in mute wonder at its ceaseless change: "The music went on and on, minute after minute, with astonishing variations, never once repeating itself. . . ." And their absorption in this natural difference leads the different lovers into mutual absorption, a state in which, paradoxically, all difference, all distinction seems to disappear:

> But by degrees the flood of music drove all speculations out of his mind. It was as though it were a kind of liquid stuff that poured all over him and got mixed up with the sunlight that filtered through the leaves. He stopped thinking and merely felt. The girl's waist in the bend of his arm was soft and warm. He pulled her round so that they were breast to breast; her body seemed to melt into his. Wherever his hands moved it was all as yielding as water. Their mouths clung together; it was quite different from the hard kisses they had exchanged earlier.

All is melting, "liquid," "yielding," "soft and warm." This experience of timelessness and mindlessness, this spreading ecstasy, begins the lovers' life together; and later, after a second moment of such ecstasy, the lovers' union violently ends. As the thrush did initially, the washerwoman outside the pawnshop later accompanies the lovers' trysts with endless song; and Winston, as he contemplates her stolid form, discovers her difference—" 'She's beautiful,' he murmured"—and then, as with the thrush, loses himself in his experience of that difference, then loses too the sense of difference altogether, as he turns visionary, apprehending an eternal, universal counterforce:

> The mystical reverence that he felt for her was somehow mixed up with the aspect of the pale, cloudless sky, stretching away behind the chimney pots into interminable distances. It was curious to think that the sky was the same for everybody, in Eurasia or Eastasia as well as here. And the people under the sky were also very much the same—everywhere, all over the world, hundreds or thousands of millions of people just like this, people ignorant of one

another's existence, held apart by walls of hatred and lies, and yet
almost exactly the same—people who had never learned to think
but were storing up in their hearts and bellies and muscles the
power that would one day overturn the world.

And right after this exhilarating vision, the Thought Police
close in.

Winston's momentary ecstasies would seem to represent a
real act of defiance, inasmuch as they envision something utterly opposed to Party rule; and, as O'Brien puts it, "It is
intolerable to us that an erroneous thought should exist anywhere in the world, however secret and powerless it may be."
Certainly, those ecstasies do seem a marked departure from
Winston's ordinary frame of mind. Constantly afraid and isolated, suffering "in the locked loneliness in which one had to
live," Winston has discovered "a feeling," as Freud puts it, "of
an indissoluble bond, of being one with the external world as
a whole." That is, Winston now enjoys (to continue quoting
Freud) "a sensation of 'eternity,' a feeling as of something
limitless, unbounded—as it were, 'oceanic.' "[5]

Now the nightmare suddenly seems worse, implicating even
its opponent. When Winston Smith enjoys his "oceanic" state,
does he really contradict his Oceanic State? Or is there, in fact,
no difference between the "oceanic" and the Oceanic, since
each one makes no difference? To think that "the sky was the
same for everybody," and that "the people under the sky were
also very much the same," were, indeed, "almost exactly the
same," is to imagine, albeit in a spirit of benevolent resistance,
the Party's own malevolent ideal, "three hundred million people all with the same face."

In fact, Winston's opposition is no opposition, because his
imagined methods of subversion are also the Party's actual
methods of oppression. Like any radical, he believes in tearing
down the hateful system, which he conceives as largely a fa-
cade, "a sham concealing iniquity," and dedicates himself to its
collapse: "Anything to rot, to weaken, to undermine!" He in-

vokes apocalyptic forces to cleanse the world of this detested structure. At first, impressed by Julia's promiscuity, he has high hopes for the libido as a means of liberation—"the animal instinct, the simple, undifferentiated desire: that was the force that would tear the Party to pieces." Then, calmer about sex, and influenced by O'Brien's rhetoric ("We are the dead"), he abandons the Reichian platform, and believes instead that the proles contain, deep down, "the power that [will] one day overturn the world."

However, no subversive tactics can succeed against the Party, not because the Party has proscribed them, but because it has itself become the most subversive agent in the world. Through subversion it came to power in the first place, and through subversion it remains in power now: "Anything to rot, to weaken, to undermine!" Such is the failed creed of Winston Smith, the would-be traitor, and such also is the policy of O'Brien and his unseen colleagues, who implement that policy against the citizens of Oceania, in order to remain in power, and make no difference.

Are Winston and O'Brien, then, no different?

"You are prepared to commit murder?"

"Yes."

"To commit acts of sabotage which may cause the death of hundreds of innocent people?"

"Yes."

"To betray your country to foreign powers?"

"Yes."

"You are prepared to cheat, to forge, to blackmail, to corrupt the minds of children, to distribute habit-forming drugs, to encourage prostitution, to disseminate venereal diseases—to do anything which is likely to cause demoralization and weaken the power of the Party?"

"Yes."

"If, for example, it would somehow serve our interests to throw

sulphuric acid in a child's face—are you prepared to do that?"
"Yes."

Later, during the "second stage" of Winston's "reintegration," O'Brien plays back a tape of this exchange, to repudiate Winston's claim that he is "morally superior" to the Party. And yet this seems almost too obvious, as Orwell implies: "O'Brien made a small impatient gesture, as though to say that the demonstration was hardly worth making." For what makes this gruesome catechism seem especially insidious is not simply that the Party taped it surreptitiously, in order to incriminate Winston later on (hardly a necessary precaution in Oceania); but that, by getting Winston Smith to pledge himself to such grotesque obedience, the Party utterly undoes his moral difference, by demonstrating that his righteousness is merely the precondition of their power. For, during this exchange, Winston sounds exactly like the dedicated revolutionaries of the past, those who gave up all personal feelings and associations in order to advance the Revolution, and who thereby actually brought closer not the hoped-for age of justice and equality, but the undeluded Party, the machine that makes no difference. Thus Winston, O'Brien's eager follower, speaks here as O'Brien's ancestor; and so even temporal difference is uncertain in this nightmare world: "What was happening was only the working-out of a process that had started years ago," thinks Winston at one point. "The end was contained in the beginning."

And O'Brien is, in a sense, contained in Winston, even if Winston thinks that O'Brien's "mind contained Winston's mind." For Winston, "a smallish, frail figure," is the outcast intellectual, the defunct humanist, the last of Orwell's marginal protagonists, and the last too of those spectral wanderers who haunt the Unreal City of the modern landscape; whereas O'Brien, with his "solid form" and "powerful grip," his "urbane manner and his prizefighter's physique," is all that Winston cannot be, a fantastic combination of intelligence and might, a thinker (or doublethinker) at the center, in control.

Although broadly different, they are convolved, and, in some way, no different. "Your mind appeals to me," O'Brien tells his alter ego. "It resembles my own except that you happen to be insane."

Through the interrelationship of Winston and O'Brien, Orwell dramatizes a deep confusion at the very center of the nightmare, a contradiction that had long troubled him. "I believe," he wrote to Francis A. Henson of the UAW, "that totalitarian ideas have taken root in the minds of intellectuals everywhere, and I have tried [in *1984*] to draw these ideas out to their logical consequences." In fact, Orwell perceived a totalitarian tendency in all of modern intellectual culture, a tendency inextricable from that culture; and O'Brien/Winston represents the grim fulfillment of that tendency.

> O'Brien was a large, burly man with a thick neck and a coarse, humorous, brutal face. In spite of his formidable appearance he had a certain charm of manner. He had a trick of resettling his spectacles on his nose which was curiously disarming—in some indefinable way, curiously civilized. It was a gesture which, if anyone still thought in such terms, might have recalled an eighteenth-century nobleman offering his snuffbox.

Although that image of "an eighteenth-century nobleman" could have no resonance whatever in the Oceanic world (as Orwell makes clear), it does have resonance for us; and its function is not simply to evoke a visual image, but to locate the historical origins of O'Brien's relentless subversiveness.

In his review of Malcolm Muggeridge's *The Thirties,* Orwell discusses the disappearance of "religious belief," a disappearance both inevitable and deadly. "It was absolutely necessary that the soul should be cut away," because the fiction of the soul was at the service of "a lie, a semi-conscious device for keeping the rich rich and the poor poor."

> Consequently there was a long period during which nearly every thinking man was in some sense a rebel, and usually a quite irre-

sponsible rebel. Literature was largely the literature of revolt or of disintegration. Gibbon, Voltaire, Rousseau, Shelley, Byron, Dickens, Stendhal, Samuel Butler, Ibsen, Zola, Flaubert, Shaw, Joyce —in one way or another they are all of them destroyers, wreckers, saboteurs.[6]

"Anything to rot, to weaken, to undermine!" The subversive impulse, conceived as a humane and liberating force, first gained cultural currency in the age of Gibbon, Voltaire, and Rousseau; and although that long rebellion soon accomplished its immediate objectives, discrediting Church and Kingdom, deposing God and His obscurantist henchmen, that impulse persisted as an intellectual reflex, outlasting the Enlightenment, and gradually itself becoming an oppressive orthodoxy, as it turned against the very values once used to justify it. In this century, the subversive impulse, although still considered both the proof and means of liberation from a cruel, coercive system, has at the same time enabled the powerless intellectual to express his thwarted will to power; so that, through this very impulse to subvert, he can behave as cruelly and coercively as that same hated system.

"Without another word I pulled her off the bed and threw her on the floor. And then I fell upon her like a tiger! Ah, the joy, the incomparable rapture of that time! There, *messieurs et dames,* is what I would expound to you; *voilà l'amour!* There is the true love, there is the only thing in the world worth striving for; there is the thing beside which all your arts and ideals, all your philosophies and creeds, all your fine words and high attitudes, are as pale and profitless as ashes. When one has experienced love—the true love —what is there in the world that seems more than a mere ghost of joy?

"More and more savagely I renewed the attack. Again and again the girl tried to escape; she cried out for mercy anew, but I laughed at her. . . . Ah, how she screamed, with what bitter cries of agony. . . .

"And so, just for one instant, I captured the supreme happiness,

the highest and most refined emotion to which human beings can
attain.'"[7]

Thus Charlie, one of the narrator's companions in the bistro
in *Down and Out in Paris and London,* describes, with the
Bohemian's tiresome and deliberate perverseness, an instance of
"true love" that was, in fact, a case of rape. Such perversity
represents the old subversive impulse in degraded form, deprived of an appropriate object; and, as it derives from and
distorts an earlier rebelliousness, so is this subversiveness, in
turn, distorted further within Orwell's projected history, made
even crueler and more dangerous, as it becomes less marginal,
as it ceases as a method of attack on some official policy or
ideology and itself becomes both policy and ideology.

Charlie's willful contradiction of the phrase "true love" an-
ticipates the contradictory formulas of Ingsoc; and Charlie
himself, with his cruel and sophomoric ironies, prefigures the
subtle ironist O'Brien, crawls out, as it were, out of that Pari-
sian cellar to become a perfect weapon of the Inner Party.
O'Brien is the end result of that long tradition of subversion,
the last of the "destroyers, wreckers, saboteurs," as he gives up
all illusion, mediation, sublimation, in favor of the thing itself,
"pure power." "Power is not a means; it is an end," he tells the
prostrate Winston. "The object of power is power." Like his
predecessors, O'Brien too sees through the fictions of the past,
would also sweep away the pompous, useless structures of the
world before his time. Yet the end of such promiscuous decon-
struction is not some vague final liberation, but the total opposite of liberty, as that necessary insurrection against God and
Church, begun with the Enlightenment, necessarily creates the
final darkness:

> For two hundred years we had sawed and sawed and sawed at the
> branch we were sitting on. And in the end, much more suddenly
> than anyone had foreseen, our efforts were rewarded, and down we
> came. But unfortunately there had been a little mistake. The thing
> at the bottom was not a bed of roses after all, it was a cesspool filled
> with barbed wire.[8]

When Orwell wrote these words in 1940, he had in mind the terrorist regimes of Germany and Russia, whose captains, however monstrous, had still not yet attained the iron self-awareness of the Inner Party leadership: "We are different," O'Brien points out, "from all the oligarchies of the past in that we know what we are doing." In this last difference rests the end of difference. Undistracted by ideals of racial or doctrinal purity, the Party is now ready to fulfill and terminate the process unwittingly begun by those well-intentioned rebels against God.

For that rebellion, which has made the greatest difference, has also made no difference. However stifling His long reign, God still functioned as the guarantor of difference, keeping the elements of all creation lucid and distinct within His reassuring Book of Life. As long as God remained believable, so too did that great universal registration, whereby the apparent differences between the species, sexes, classes, races, nations, notions were established as eternal and correct. But "every thinking man" had to reject the Book of Life along with its exhausted author; and all the scientific progress of the last few centuries arises from and reconfirms the loss, each irrefutable discovery canceling out some ancient body of distinctions. We have learned that men share common origins with the other animals, that all men and women harbor common drives, that class is not an absolute, but an historical determinant, that culture is the author of identity, and so on. Thus disabused of God's arrangement, we are now forced to allow the possibility that every seeming "difference" may be a mere linguistic fabrication, a possibility repeatedly advanced in the various texts and artworks—Nietzschean, Borgesian, Foucaultian—of postmodernism.

However, while it is one thing to entertain this thesis in the classroom or the armchair, it is quite another to accept its consequences as an ideology. The old scheme of differences is certainly untenable and so, necessarily, is "man" as that scheme formerly exalted him. Therefore, our attack on metaphysics, our rejection of the category "man," our subversion of such notions as "identity" and "selfhood," and so on, would all seem to promote the righteous disestablishment of an archaic world view. But once the State also dispenses with the myth of man's superiority and privilege, once it too jettisons the creaky values of the Enlightenment, it becomes a force disastrous and invulnerable, its neutralizing impulse now uninhibited by a regard for any metaphysical hierarchy. For the will to power, once unsheathed, also cuts through and abolishes all differences, and does it more efficiently, more sweepingly, than any argument—not for the sake of truth, or liberation, or aesthetic pleasure, but only for the thrill of total domination. "We shall squeeze you empty," says O'Brien, "and then we shall fill you with ourselves." And why not? What natural plan or heavenly design would such a program violate?

Modern politics itself, in other words, has become an endless avant-gardist process, having finally translated the disruptive yearnings of the "destroyers, wreckers, saboteurs" into annihilating practice. This is Orwell's great perception, the idea that animates and darkens *1984* and that other penetrating vision of his final years:

> Twelve voices were shouting in anger, and they were all alike. No question, now, what had happened to the faces of the pigs. The creatures outside looked from pig to man, and from man to pig, and from pig to man again; but already it was impossible to say which was which.[9]

At Animal Farm as in Oceania/Eurasia/Eastasia, the triumphant force of modern politics shatters old distinctions, unmakes vital oppositions, thereby transforming life into a public dream. And yet that dream has nothing in it, nothing even to define its own clear-sighted managers, who, also trapped within the dream, are also nothing. Once the corporate will to power, embodied in the Party, fills the vacuum left behind by God, all of life's differentiating fictions, theories, patterns, myths, principles collapse and disappear into the obliterating current of the Oceanic State: "If you want a picture of the future," O'Brien suggests, "imagine a boot stamping on a human face—forever."

Yet even this horrific forecast evokes a difference that has also
been wiped out, for O'Brien's "picture of the future" is itself
another torment in the hell that Winston and O'Brien now
inhabit. Here "the future" and "the present" are inseparable,
just as "the end [is] contained in the beginning"; and in this
temporal chaos it becomes impossible even to tell the essential
difference between Winston Smith, the tortured subversive, and
O'Brien, the subversive torturer.

This, then, is the real horror at the heart of *1984*—not that
the Party is too devious, or too thorough, or too well-protected
to be seen through, but that it sees through everything itself,
even sees through itself, so that any effort to subvert it can do
nothing but resemble it. Thus Orwell's narrative, despite its
seemingly distinct events and characters, seems ready to im-
plode into one eternal, brutal moment; and this implosiveness
takes with it all of modern cultural history, blurring "fact" and
"fiction," "good" and "evil," "us" and "them," as we discover
no absolute criterion to separate the earnest *philosophes* of the
Enlightenment, or the great iconoclasts of modernism, from the
undeluded Inner Party. All seem stuck within the same ineluct-
able progression toward erasure. History will be wiped out by
the intellectual descendants of those same reformers who had
once hoped to redeem it. "History has stopped," says Winston
Smith, whose very name suggests the dissolution of a specific
vivid past into an encroaching sameness.

This would seem to be as far as we can go; and yet the truth
of *1984* becomes manifest, not in the book's reflections on the
past, but in its reception here and now. For, finally, this vision
of a world that makes no difference makes no difference. Although it once stood out, this "most terrifying warning" cannot
now terrify or warn as it once did. It cannot warn because the
state it warns us of is here already—the state that terrifies us,
if at all, for just a moment; the state in which the novel's vision
of annihilated history can make no difference, since our state
too annihilates its history, as it has annihilated *1984*.

Our state, however, is not supervised by any single-minded

oligarchy, but rather is pervaded and determined by the process of consumption, which makes no difference as successfully as the deliberate program of the Party. In many subtle ways, we are all forced to consume, as ruthlessly as the citizens of Oceania are all forced to obey, betray, and hate. In our state, this consumerist imperative is a force of enormous neutralizing power, a force now mightier than ownership, or class, or anti-Communism, because, precisely like the Party, it has attained its universal sway, not by establishing itself overtly, but through continual subversion and denial.

Of course, consumption must rely on the manipulation of desire, while the Party's dominance is based on pain and terror. Moreover, our system seems to lurch along all by itself, decentralized and pluralistic, whereas the Party's program is intended, highly organized, the meticulous daily work of careful rulers and police. And yet, while the novel's world thus seems, at first, entirely different from our own, the novel's fate should be interpreted as rigorously as we should read the text, because such interpretation will reveal the possibility that these two worlds may be, in effect, no different.

The novel has been vaporized, first of all, by its inclusion into that morass of failing stimulants that finally constitutes our culture. Whereas the book could and did originally command the critics' shocked consideration, such a difficult response today seems unimaginable, now that 1984 is that dead thing, a "modern classic," and "1984" a mere catch phrase. The effects of such inclusion demonstrate at least one major similarity between the novel's world and ours.

In 1984 as in 1984, the state that makes no difference works by maintaining a monotonous and trivial public frenzy. In Oceania, nothing stands out. Doublethink nullifies thought itself; Newspeak replaces the expressive differences of language; all wear the same outfit, eat the same food, speak the same slogans, watch and hear the same things on the telescreens. And yet the world of 1984 is not made tranquil by this sameness, nor is this sameness, certainly, the result of calm. Although approaching perfect stasis, Oceania does not approach a state of rest, but is explosive, noisy, frantic, hectic, making no difference through excessive pseudo-difference: bombardments, torture, daily bouts of managed hate, sudden "bulletins," wild parades, unceasing panic, music, celebration, war, rallies, and so on.

And now, within our rushing public spectacle, *1984* itself is made to seem as flat as any non-event in Oceania. The novel's vision has become commoditized, simply one more celebrated ugliness among so many others, including nuclear destruction, *Psycho,* Beckett's works, the Holocaust, child abuse, *A Clockwork Orange,* toxic waste, assassinations, and so on, each processed into simple images and sold for an instant's titillation; and there has emerged, to sustain this market for vicarious horror, a journalistic rhetoric of extremity, as pervasive now as the rhetoric of Progress was a century ago. Critics and reviewers now routinely mention "panic," "survival," "upheaval," "agony," and often use as metaphor such realities as cancer and "the Front." Such commonplace public language, equivalent to the incessant blasts and screams in Oceania, creates an atmosphere in which the consumer/viewer cannot respond to *1984,* but only flinches at it, or ignores it.

In other words, *1984* is something known about, not known, its title and its famed devices having long since dwindled into mere code words, tossed off with uncomprehending ease by the members of the media, our inadvertent Ministry of Truth. "1984," "Big Brother," "doublethink," "Newspeak" are each themselves bits of our unplanned Newspeak, words that make no difference, obscuring those very cultural and political realities that Orwell meant them to expose.

However, it is not simply in its trivialization of this text that our world seems no different from the world within the text. As our system reduces every meaningful creation to an image, meant for a quick, oblivious ingestion, so must it similarly empty and reduce ourselves, making each of us appropriately inattentive, ravenous, and shallow, unable to be gratified within the crammed emporium, yet powerless to move outside of it, or even to imagine any decent world unlike it. We must, in other words, become *consumers,* beings who can only long for that next, "different" mouthful, even in the very act of chewing. As in the Oceanic State, so here has the predominating system really worked, not so much through coercion as through inculcation, through that process which *the book* calls "molding the consciousness." In short, we must internalize the state, so that its overwhelming influence seems imperceptible, as its one unnatural message starts to seem the prompting of our own unbridled nature.

It is a similar process of internalization that makes no difference within Winston Smith. Even before his hideous "reintegration," Winston Smith, although supposedly "the last man," already resembles that same Party which he would oppose—indeed, resembles it most closely in opposing it. And once his futile animus against the Party is extinguished, he is the Party's creature through and through, knowing and believing only what the telescreens present to him, their meaningless alarms and promises suffusing him with bursts of "undifferentiated excitement." His mind now broken, he is finally able to contain/eliminate whatever "facts" the Ministry of Truth invents/erases, nor can he glean significance from his murky, random memories of the prior world.

Our state too recurs within the minds of its inhabitants, but in this the similarity seems inexact—for our system may "mold the consciousness" even more successfully than O'Brien and his comrades could imagine: "We shall squeeze you empty, and then we shall fill you with ourselves." This promise, which O'Brien makes explicit, also expresses the unspoken plan of our corporate advertisers, who work diligently, brilliantly, to break down all individual resistance, all integrity, all selfhood, in order to complete the transformation of our once-puritanical workers into an ever-hungry, malleable mass. And in ways far too diverse and subtle to be comprehended here, our other institutions are now variously structured and administered to induce the same dependency, through, for example, the liberal

use of "counseling" and the cult of "expertise." Under the
enervating pressure of these forces, and under the congruent
influence of television, the consumer is intended to end up
gaping, wide-eyed and open-mouthed, at his "advertising sup-
plements" and video screens, turned just as infantile as those
Party members at the end of the Two Minutes Hate, with their
"deep, slow, rhythmical chant of 'B-B! . . . B-B! . . . B-B!'"

Our system works seductively, not through abrasion, im-
planting itself perfectly within the minds comprising it.
Whereas Winston Smith will always remain fundamentally
aware of the Party that has snuffed him out, the consumer
yearns and buys and yearns as if responding only to his heart's
desire—a desire more than half-created by the very system that
keeps promising to satisfy it. With our habits, affects, appetites,
and principles, our beliefs, anxieties, opinions, and desires all
continually redirected toward, determined by consumption, we
bear the system in our very nerves; and so there is no need, in
1984 and after, for an elaborate machinery of torture and surveillance, nor is it incorrect to say that our state is "decentralized." Even without a single-minded Party, we may well be as
paralyzed as Winston Smith, since, in our fragmentary culture,
there is virtually nothing anyone can do except consume, and
does so at the service of those few conglomerates that override
us, and that are themselves overridden.

And there is still another way—the crucial way—in which
our state is Oceanic. Like the Party, which is impossible to
undercut because it has already undercut itself, automatically
subverting every effort to subvert it, consumption too has risen
into dominance, not by representing some overt and positive
example, but through a process of continual negation. We are
encouraged not so much to taste as to rebel; not so much invited
to take on some gleaming object, as incited to throw off some
prior inhibition or constraint. Because consumption is no
longer based on need, the ads must break apart those inner
barriers that would obstruct our total self-indulgence, and so
they promulgate a kind of permanent revolution, making every

purchase seem a blow against the dreary past. Whatever its alleged deliciousness, the product is desirable primarily because it sets you free from something old and therefore stifling—oppressive attitudes, or messy chores, or crude beliefs, or clumsy tools, or awkward customs, all now to be consigned, as it were, to the trashmasher of history.

And yet that image of the past refers to no real pre-existing moment, but rather to the buyer's own internal hindrances, which comprise the major obstacle to a life of full consumption. Because the ads repeatedly exhort us to remove this obstacle, to free ourselves of our own guilts and inhibitions, they seem to crave our utter liberation, to oppose whatever might oppress and bully us; so that it seems impossible to demonstrate that the ads themselves are bullying, oppressive, canceling our freedom precisely through the act of calling for it. And this problem is compounded by our collective self-conception as "a free society," so that all this inescapable, enforced consumption goes on in the name of liberty, throughout "the free world," in the precinct of "free enterprise," where our newsmen, in between commercials, attest, with shining eyes, to our complete autonomy. In such a state, we manifest our "freedom" by discarding everything, including *1984,* which would reveal to us the fact of our imprisonment.

And so the fate of *1984* is proof that *1984* is deeply accurate. Is there, then, no difference between the world of Orwell's novel and our own? Or is there still one crucial difference, implicit in the book's existence? For Winston Smith, immured within his Oceanic state, can't tell its automatic voices from his own, is unable to interpret his blank history, or discern the fatal basis of the similarity between O'Brien and himself; whereas we have no choice but to do otherwise. As *1984* moves into 1984, and vice versa, all differences between, within them growing ever more unclear, we are obliged to try somehow to stand outside this spreading dream, and read it.

Elaine Hoffman Baruch

3 "The Golden Country": Sex and Love in *1984*

Early in *1984* Winston Smith has a dream:

> Suddenly he was standing on short springy turf, on a summer evening when the slanting rays of the sun gilded the ground. The landscape that he was looking at recurred so often in his dreams that he was never fully certain whether or not he had seen it in the real world. In his waking thoughts he called it the Golden Country. . . . In the ragged hedge on the opposite side of the field the boughs of the elm trees were swaying very faintly in the breeze, their leaves just stirring in dense masses like women's hair. Somewhere near at hand, though out of sight, there was a clear, slow-moving stream. . . .

A girl with dark hair comes toward him across the field and with a single movement tears off her clothes. "With its grace and carelessness it seemed to annihilate a whole culture, a whole system of thought. . . ."

Later, the dream comes true.

There are precedents for Orwell's "Golden Country." In Huxley's *Brave New World,* it is the reservation that preserves the green world of nature and wildness. In Yevgeny Zamyatin's *We,* which Orwell knew and praised highly, it is the land beyond the Green Wall that represents freedom and forest. And, of course, long before that, there was Arcadia . . .

Author's note: I would like to thank the National Endowment for the Humanities for enabling me to pursue the research for this article.

It is not only the external world of nature that provides a setting for love in anti-utopia. There are internal shelters as well. In Zamyatin, it is the house of antiquity with its blazing colors unlike the glass architecture of the rest of the One State. In Orwell, it is the room above Charrington's junk yard that is the twentieth-century love grotto. It contains that ancient shrine, a double bed. In anti-utopia, ordinary life itself becomes utopia—utopia, that is, in the sense of a longed-for ideal.

Anti-utopians believe that there was a union of passion and thought before the state takeover. They have none of the overt critique of dualism in our culture that is found in feminist utopias, Marge Piercy's *Woman on the Edge of Time*, for example. Anti-utopian authors locate the source of freedom from the state in romantic love. Here too they differ from feminist writers, who often see it as a source of oppression—for women. Winston says, "Not love so much as eroticism was the enemy. . . ." Women too sometimes see eroticism as the enemy, not because it is a threat to the state, as in *1984*, but because it is a threat to the self.

But just how erotic is Winston and Julia's relationship? Of their first meeting in the wood, we read:

> She stood looking at him for an instant, then felt at the zipper of her overalls. And, yes! It was almost as in his dream. Almost as swiftly as he had imagined it, she had torn her clothes off, and when she flung them aside it was with that same magnificent gesture by which a whole civilization seemed to be annihilated. Her body gleamed white in the sun.

Enough to please a Lawrence—and with the emphasis on the woman for a change. But then what do we hear? " 'Have you done this before?' " asks the hero.

Consistently, there occurs a deflation of the erotic. When they make love again, Orwell writes: "He pressed her down upon the grass, among the fallen bluebells. This time there was no difficulty." And another time: " 'It's all off,' she murmured as soon as she judged it safe to speak. 'Tomorrow, I mean.

. . . It's started early this time.' " It is hard to believe that so trivial an impediment as menstruation would deflect such supposedly passionate lovers.

How much more dionysiac is the experience of Zamyatin's hero: "Lips unbearably sweet . . . and then a swallow of searing poison was poured into me—and another—and still another . . . I took off from the earth and, as an independent planet, rushed down, down, following an uncharted orbit."

There is much that is bourgeois about Orwell's romance—perhaps working class is a better term. That is where Winston's sympathies lie, after all: with the proles. The lovers remind us of the early days of the first Orwell marriage, as Bernard Crick describes them: "George had furnished the cottage gauntly with a table or two, a few chairs and two bedframes . . . the chimney smoked, the kitchen was bitterly cold even in June. . . ." Another telling detail: " 'People think they are rats,' " George said about the birds that nested between the chimney and the roof.[1]

Yet what is amazing is how much feeling the understated passages in *1984* are still able to carry. And no doubt that was part of Orwell's point:

> [Winston] wondered vaguely whether in the abolished past it had been a normal experience to lie in bed like this, in the cool of a summer evening, a man and a woman with no clothes on, making love when they chose, talking of what they chose, not feeling any compulsion to get up, simply lying there and listening to peaceful sounds outside. Surely there could never have been a time when that seemed ordinary.

In his nostalgia for ordinary pleasures, Winston even glorifies the prole woman hanging up diapers and singing cheap popular songs. (How different from Orwell's earlier *Tribune* articles, which contrast the susceptibility of working-class women to "wealth fantasies" in the "love books," i.e., women's papers, with the reality of their physical pain. Now it is his hero who is sentimentalizing those very women.) In the bleak world of

1984, what Orwell gives us is a romanticization of the domestic.
No wonder feminists don't like him.

In his treatment of women and love there is much to fault
Orwell, if one is so minded. Winston has violent fantasies of
raping and killing Julia when he thinks he cannot have her. "It
was always the women, and above all the young ones, who were
the most bigoted adherents of the Party, the swallowers of
slogans, the amateur spies and nosers-out of unorthodoxy."
Later he not only dreams but is able to live out the ancient
fantasy of having a beautiful young creature declare that she
loves him before he even knows her name—he with his varicose
veins and false teeth—and then be utterly unresisting. "He could
do what he liked with her." We never do learn what her last
name is, although we get much detail about her use of cosmetics
and desire to wear silk stockings and high-heeled shoes.
" 'You're only a rebel from the waist downwards,' " Winston
tells Julia. As if to prove it, she falls asleep when he reads
excitedly from Emmanuel Goldstein's revolutionary manual.

But matters aren't so simple. Winston's initial murderous
fantasies are all too explicable in the light of Wilhelm Reich's
The Mass Psychology of Fascism, which notes that "every inhibition of genital gratification intensifies the sadistic impulse."[2]
Reich also makes clear why Winston's charge that women are
politically orthodox is less that of a sexist than a realist: women
and adolescents are always willing to heed political reaction,
says Reich, because they are so sexually repressed. Since the
main thrust of the anti-sexual conditioning in *1984* is directed
to the women, those bearers of the red sash of chastity, Julia,
who provides a deliberate foil to Winston's absent and sexually
impoverished wife, is all the more remarkable in her rebellion.
Like Zamyatin's I-330, Julia rejects the uniform and pallor of
the Party. The use of cosmetics, like the sex act itself, can
represent either bondage or liberation, depending on the norms
of the society. In Tommaso Campanella's seventeenth-century
utopia, *City of the Sun,* wearing cosmetics or high heels is
punishable by death. Severe restrictions seem to apply in *1984*

as well. In such a society, to wear makeup represents an act of freedom, not the capitulation to patriarchy it might be in ours.

Sex is unquestionably the key political issue in *1984:*

> Unlike Winston, she had grasped the inner meaning of the Party's sexual puritanism. It was not merely that the sex instinct created a world of its own which was outside the Party's control and which therefore had to be destroyed if possible. What was more important was that sexual privation induced hysteria, which was desirable because it could be transformed into war fever and leader worship.

Religions and tyrannical political systems, as Reich points out, provide excitement that is both anti-sexual and a substitution for sexuality. Julia recognizes this before Winston does.

Finally, Julia's identification with sexuality may have less to do with woman's traditional association with the body than with something more important. It is not only dystopias that repress sexual love; most utopias do also. Even when they allow promiscuity, they do so to reduce the claims of individual passion against the state. The psychoanalyst Martha Wolfenstein asks why romantic love is taboo in utopias and concludes that the indoctrination, the "constant surveillance and deception practiced by authorities, regimentation of all aspects of life, proscription of art and adornment, the cultivation of diffuse esprit de corps in place of intense personal attachment" correspond to the latency period.[3] There is much truth in this theory, it seems to me. In traditional utopias, the characters never reach a state of complete individuation. It is the giant state that is the main character, like the parent or parent surrogates of one's childhood. Utopia represents a state before adult genitality. In such a world, sexual rebellion, if it ever occurs, constitutes separation from authority figures, the mythic journey to adulthood, growth of consciousness, and total individuation. The more severe the prohibition overturned, the greater the heroism. In this light, there is no question that the most courageous and admirable figure in the society of *1984* is Julia.

Eugen Weber has said:

Insofar as the anti-utopian allows us a glimmer of hope, it lies in the instincts, in fantasy, in the irrational, in the peculiarly individualistic and egotistic characteristics most likely to shatter any system or order. This accounts for the importance of basic feelings—sex, love, selfishness, fantasy which all utopian planners try to control and in which all anti-utopians seem to put their faith insofar as they have any faith.[4]

Not all utopian planners exclude these elements. Women's utopias, which are anarchic rather than authoritarian, do not see a split between the individual and the community. They are much more inclusive of feeling, of fantasy (although not the traditional kind), and art—as, for example, in Doris Lessing's *Marriages Between Zones Three, Four, and Five.* Why these differences? Perhaps because the Oedipus complex operates with far greater force among men, the traditional male utopia is confining, constricting, rigid. In male utopias, women are deprived of their ancient power. In dystopia, they are granted it back again, with approval.

Despite the attempt of the mathematical world of Zamyatin's *We* to eliminate the unconscious, all the old mythology is apparent in the hero's responses to women. Like much of Western culture before him, he splits the sexual object, and has two lovers: O–90 and I-330.[5]

Although the roseate O–90 with her eyes of blue crystal has an appealing sensuality—she talks of spring when the hero speaks of formulas—there is no doubt that she comes from a long line of childlike, submissive heroines. Yet she too is subversive in that she insists on becoming an illegal mother. Then there is the ambiguous I-330, who is fire and ice, a sting and honey—and brilliant, a rebel against the existing order intellectually as well as physically. Unquestionably, D is afraid of her, and her seductive enchantments as well as her intellect, her ability to overpower him, to erase thoughts of all else in a kind of drowning. She comes from the *femme fatale* tradition of dangerous and alluring sorceresses. She represents freedom from the state but also erotic enslavement. Yet it is I-330 that D prefers—here in dystopia in a way that he perhaps would not feel free to prefer her in the real world, where the O's tend to win out. At the end, however, he is saved for the One State by a fantasiectomy—the operation that removes imagination.

Orwell, in contrast, treats only one woman. He doesn't split women into the good versus the seductive, the antithesis that Freud treats in his "On the Universal Tendency to Debasement in the Sphere of Love" (unless Winston's shadowy wife should be considered one side of the split). Yet in reversing the values of the old sexual definitions—"I hate purity, I hate goodness" —is he not tied to the old mythology after all? At least Winston can be congratulated on rejecting the tradition of the seduced and abandoned heroine: "The more men you've had, the more I love you." "Not merely the love of one person, but the animal instinct, the simple undifferentiated desire," is what he says delights him in Julia. Actually, the relationship of Orwell's lovers is as faithful as anyone of the old world could have wished. Would Winston have responded with the same fierce jealously as the Savage in *Brave New World* had he found Julia with someone else? Probably not, though it is doubtful that he actually wants the promiscuity of *Brave New World.* His desire that everyone be corrupt to the bones has meaning only where it is impossible of fulfillment. Sexual freedom in *1984* is a political act. In a state of sexual permissiveness, it would cease to be that, indeed, would become a sign of submission.

Part of the significance of Orwell's treatment of love is that, once consummated, it doesn't depend on fantasy. In fact, it is as if Winston has had a fantasiectomy himself. He has none of D's dependence on dualistic images of woman as child/mother or temptress/destroyer. Since so many feminists are trying to eliminate these polarities, perhaps they should praise Orwell, who keeps nothing of the sado-masochistic elements of the *We* lovers either. But while Orwell eliminates the dangerous lure of I's sexuality in his treatment of Julia, he also eliminates I's intellectuality, and this women will not be so quick to forgive.

It is of particular interest that in a short review of *We* that Orwell wrote for the London *Tribune* on January 4, 1946, he was at pains to quote a passage that very forcibly indicates the political consciousness of I-330. It is she who is a member of the underground resistance that actually seems to exist in *We*, and she who leads the hero to a momentary political rebellion.

It is this relationship between the sexes that Orwell reverses, when he might have equalized it. Why? Is it because, despite his rejection of fantasy, Orwell is a sexist after all? Or because Winston Smith is the outsider from the beginning, the man with political consciousness unlike Zamyatin's hero, who starts out as the good man of the One State, gifted in mathematics but something of a naif otherwise? Or because such a shift makes more poignant Winston's betrayal of Julia at the end, his regression and defeat?

In Orwell's depiction of a world that combines Nazi barbarism and Stalinist tyranny, many readers hear a poignant counterpoint, that of the early dream of socialism. Was Orwell aware that that dream had as much to do with the transformation of love as with economics? Whether utopian or scientific, socialism wanted to change the bourgeois ideology of love, with its obsessive desire for possession, into something free and liberating. Only after the economic independence of women can there be true and individual sexual love, proclaimed Engels, who anticipated the appearance of authentic romantic love in the new order. Perhaps most touching, Alexandra Kollontai, Bolshevik leader and contributor to the International Women's Movement, spoke of the "love-solidarity" that would develop in socialism:

> In the new collective society, where interpersonal relations develop against a background of joyful unity and comradeship, Eros will occupy an honourable place as an emotional experience multiplying human happiness. . . . Modern love always sins, because it absorbs the thoughts and feelings of "loving hearts" and isolates the loving pair from the collective. In the future society, such a

separation will not only become superfluous but also psychologically inconceivable.[6]

I don't think that Orwell had in mind this ideal. What his
treatment of love and sex in *1984* indicates is that he would
have been happy with traditional love. But this is not an option
that remains. The only love that is allowed in *1984* is the love
for the leader. What Freud said about the attraction of the
group to the leader of the Church and the army applies to the
leader of the totalitarian state as well. It is a libidinal tie,
grounded in the child's love for the father. Instead of being an
object relationship, it is a regressive bond, an identification,
which is something far more primitive and therefore potentially
dangerous. Recently, some critics have indicated that Orwell's
sexism prevented him from seeing that the power relationships
in *1984* are based on the model of sexual polarization.[7] I would
make a different claim: The domination of male over male in
1984, that of O'Brien over Winston, for example, is far more
severe than the domination of male over female. Polarization
need not be sexually based; indeed it is not in *1984,* where the
opposition is between the ruling class and the ruled, and ultimately between one leader and his followers. Here the basic
model is not male/female but rather parent/child, as it is in
most political groups. Winston is passively masochistic and
submissive to O'Brien in ways that Julia never is to her lover.
Whether we like his depiction or not, Orwell's sexual love
provides the only escape from male domination of males in
1984, the only escape from the reversion to Freud's primal
horde. Insofar as Winston and Julia are able to meet "for the
purpose of sexual satisfaction, in so far as they seek for solitude,
[they] are making a demonstration against the herd instinct, the
group feeling," in Freud's terms.[8]

But by the end of *1984,* there is no idyllic nature (there is no
mother in the old sense), and there is no sex, let alone sexual
love. Now it is just possible that we could get rid of these
traditional sources of pleasure and still remain human. Pascal

said: "There is nothing that cannot be made natural. There is nothing natural that cannot be lost." Then too what seems utopia to one sex might well be dystopia for another. It is surely of some significance that the loss of home, marriage, romantic love, and the replacement of motherhood by *in vitro* reproduction that Huxley so deplores in *Brave New World* are posited as the very terms of liberation in Shulamith Firestone's *Dialectic of Sex,* one of the most influential books to come out of the women's movement.[9] The crucial questions are: To what use would a society put these changes, and what kind of society can we expect?

The answer Orwell gives is horrifying. In his review of Zamyatin, Orwell claimed that *We* was superior to *Brave New World* because of its "intuitive grasp of the irrational side of totalitarianism—human sacrifice, cruelty as an end in itself, the worship of a Leader who is credited with divine attributes. . . ." In *1984,* O'Brien says: "the old civilizations claimed that they were founded on love and justice. Ours is founded upon hatred." Not quite so. There is an affective tie that remains and Winston confesses it at the end: "He loved Big Brother." He is therefore able to participate vicariously in the power that intoxicates the Inner Party. Traditional sexual love has been transformed into a sublimated homosexuality, which may in fact be part of all patriarchal institutions—but which is here pushed to its furthest extreme. Looking at such a world from the outside—and we are still outside, even if getting closer —who would not lament the loss of "the Golden Country"?

Bernard Avishai

4 Orwell and the English Language

"The best books," Winston Smith perceived, "set your scattered thoughts in order . . . are those that tell you what you know already."[1] That may be so, but we should now find it hard to have the thoughts George Orwell wanted to order in his readers when he invented Winston Smith. The details of Stalinism and fascism have faded from view since *1984* took shape; Orwell's youngest admirers from then would now be in their fifties. I suspect that other educated Americans will not easily recognize Trotsky's style in Emmanuel Goldstein's historical materialism, or recognize the GPU's brutality—and talent for euphemism—in the comportment of the Thought Police. Still less are we likely to ponder the revolutionary potential, if any remains, of the proles.

Yet *1984* delivers a shock of recognition today, and not only to political historians. In part, this is because of Orwell's way with our scattered anxieties about love and death. Any man can share Winston's passion for Julia—at first self-canceling, then clinging. The threat is carefully constructed. What Orwell calls "dignity of emotion" is tenderly reciprocated by her, moreover. Julia cannot articulate the systematic extinction that obsesses Winston, but she wards this off more forcefully, Winston thinks, with the mere gesture of flinging aside her clothes. Love seems to "annihilate" the whole tyranny—of marches, flags, and imbecile enthusiasms which seem to her nothing more than "sex gone sour."[2]

Still, that tyranny outlasts our lovers. So it is Winston

Smith's political imagination, not Julia's sensuality, that has
had to keep the novel fresh. Orwell conceded this in advance.
"Their embrace had been a battle," he wrote, "their climax a
victory . . . a political act."[3] Civilized rights are always at stake,
not—or not only—solace. And if rights come across deeper and
sweeter as a condition of lovemaking, they depend less on desire
than on feats of civilized culture.

I

The words Orwell considered crucial to a civilized outlook—
"honor, justice, morality, internationalism, democracy, science,
and religion": words he expected to be banished from Newspeak[4]—have struggled for existence against primal forces in
the past. More common, Orwell wrote, was an outlook similar
to that of the ancient Hebrew "who knew that all nations other
than his own worshipped false gods. . . ." Without training, any
man would rush to deny other gods. "The less he knew about
them the better for his orthodoxy." Orwell's distaste for such
closed-spiritedness was hard won. He was born in Bengal and,
after Eton, returned to Burma to do a stint with the Indian
Imperial Police. This was, as he put it, the only time in his life
that he was important enough to be hated by a large number
of people. He recalled seas of yellow faces, pressing their wills
against his own, transforming him into a "hollow, posing
dummy, the conventionalized figure of the sahib."[5] Yet unlike
Rudyard Kipling—some of whose attitudes he considered "sadistic"[6]—Orwell could not imagine imposing more nearly universal values by force. He could see himself, or a part of himself,
in the rushes of the tribe. The Burmese reminded him of an
English football crowd, eager for rough sport—fellowship and
the promise of power. Nobody wants to be left out or thought
a fool. So there was no use throttling a man's magic for the sake
of his emancipation. "Nothing is possible, except to extend the
area of sanity little by little."[7]

Orwell was probably thinking of the limits of imperialism,
not of Winston Smith's conspiracy, when he wrote that line.

But he was also troubled by the ways resistance to tyranny may itself be suspect. What else are we to make of Winston's declared willingness to throw acid in a child's face in order to extend his own area of sanity?[8] Then again, uncertainty about the political means to determine the fate of enlightenment was by now old hat. It was a Victorian problem, and Orwell knew how it afflicted Dickens—and Spencer and Cobden. Even John Stuart Mill had to admit limits: "Liberty as a principle has no application to any state of things anterior to the time when mankind have become capable of being improved by free and equal discussion."[9] For an advocate of liberty, this was a bitter pill. Of course Mill had himself made a career from imperialism, in the East India Company. But here he was trying to be careful about where in the world his libertarian arguments might stand a chance.

Orwell took to such cautions like a sahib to rifles. He agreed that restricted principles such as "justice, democracy, science, etc.," are deeply rooted in English history and culture, strong even in the lower middle class as well as in the working class. They cannot be exported like bicycles and gin. "The gentleness of the English civilization is perhaps its most marked characteristic," he wrote in 1940. "It is a land where the bus conductors are good tempered and the policemen carry no revolvers. In no country inhabited by white men is it as easy to shove people off the pavement. And with this goes something that is always written off by European observers as 'decadence' or hypocricy, the English hatred of war and militarism." Self-mocking English postcards and jokes were, for Orwell, "a sort of diary upon which the English people have unconsciously recorded themselves." He noticed that, even in the Great War, the soldiers' songs took the sergeant major for the enemy:

> I don't want to join the bloody army,
> I don't want to go to war;
> I want no more to roam,
> I'd rather stay at home,
> Living on the earnings of a whore.[10]

Just how many such songs the uninitiated would have to learn to get a grasp of English tolerance Orwell could not say. (The Irish might want to dispute the value of the education.) And given his own distaste for imperial fiat, his sense of its futility, one suspects that Orwell was afraid of the question. On the other hand, he could not condemn Kipling's condescending attitude toward illiterate peoples. Kipling, at least, had a "grip on reality," a "sense of responsibility." Kipling also saw that men "can only be highly civilized while other men, inevitably less civilized, are there to guard and feed them."[11]

Orwell skillfully works over this connection between politics and improvement in *1984*. Like one of V. S. Naipaul's half-initiated natives moving forward to London, Winston Smith moves back—to a secret, cherished world of artifacts that embody individual wills. Taking leave of O'Brien, in whom he misplaced his trust, Winston cannot bring himself to speak generalities about freedom. Instead, there comes to his mind a picture of illicit pleasures: a memory of his mother's nurturing, a private room, a crafted paperweight, a steel engraving in a rosewood frame. Then he asks O'Brien to help him piece together a submerged nursery rhyme—" 'Oranges and Lemons' say the bells of St. Clement's; 'You owe me three farthings' say the bells of St. Martin's"—suggesting Church, trade, play. It is a mysterious and touching moment. Then a horrible one. For it is then that we share with Orwell the knowledge that Mill, steeped in Victorian science and triumphalism, could not. Where books were once burned, now rhymes are blotted out. If liberty as a principle does not apply to a time before men can be improved by free discussion, it does not apply either to a time after this is so.

In Germany and Italy, the past had been erased for a generation. In Russia, the erasure was already forgotten. So Orwell had grounds for thinking it especially important to preserve English culture and he said so: "The world is sick of chaos and it is sick of dictatorship. Of all peoples, the English are likeliest to find a way of avoiding both."[12] The English would first have to think more deeply, get rid of their snobbishness and anachronistic class distinctions, and pay more attention to the world. But the civilized part of the world would continue to need them.

II

This was not sheer patriotism. For Orwell, the English had never been "gifted," not as musical as Germans or Italians, not as good at painting or sculpture as the French.[13] They were certainly not brilliant intellectuals. And when it came to the grasping jabber of Soho—reproduced in *1984*'s pubs—Orwell remained the mocking product of the British public schools. ("I arst you civil enough, din't I? You telling me you ain't got a pint mug in the 'ole bleeding boozer?") What Orwell was developing here, as good-natured nationalism, is a serious theory about the way English literacy works on the English nation. Consider what, of all things, was on his mind as the Allies drove toward Berlin: "The greatest quality of English is its enormous range not only of meaning but of *tone*. It is capable of endless subtleties. . . ." English, indeed, is not a science but an "art." It is old and vast. It has no reliable rules, but is terribly irregular— something that delighted Orwell and also daunted him: "Whoever writes English is involved in a struggle that never lets up for a sentence. He is struggling against vagueness, against obscurity, against the lure of decorative adjectives, against the encroachment of Latin or Greek, and, above all, against the worn-out phrases and dead metaphors with which the language is cluttered up."[14]

So there are three important *moral* consequences for anyone gaining literacy in English. First, and least important, is that the language includes the restricted terms of civil life. It contains Greek and Roman universalism. One can mine it directly for words like "individual" or "freedom," which already mean individual freedom in the political sense. A child of English culture should therefore have a privileged feel for civil society. (In contrast, Orwell did not know but would not have been

surprised to learn that the word for "individualism" in modern
Hebrew, *enochiyut,* also means selfishness. In Vietnamese, "I"
is conventionally expressed as "your brother, your mother,
etc.")

Moreover, the size and suppleness of the English language
promotes the practice of freedom that the English word for
freedom connotes—our reward for involving ourselves in a
struggle "that never lets up for a sentence." To become literate
in English, to master it, one must constantly make discrimina-
tions, as would an artist, about tone and color, archaisms and
clichés, science and cant, appropriate allusions and distracting
ones. This is a kind of training ground for individuals.

Finally, however, the historic virtues of English are dangerous. Its familiar phrases and metaphors can be so impressive
that they reassure unsuspecting readers. English is therefore a
perfect vehicle for demagogy. Political language can make "lies
sound truthful, murder respectable, and give an appearance of
solidity to pure wind."[15] To prevent this, writers have the moral
obligation to simplify their thoughts and express them plainly.
This is not to say that English should itself become simple; only
that, having ridden its twists and turns, writers ought not to get
carried away: "If you simplify your English, you are freed from
the worst follies of orthodoxy. You cannot speak any of the
necessary dialects, and when you make a stupid remark its
stupidity will be obvious, even to yourself."

One must be on guard as much against vivid catchwords—
"jackboot, Achilles heel, hotbed, melting pot, acid test, veritable inferno"—as against failures of logic and evidence. Catchwords give relief from the struggle to make sense, one's own
sense, and leave one possessed of contradictions which must be
suppressed—either in imagination or by force. Authoritative
jargons especially annoyed him for the way they obscure moral
contradictions. "To accept an orthodoxy is always to inherit
unresolved contradictions," he wrote in 1948. "The normal
response is to push the question, unanswered, into the corner
of one's mind, and then continue repeating contradictory catch-

words."[16] (In *1984,* Orwell called this "doublethink.") We are revolted by industrialism, he noted, yet welcome the conquest of poverty. To come down unequivocally for "growth" needs an economist's jargon—"productivity of labour," "lagging indicators"—that conceals cruelties of all kinds. To oppose industrial expansion needs a jargon of utopian fellowship. Orwell could not buy into either.

And however we view his claims for and against English literacy, Orwell has hit on a simple premise that can hardly be denied: political freedom, freedom as a way of life, is of use only to people who, unlike Julia, have complex thoughts which they can articulate. Writing the English language well does not assure democratic values, but the general collapse of literary skills will sooner or later bring on political degeneracy. "The English language becomes ugly and inaccurate because we have foolish thoughts, but the slovenliness of our language makes it easier to have foolish thoughts."[17] If the language gets flatter, coarser —more regular or perverted by orthodox catchwords—then the challenge of literacy is diminished. But so, then, is the chance to deserve civil liberties.

III

It seemed crucial to Orwell that we write less to say what we think than to discover what we think. We cannot make our thoughts serious or original without steady practice. The page disciplines the too spontaneous eruptions of mind. It needs evidence, logic, rules, precision, and calm. It gets the attention of skeptical readers who can track back and forth along one's words and call one's bluffs. Orwell could not even imagine giving a serious reading to some text without writing prose in response. He thought every citizen should keep a journal: "To see what is in front of one's nose needs a constant struggle."[18]

But Orwell's chain of deduction—from improvement to literary idealism—begins in a thoughtful philosophic theory. There is no other activity quite like writing because science is not "the mere piling up of facts" but a "rational, sceptical, experimental habit of mind."[19] Essays and fiction are only freer expressions of these scientific habits. Furthermore, the social nature of reading and writing betrays how even scientific doubt is impossible without a community of literate people. A man may see the truth, or a part of it, but he is helpless to establish it by himself.

What dawns on Winston Smith, certainly, as part of his capitulation, is the futility of trying to examine truth in isolation: O'Brien claims to float away like a bubble. Winston first denies this and then catches himself: "The fallacy was obvious. It presupposed that somewhere or other, outside oneself, there was a 'real' world where 'real' things happened. But how could there be such a world? What knowledge do we have of anything save through our minds? All happenings are in the mind. Whatever happens in all minds truly happens."

The freedom to say two plus two equals four, Orwell implied here, is a social achievement before it can be demanded as a political right. The mathematical formula is not impressed on every child's senses by the world outside. Mathematical terms are first established in discourse. Writers and speakers—fathers and mothers—establish the categories of imagination in language; scientists discipline and augment their senses to ratify the claims that categories have given them the wit to conceive. So no complex fact is self-evident. A fact needs a community. It will also need a public realm in which evidence—such as that photograph which Winston Smith frantically shoved down the memory hole—can be debated, filed for retrieval, reproduced as history.

Orwell came down hard in *1984* against what philosophers call mechanistic theories of knowledge, against the view that the motions of the world report to every man's senses in uniform ways. Thomas Hobbes—to whom Bernard Crick recently compared Orwell—held the opposite view, believed that all thinking is the product of inertial collisions. Hobbes called ideas "decaying sense" and supposed that the names we fix to our ideas are just arbitrary. In contrast, Orwell tried hard to deny that words just capture what is necessary. He thought that knowledge of the world is inseparable from particular language, which is not "a natural growth" but an "instrument we shape for our own purposes."[20]

Though we have no evidence that he had even heard of them, Orwell is much closer to the Cambridge philosophers of his day than to Hobbes, closer to Ludwig Wittgenstein's emerging ideas about "language games" constituting and limiting political reality for us: "Politics is a sort of sub-atomic or non-Euclidian world where it is quite easy for the part to be greater than the whole or for two objects to be in the same place simultaneously."[21] Two plus two do not make four where people lack the words to imagine how this must be so. (Think again of little children.) That is a sobering conclusion and one we should not want tyrants to figure out. Unfortunately, the totalitarian state has already done so: "It declares itself infallible and at the same time attacks the very concept of objective truth."[22] And the totalitarian state can scotch the process of truth at its source. It can tamper with the rules of language for its own purposes —legislate simplicity of form and spin off the litanies of orthodoxy. But easiest of all, the state can destroy words, and along with words, their precious "shades of meaning."

The virtue of Newspeak—sincere, doomed Syme expostulates with Winston Smith—"is the beauty of the destruction of words."[23] Why have complex people when simple-minded ones give promise of greater harmony? "Every year, fewer and fewer words and the range of consciousness always a little smaller. . . . The Revolution will be complete when the language is perfect." Ingsoc will be belly-felt. And along with Oldspeak, ironically, it will be necessary to obscure the very philosophical principles that have to be true for the totalitarian state to succeed. The "C vocabulary" of Newspeak preempts the study of philosophy with the "scientific and technical terms" of pragmatic specialists that give no clue to science as a habit of mind or method of thought. Science, correspondingly, degenerates into a routine manipulation of external conditions—conditions that seem as purely uniform and predictable as Newspeak has made men. Behaviorism cannot be right. But Orwell understood that it can win.

It is as satisfying as ever to read how Winston's struggle to write English with individual force gives the lie to behaviorism. Once he starts to keep a journal, he becomes unpredictable. Still, Winston's gathering talent reveals the distance that is traveled from routine literacy to literacy in Orwell's active and ambitious sense. In *Animal Farm,* this is the extreme distance from the horses to the pigs. Even a writer's "style" is not trivial in that it insinuates the kind of civilization in which we are supposed to fit the rest of our capacities. Orwell wanted democratic conceits between the lines.

He put this case sharply in "Politics and the English Language." Prose gets to be ugly—and ominous—when writers reproduce "metaphors, similes, or other figures of speech which we are accustomed to seeing in print." Demagogues are never stylish writers just because their familiar euphemisms ("memory holes"), nicknames ("Miniluv"), and slogans ("WAR IS PEACE") are meant to frost over the reader's curiosity. But less insidious writers corrupt thought by using foreign phrases and technical jargons, long words "when a short one will do." If the reader must be intimidated, then something is wrong. All writers know when they're being judicious.

The most intriguing rule of style Orwell suggests in the essay has to do with voice. "Never use the passive where you can use the active."[24] This is nothing if not a call to the kind of responsibility he admired in Kipling. Active subjects of sentences describe people who are—or should become—the conscious agents of their actions. The passive voice implies a version of social history that unfolds regardless of human will. For example, in Samuel Sillen's review of *1984* in the Communist monthly *Masses and Mainstream,*[25] we find this pretty sentence: "In short, Orwell's novel coincides perfectly with the propaganda of the National Association of Manufacturers, and it is being greeted for exactly the same reasons that Fredrick Hayek's *The Road to Serfdom* was hailed a few years back." Orwell had in fact written a critical review of Hayek's book. Had Sillen been required to specify just who was doing all this greeting and hailing, things would have gotten dicey for him.

IV

The notion that mankind makes the world with language—and a democratic world with high standards for literary "style"— does not appeal to common sense. It is even less obvious than the notion of science as a skeptical and experimental outlook rather than a pile of facts. Yet Orwell hoped that every child's mind could be led through such reversals of imagination. "There is always hope for the individual human being if you catch him young enough."[26] And here is the source of *1984*'s power today: one cannot put it down without wondering if American schools and households are doing much "catching." Every child in this country would know enough to endorse freedom in some vague sense, and know better how to back up the claim with impatience of appetite. But students are reading fewer books than ever before, and what they read is often specialized jargon. Anyone close to university life today knows that students write badly.

The decline of literacy can be blamed on the high schools but also on trends in the public culture which Orwell had the guile to fear in his novel. He especially feared television. "With the development of television," Emmanuel Goldstein wrote, "private life came to an end."[27] Orwell wanted to acknowledge the government's growing power of surveillance. Yet the first thing Orwell chose to tell us about Oceania's telescreens is not that they can spy on people, but that they could never be shut off. The sound could be reduced slightly, never entirely.[28]

Here is a shrewd point, and an increasingly urgent one, since there are millions of American families who would not take a permanently lit TV screen to be a hardship. In Oceania, television degrades private space—first by promising some more compelling public realm, and then by eroding the skills that need privacy and make it worthwhile. Reading and writing are obvious casualties, but the problem is compounded. For Oceania's telescreens provide only an illusion of public life. People lack the constancy of family or political association—they have nobody—and cannot resist what feels like simultaneous sentiment with everybody. Winston Smith does not trust the political claims that are flashed before him during the Two Minutes Hate. But chanting curses with everybody else never fails to evoke his animus. "Within thirty seconds, all pretense was unnecessary."[29]

In putting private life to an end, the telescreen transmissions also put an end to the way people get at the truth. They intensify disconnectedness. They flash images that cannot be inspected or reviewed. And since everybody learns the telescreen's claims all at once, no individual can feel bold enough to challenge them. What is commonly seen takes on the force of truth; evidence burns or melts into air. Few who get this steady diet can remain much concerned about getting at the truth, anyway. The telescreens are filled with sadistic and salacious stuff that brings out the worst in everybody—desires for conquest, skin, revenge.

There is an obvious temptation to draw parallels between Oceania's telescreens and America's television. V. S. Naipaul once joked that the American version of the "Bush" consists of a thicket of antennas. But who can read Orwell's account of Oceania's violent and pornographic telecasts without thinking about American crime shows, the soaps, the Big Events and the commercials that interrupt them? I am sure that the commercials would have struck Orwell as particularly obnoxious, for they have a pacing and a tone that seems just right to capture the attention of children. The jingles are easy to learn, and they are full of handsome grownups who make a big show about having this or that. I am told, by the way, that advertising executives refer to cleavage as "eye-candy"—a word that Syme would have wanted for the eleventh "and definitive" Newspeak dictionary.

In Oceania, Big Brother won't let you turn the set off. In America—little brother. One recent study revealed that the average American child will have seen some 75,000 thirty-second advertisements by the age of ten.[30] The same study determined that most of these kids assume that those handsome grownups are usually lying. There is some—not much—consolation in that finding. But what child will see the lie in the phrase: "part of a nutritious breakfast"? Orwell, it should be said, was not hostile to the potential of new media further to educate an already educated public. He saw great possibilities for radio and film and—"if it could be freed once and for all from commercial interests"[31]—the press. But his reservations about the commercial press can certainly be applied to American commercial television. How good it would be to have had Orwell around since *1984,* all this time, especially during elections. What would he have made of serious journalists debating whether or not the President can "stay the course"? Felix Rohatyn, the chairman of New York City's Municipal Assistance Corporation, observed that his city would never have been able to pull out of its financial crisis during the late seventies were it not for publications such as the *New York Times.* "The issues were too difficult for thirty second spots." But the issues are not less difficult where the press is not so honorable and clever. What official can resist pressing the advantage when he knows that voters may turn him out of office in the same spirit that we change channels? The Environmental Protection Agency now calls acidic rain "poorly buffered precipitation." The President calls new taxation schemes "revenue enhancement measures."

The print media have not been immune to television's standards, of course. In *Time* and *Newsweek,* writers take for granted a democracy of shifting perceptions. Their relentless polls imply that simultaneous opinion is our only hard fact. Thus, for example, the question of whether Israel was responsi-

ble for the Beirut massacre is transformed into a question of
whether "a majority of American Jews feel Israel must bear
'partial responsibility' for the massacre."[32] ("Whatever happens
in all minds," Winston coached himself, "truly happens.") But
the automatic style of television reporting has reinforced more
traditional failings of print, especially our reliance on empty
phrases and metaphors that might be forgiven in conversation.
The *Boston Globe* recently printed this account of the effect of
President Reagan's peace plan on the Hashemite Kingdom of
Jordan: "In Jordan, it has unleashed a process of internal discussion and political debate that is rubbing up against the very
core of this small nation, which has existed in a state of domestic political suspended animation since its founding some sixty
years ago."[33]

I think that advances in technology, in computers and communication, are also revamping English for the worse. This is
not an original observation, but my reasoning bears on Orwell's
shrewd apprehensions. Winston Smith used a "speakwrite" on
the job, a machine that took dictation and recorded his
thoughts without giving him a chance to work up a draft. A
good many memos that course through executive and government offices read as if they were dictated in a similar fashion,
and we are apparently getting close to building machines such
as the one Orwell describes. Yet more essential technological
habits have also affected English. Recently, I heard a NASA
official announce that the "Columbia spacewalk would be up-
scheduled in terms of one day." It dawned on me that he
thought a computer might be eavesdropping. Our educated
classes do speak FORTRAN or COBOL more and more these days,
and, more and more, treat English as if it were also some
conveyor for "information bits." Think, now, of Newspeak's "B
vocabulary"—*goodthing, goodthinkful, goodthinking.* Computers have needed such compound words as fit into strictly regular sentences. As with Newspeak, any word should be available
as noun, adverb, adjective, or verb, depending on how it is used
or combined with other prefixes and suffixes. Remember that

Newspeak's syntax was expressly invented for simple minds, so it gave priority to regularity and to "almost a complete interchangeability between different parts of speech."

There is nothing wrong with getting digital machines—our new population of simple minds—to do tedious work for which men and women are emotionally unsuited. Still, when Edward Kennedy confessed to Roger Mudd that the assassination of his brother "impacted his life," I thought of Orwell's belief that colonial masters may succumb to the culture of backward laborers. And how about this, from J. D. Singer's *Quantitative International Politics:* "If we think of interactions among nations in scientific as well as normative terms, it becomes evident that *some* portion of the variance is accounted for by factors having little to do with the conventional warlike versus peaceful classification of the national actors."[34] The danger from computers is not that they will eventually get as smart as men but that we will meanwhile agree to meet them halfway.

Orwell's dark vision for *1984* is about more, of course, than the connection between literacy and democracy. Even the most cultivated man may be a barbarian: O'Brien knows the arguments against the Party and loves its power all the more. But our permanent interest in Orwell does derive from his elaborate despair over the corruption of English. His great novel is full of exaggerated lines of thought; like Picasso's brushstrokes of Gertrude Stein, they've got truer as we've aged.

Luther P. Carpenter

5 *1984* on Staten Island

To figure out what *1984* means today, it is important to look at the responses of ordinary readers. Orwell wrote for them; he hoped to affect them politically. Does *1984* still move these readers, two generations after he wrote? If so, what do their responses tell us about their political and personal values? Does America feel like *1984* to them? Could they be made into "proles" or Party drones?

I assigned *1984* to an introductory history class in the evening session at the College of Staten Island in September 1982. The College of Staten Island, a branch of the City University of New York, is a commuter college, located on an expressway about two miles from the Verrazano Narrows Bridge. To it comes a self-selected portion of the people whom Orwell called working class but who now call themselves middle class. They are office workers, housewives, meter readers, part-time retail clerks, sanitation men, police, construction workers; or they are the children of those people. Some of them have already worked "up" to the lower edges of middle management; all seek to "get ahead," either in their current companies or by obtaining credentials in computer programming or nursing or business. Yet their careerism is often mixed with a pleasure in thinking and learning. Occasionally that pleasure takes over completely, as in the case of a fifty-year-old subway motorman who could not afford to go to college when he was young. His ultimate goal is a Ph.D. in philosophy for the sake of enlightenment and self-esteem.

These are not traditional students, but they tell us something about how American education has changed, as public universities and community colleges have grown to incorporate returning adults and the children of the stable working class. My students are also representative in another sense: Staten Island sees itself not as part of "the City" but as part of "Middle America." It is miles from the Lower East Side and years from the old working class of immigration and depression. Nonetheless, we also have a portion of the new immigrants and the new unemployed.

When our class met for the first time, I learned that virtually all the students were working adults. Most appeared to be between twenty-five and forty years old. Women made up two thirds of the group. About half had Italian-American surnames, as is common at the College; five out of forty-nine were black. Although they were taking an introductory course, four of the first thirty-nine registrants had completed three years' work. Only eleven had completed sixteen credits or less. The latecomers probably had put in less time, but as a whole they were an experienced group of students. Nine were taking a nursing degree and nine a general liberal arts associates degree. The rest were scattered among business, technology, and science—with one lone English major.

The course they took is an introduction to thinking historically, organized around a basic theme. I made *1984* the theme of the course, spending five weeks on it and postwar Europe, and then seeing whether its projections were confirmed in the recent history of Poland and in the way that Brazil has tried to develop the Amazon region. This article is drawn only from the experience of the first five weeks.

On the first evening, I told the class that I would write this article and asked them to keep a journal of their responses as they read *1984*. I collected their journals in the third and fifth weeks, but did not grade them or make comments approving or criticizing their entries. Their journals are my main source. Most of the students' names are fictitious, but a few wanted to use their real names or initials. I promised that no one would be quoted without permission. I have kept their exact words, so that you may get a more personal feeling for them; you will notice some errors in grammar, but I hope these will not distract from the evident sense that they make. I have drawn quotations primarily from early journal entries, when my opinions cannot have influenced the class significantly. To avoid steering their responses, I did not give a background lecture until the fifth week. I believe that they did not know enough about me to be influenced.

They also brought few preconceptions about Orwell to the book. A quarter of the students said they had already read it. Two or three proudly announced they had read it on their own, rather than for school. Those who had read it in high school felt quite distant from that experience. Ruth O'Neill read it twenty years ago. "Being an impressionable teenager at that time, I can remember that the big thing was to destroy or stop Communism from expanding." Cari came through high school ten years later. "I can remember thinking of it as science fiction. It didn't have any impact on me at all. The contrast between their memories suggests how the 1960s affected our high schools.

The first, basic response of the class was that they hated the book. That may seem an obvious, elementary remark, but I am glad to be able to make it. No one visibly enjoyed O'Brien's cruelty and sadism.

They hated *1984* because it hurt them. This pain was an obstacle to reading it. Joan Wood wrote: "I find it hard as a reader to get into *1984;* I don't know if its because I find the book dull, depressing or both. Maybe its the way that I've been raised, I can't even imagine a world where normal existence is completely opposite to my values." Clearly, the obstacle was not really boredom. Instead of feeling nothing, she had felt too much and had to protect herself. She went on to affirm "the family unit, love for my fellow man, value of human life and free thought. . . ."

Holly Dellolio attacked both Orwell and the course. "I really don't like George Orwell. I don't like his book *1984.* I would rather read a book about history than to read a book and discuss its political overtones. I can't say that I'm apolitical but sometimes I am. And I can say that after 2 classes, I feel that I registered for a political science class." She charged that Orwell was anti-Semitic, sexually frustrated, and paranoid. Many students reported moments when they felt like Holly or Joan and could read no farther. Most (including Holly and Joan) got past the obstacle as they saw that they didn't have to like it or agree with it and could invent other reasons for reading. Even though they learned this, the book still continued to upset them.

Of the forty-four who turned in journals, only six showed no strong emotion. These six listed details of Oceania's society without trying to integrate them with one another and without giving a clearcut personal response to them. These students may have felt that they were being properly "objective" by keeping themselves out of the picture; but it is just as likely that they were disoriented by the culture shock Joan Wood described.

At least ten were moved by Orwell as they would have been moved by a thriller or a romance: they took sides. Ruth Leigh-Johnson wrote: "My general feeling is disgust or depression. . . . The only positive thought that comes to mind is that Winston might possibly come through as a revolutionist." L. T.-C. was "not surprised at Winston's willingness to risk death or imprisonment in order to air his inner feelings. If I were in his position I might take the same risk." Annmarie Della-Torri used empathy, a capacity that is valuable to a democracy. "I feel sorry for Winston and the people who may be like him who are being brainwashed and forced to live in poverty and illiteracy. I find it very hard to believe that people will let such a thing happen to them. I try to put myself in that position and think to myself how in the world would I keep my mouth shut—I would probably be 'vaporized.' " Clearly, Orwell still has the capacity to move readers.

Specific Reactions

Which of Orwell's nightmares have retained the greatest power
to shock this audience? They responded to many things, with
great diversity.

In their comments on the early part of the book, two basic
patterns emerged. One group reacted most strongly to what had
happened to the family and personal relations, while another
group was troubled primarily by thought control. Within these
basic patterns, you will see plenty of individual interpretations
and emphases, but these patterns are the starting point for
getting closer to the students.

Staten Islanders are family people, and the family was often
the first detail they reacted to, instead of just listing. Lizann
Cutter wrote: "The family structure, as we know it, has broken
down completely. Children eavesdropping on their parents and
turning them in to the Thought Police. The future of modern
society as we know it lies in our children, how sad that this
society has used this principle so fully for its own end!" Nine
people had this kind of family-centered reaction. Their reaction
was not confined to changes in family structure; they objected
broadly to the absence of trust and love in 1984. Images of
violence and inhumanity caused them pain. Several journal
writers commented on the Parsons children demanding to view
executions and the crowd laughing at films of war victims.

Interestingly, in a time when the Moral Majority is active in
places like Staten Island, five of these nine readers objected
specifically to the Party's debasement of sexuality. In our discussions, the class as a whole concurred. They found the role
of sex in 1984 to be arbitrary and not integrated with the rest
of Orwell's vision. They understood that Orwell wanted to
attack Victorianism. They understood that sexual frustration
could store up energy for hatred and aggression—Freudianism
has become a given for many of them—but they could rarely
agree that a ruling class would find it necessary or desirable to

use this technique. Sexuality is so natural for them that they did not notice the Party's belief that unfettered sexuality could be a way to tame and degrade the proles.

Two other points support my impression that many working people believe in, and would defend, families, but not in an intensely ideological way. Only one of these nine readers drew a connection between *1984* and the problems of American families—even though five of them said that other parts of Orwell's predictions are coming true. Secondly, at least five members of the class used feminist concepts. They criticized Julia's lack of political consciousness as stereotyping on Orwell's part or a feminine problem on hers. Cutter responded to a passage in which Winston recalled taking food from his mother and sister: "Was he destined to be a Party member from childhood and his mother and sister were proles? Was this passage a comment by Orwell about male superiority and female submissiveness?"

Thought control was the focal point for half the journal writers—twenty-two people. To these twenty-two we must add the three who took solace from Winston Smith's heroic early success at maintaining an inner core of personal thought. These students have a visible commitment to free thought and education. They saw that the horror of mind control went beyond physical coercion and took away a person's essence. Fred Siracusa grasped it almost immediately: "P. 16. Orwell has me convinced that with proper condition and absence of truth I could be made to rationalize or could be made to hate that which is good." Cassie Bari and Cari said that they would go insane under the pressure of mind control. Several agreed with Orwell that altering language could destroy ideas. As a historian, I was especially pleased that at least six students spontaneously emphasized the disorientation that would come from being deprived of history. Cassie Bari summed up the theme succinctly: "Orwell's message: Government can totally take over a person's life, mind and body. They have ways and means of 'persuading' you to give up your way of life, your thoughts to their thoughts. To live for the future is one thing, to forget the past is another."

Bari's summation is noteworthy for looking beyond the control to the controller. Six other students centered their reading directly on Oceania's class structure or political system. Jerry Septoff said: "I feel that it is Big Brother and the inner party that broke the trust the people had put in them. I see in the rise of the party a platform based on peace and prosperity, democratic in nature. . . . I believe it is an outgrowth of the cliche, 'Absolute power corrupts absolutely.' " Constance Robinson found *1984* "truly obscene, so much power in the hands of one or a group of people." In class discussions, she explicitly used class analyses.

However, most of the students, perhaps like most Americans, did not analyze the Party until they had to in our discussions. At least two confessed that they never paid attention to politics. A third student, E.T., investigated her feelings by identifying with Julia:

> She appears to live for here and now! This is probably good in one sense but without *any* thought or plan for the future life isn't too worthwhile. . . . Maybe she felt like me—if you didn't know anything about what's going on, you can't be involved and it really can't be too important. . . . I guess that's why I don't like the news.

By the end, she had vowed to change. Holly Dellolio and Joan Wood, whom I quoted earlier, also help us understand the non-political feelings of middle-income Americans. Wood wrote:

> I do read material such as the newspapers and listen to the news on radio and television and often I am appalled by many things that are going on in the world; But as a middle class housewife and student in a Democratic society, I feel I have enough problems trying to maintain my and my family's existence within this society without really doing something to correct or lend support to those

who may be doing something to correct these ills which exist throughout the world.

Politics, to her and to many others, threatens to take time away from family and career. Rather than assist those parts of her life, it threatens to overwhelm them. I am reminded of an aphorism by G. D. H. Cole: "Our problem in face of all these formidable difficulties . . . is to find democratic ways of living for little men in big societies."[1]

Ignore the slight condescension and sexism in "little men"; the problem remains. Orwell did not help my students with it. Several hoped that the Brotherhood would provide an alternative, but they recognized (sooner than Winston did) that it was just the same thing. Small wonder that they were then thrown back onto personal relations or personal moral values as the only source of meaning. Florence Fidelio, for example, struggled to make sense out of the Party's nonsensical slogans. Next she tried to side with the Brotherhood. When Winston finally broke and betrayed Julia, she commented: "I feel that he is a goner. One is 'lost' without love!" Her last words are both significant and funny:

> I enjoyed reading this more as a moral story than a
> political book.
> The moral of this story is:
> Never Trust a Man who Whispers to you in the Dark![2]

In this way, Orwell can confirm anti-political feelings or make readers even less political than they previously were. However, at least six of the forty-four drew just the opposite conclusion, as E.T. had done. "I think I learned something!" she wrote. "Don't have a blaisé attitude about politics."

In our class discussions, while the students did a good job of analyzing the Party's grasp for total control, they resisted the full horror of Orwell's vision. They emphasized semi-rational motives for desiring control—consumption of luxuries, compelling respect from ordinary people, and not losing the status one has—rather than the sadistic enjoyment of power as an end in itself. In interpreting power this way, they were not just being apolitical; they were protecting their basic *niceness* against Orwell's despair. Marlena Friscia's journal illustrates how they struggled past their assumption of human decency:

> I can't believe that they set people up so they can torture them. . . . But then again I do know people who would intentionally play mind games and scheme to hurt other people emotionally. Most of these people have low self esteem and are on ego-trips. They want power and they manipulate anyone to get what they want.

Only a few of them speculated that our ruling class may have this drive for power; it is probably necessary for many to protect the assumption that our own rulers are rational and somewhat benevolent or fatherly.

It Can't Happen Here

The need to protect their niceness did not prevent a substantial number of students from saying that parts of Orwell's predictions are coming true in the United States. Nineteen out of forty-four said so explicitly; in arriving at that number, I excluded several rhetorical questions or hints that weren't connected to specific parts of Orwell's analysis. It is interesting that slightly fewer students—fifteen—connected details of *1984* to the Soviet Union in their journals. Only one of those students gave the kind of full-blown anti-Communist reading that was so common in the 1950s and early 1960s. Three others drew conservative conclusions; I will cite two of them so that you may see the twists that they gave to conservative thinking. Diane Marciano said: "I think this book . . . shows how things might be if we let the government take control of everything." But then she added: "Pretty soon I think that we will need the type of economy they have in this book—they have a socialist economy." Fred Siracusa saw "a warning to the reader. Revolution can be more dangerous than no revolution." Staten Island sees itself as a pretty conservative place, but the absence of hard-line conservatism in these quotations and in their comments on the family can be seen as confirming Andrew Levison's view that "working-class conservatism" is an overblown myth.[3] These students have the justifiable perception that the Soviet Union is a grim place to live, without being led into unthinking approval of everything American.

The connections they made between the United States and *1984* were thoughtful and specific, not overblown and feverish. Some could only approach the comparison jokingly, through a minor symbol. Three journal writers compared the compulsory calisthenics on the telescreen with Richard Simmons, for example. I didn't count these responses among the nineteen who made connections, but I would say that these readers were trying to come to terms with the fear that their thoughts are controlled. Half of the people making connections dealt with this theme. Judy Amalfitano likened the Two Minutes Hate to a pep rally. Cassie Bari found Hate Week "typical of USA freedom. People expressing what they want, when they want, about each other. Police patrol, snooping into everyone's affairs —reminded me of Watergate." (I'm not sure whether her last clause referred to Nixon's wiretappings and burglaries or to the intensity of the Watergate investigation.) Rachel Archer also felt watched and controlled: "I can certainly see some forms of Big Brother in my own life; especially in my family and my job. One not only *has* to do what one is told—but we must do it with a smile on our faces." Laura Castiglione "was thinking—I work for a hospital":

> *They* are "totalitarian-istic" to some degree. (1) We have a dress code (2) We use double-think—when we are short-staffed we must say we have enough staff to do the job (3) The hospital has their catch-22 and can use "emergent situation" to suit their needs. (4) When your views & philosophy do not fit their mold [you are not vaporized] your career is vaporized.

Jackie Dee wrote extensively on computers and the dossiers kept by governmental agencies, while Fred Siracusa referred to the CIA and FBI. Jackie Dee and Cari connected advertising to thought control when they added to their journals. A final instance of thought control brought us closer to Orwell's treatment of the proles. In New York, the State Lottery has become a big enterprise. Sue Fiorenza saw that it could be used to distract her, and there was a roar of embarrassed laughter in the classroom when someone brought it up.

Six other students connected Orwell's geopolitical scenarios to the cold war. They felt that Orwell was right in saying that the nature of war had changed, so that the superpowers fought limited wars on the periphery. They also observed some of the political and economic consequences that Orwell predicted. Lizann Cutter said that our stockpiling of weapons is constricting the supply of consumer goods. This is an especially hard point for Middle Americans to admit; every class I have taught has contained a few students who argued that war is good for the economy. Constance Robinson used Orwell's architectural symbols to connect *1984* to the cold war: "The Ministry of Love sounds like, the underground city in Colorado where the president will go in case of nuclear attack." No one was ready to admit that nationalism is a way of controlling us, however.

Most were skeptical about large parts of Orwell's analysis. They found it hard to believe that Party members could really be gotten to believe the absurdities the Party put forth, or that freedom could be taken away so easily. Their skepticism may be a healthy sign, but only a half dozen took the next step and tried to argue that Orwell's predictions aren't coming true. Deirdre Ascoli and Rose Trevi said that we are not lied to in the same manner. "I believe our news is not a fabrication, merely an omission of some truth," Trevi wrote. L.T.-C. argued that we have not yet sunk to the level of laughing at death and suffering. She distinguished between our society's "semi-sanctioning" of killing in war and the Party's deliberate killing of innocents in *1984*. Finally, Audrey Speck challenged "Orwell's apparent belief that the oligarchy would be able to treat the proles (85% of the population) as a negligible factor."

Speck will have to be correct if we are to avoid *1984*. We have to hope that our working class or lower middle class can't be turned into proles. The students in my class are in a sense the class counterparts of Orwell's proles, while they desire to fill positions equivalent to those of Party members. Their responses to the proles and the Party can suggest whether they see the dangers and can resist them.

At first, none of them identified with the Party. Jack Cappaletti made the connection later. "Maybe we are the Outer Party and slaves to our jobs." I cannot tell whether he made the connection before I read out Orwell's perceptive description of the new aristocracy: "bureaucrats, scientists, technicians, trade-union organizers, publicity experts, sociologists, teachers, journalists, and professional politicians." Several of these occupations are on my students' "enemies list," which may lead to a lot of self-deception. Bureaucrats work for government, not for Con Ed. In other classes, I have found that many Staten Islanders feel they cannot oppose orders from their bosses even if they are morally wrong. However, as I noted before, many were skeptical about Winston's capacity to rewrite newspaper entries that he knew weren't wrong; so they—and thousands like them—may be able to draw a line that they won't cross.

Five members of the class identified with the proles, despite their near-invisibility in *1984*. The proles were "more normal." Rose Trevi spelled out their normalcy: "They speak of the proles as being non-human, but by my standards they are the only humans. They lead happy lives. Their families are basically normal. Their children will not have them vaporized." Fidelio, Amalfitano, and Siracusa said that if they had to live in *1984* they would rather be proles. I would not put too much weight on this particular response. In *1984*, it is already too late to make a difference. The choice lies only between an existential self-affirmation and making the best of the situation, because Orwell has excluded any political or collective response. One cannot criticize those who make the best of it; Orwell admires the prole woman who sings as she hangs out the laundry. Nonetheless, opting to be a prole may connect to some of the key vulnerabilities in the proles: their apolitical view of life, their absorption in minutia, the cleverness that limits itself to staying out of trouble. In our case, one of the three students who admitted the relative attractiveness of prole life then said that she would rather run the risk of acting like Winston and Julia. The other two were less heroic, or less romantic, even though one of them had read the book politically.

On the more hopeful side, the members of my class didn't act like Orwell's proles. They disputed points; they didn't give uniform, conditioned answers. Two of them even said that the church they belonged to, the Catholic Church, resembled *1984*. They were far more energetic than Orwell's proles. They were persistent enough to take on something they don't like—after a full day's work and despite the competing attractions of the Lottery and television. They expressed a humanity and individuality that go far beyond the remnant of sensual integrity that Orwell left to the proles.

"I always want the right to choice to make my own decisions, to always maintain mental activity, and to project love and kindness individuality is the bottom line, and freedom." In Deirdre Ascoli's self-affirmation we may see a sense of entitlement that could lead her to rebel against being herded or manipulated. For every anti-political student, there was one who saw Orwell's world in class or political terms and thus might be able to connect his/her self-affirmation to political participation. I'm not saying that their analyses were always on target; often they used codewords that indicated they could be tricked. For example, Rachel Archer feared that we could be led into "socialism" by politicians because we are so busy consuming. I don't agree with her identification of the enemy of freedom, but I think that we can safely disagree. She did not launch into a Two Minutes Hate, but instead made an individual commitment to thought and energy: "I, for one, am certainly going to live my life more calculated and to a fuller extent since I have had the chance to look at the world through Orwell's eyes." At least five other students reached this conclusion. I hope their individuality, energy, and decency can hold out.

PART II

IDEAS

Robert C. Tucker

6   Does Big Brother Really Exist?

I

I want to share some thoughts with you about a political phenomenon that has a still imperfectly understood psychological, or psychopathological, dimension, which may lie at the heart of it. This phenomenon is conventionally called "totalitarianism."

Everything about it, starting with the name, is problematic.

Whoever invented it, the name was put into currency by Benito Mussolini when he published an article in the *Enciclopedia Italiana* in 1932 in which he proclaimed himself a "totalitarian" and called the Italian Fascist state *lo stato totalitario*. That claim is widely taken by historians as more of a boast than a description of Italian Fascist reality.

In the later 1930s and after, the name was picked up by scholars, some of them refugees from the real, Nazi version of the phenomenon that took over in Germany in 1933. These refugee scholars and others who wrote tracts about totalitarianism, of which Hannah Arendt's *The Origins of Totalitarianism* is the best known and most influential, took Hitler's Germany and Stalin's Russia as the two indubitable historical cases of the totalitarian phenomenon. Arendt wrote that 1929, the year of Stalin's advent to supreme power, was "the first year of clearcut totalitarian dictatorship in Russia." Under his predecessor, Lenin, the Soviet order was, she said, a "revolutionary dictator-

Author's note: This essay was originally presented as an address to the American Psychoanalytic Association of December 18. 1981, and has appeared in *Psychoanalytic Inquiry,* vol. 2, no. 1 (1982).

ship," hence by implication, at most, pre-totalitarian.[1]

Scholars had an understandable reason for adopting Mussolini's term for their uses. They needed a word to convey what they considered a very important fact: that Hitler's Germany and Stalin's Russia represented something distinctively, even radically novel, and in Arendt's phrase radically evil, which had come into existence in the political world; something qualitatively different from the many forms of authoritarian rule, dictatorship, tyranny, or despotism that the world had seen in earlier times, all the traditional authoritarianisms.

Although I will use the term "totalitarianism" now and then, I'm not sure that it is a good one for scholarly purposes and I won't be bound by it. My real inclination is to drop Mussolini's neologism and use the phrase: "the nightmare state."

But the words we choose are ultimately of secondary importance. What matters is that the phenomenon the scholars meant to denote by the term they used has been real and may again become real; that we need to understand it better; and that this is difficult because we are dealing with something elusive.

II

The scholarly theorists seem to have sensed its elusiveness. For their writings show them seeking to define the diverse ways in which the totalitarian dictatorship, as seen in those two cases especially, differs from traditional authoritarian states.

Thus, Emil Lederer saw the totalitarian party-state as being, unlike traditional authoritarianisms, a "state of the masses," ruling in their name and possessing some sort of affinity with them.[2] Sigmund Neumann found that whereas traditional authoritarianisms have generally been conservative regimes, the totalitarian state is revolutionary, indeed, that it embodies "permanent revolution."[3]

Revolution for what? To remake the world according to a fanatically held ideological blueprint shared by the members of the ruling party (their "ideological supersense," Arendt called it),[4] driving them to create, for example, a world without Jews or a world without Trotskyists and capitalists, depending on the ideology's content. And, of course, the totalitarian state, unlike traditional authoritarianisms, sought totality of control over its subjects, including their minds, although a few scattered "islands of separateness," Carl Friedrich and Zbigniew Brzezinski allowed, might exist in the family and the Church.[5] The search for totality of control meant that the totalitarian state was a bureaucratic colossus, whose bureaucracy showed a "radical efficiency," Arendt suggested,[6] as in the operation of the Nazi death factories. Franz Neumann differed on this point, seeing a constant collision of different bureaucratic machines in the totalitarian leviathan state that he called *Behemoth.*[7]

Finally, all the theorists emphasized that totalitarian rule was terroristic in a novel way that Arendt sought to conceptualize by saying that totalitarianism pursues "*total* terror" rather than the selective, realistic "dictatorial terror" that strikes at actual or suspected enemies of a regime. Such total terror was, she said, "the very essence" of totalitarian government.[8] Agreeing, others called it "the linchpin of modern totalitarianism"[9] and "the vital nerve of the totalitarian system."[10] The source of the terror seemed to reside in the ideological fanaticism that inspired the ruling party to remake the world in its fashion.

Perhaps, by this point, you have been forcibly struck, as I am, by a certain characteristic of this theoretical thinking about totalitarianism: its utter impersonality.

In this picture of totalitarianism, a ruling party is actuated by an impersonal "ideological supersense" to practice "total terror" through institutions that are "bureaucratic machines." There are *no persons* doing things. There is, briefly, an "it," totalitarianism, which does things through persons to persons; but the subject of the action is the "it."

It will come as no surprise, therefore, when I add that the theory of totalitarianism did not treat personal needs of the totalitarian dictator as a motivating force in the radically evil behavior of the "it." The needs being fulfilled were system needs. As one of the theorists, Zbigniew Brzezinski, wrote of the terroristic purge, which he conceived as the core of totalitarianism, "it satisfies the needs of the system for continued dynamism and energy."[11] The theorists did not overlook the presence of a totalitarian leader. But they saw him as a function of the system and the fulfillment of its needs—not vice versa. Thus Arendt wrote in the first edition of her book, published in 1951, that in the view of the leader's lieutenants—which she seemed to accept—"he [the leader] is needed, not as a person but as a function, and as such he is indispensable to the movement."[12] From this perspective, *Fuehrers* have the function of assuming blanket responsibility for everything done in their names, of enabling the Eichmanns and others to perform their criminal actions in good conscience and without any sense of individual responsibility.

"Not as a person but as a function." This phrase takes us to the heart of the issue I wish to pursue. There was, I believe, a fundamental flaw in the theory of totalitarianism: however impersonal the institutional workings of the nightmare state may be, the needs being fulfilled by its radically evil behavior are ultimately those of a person—the totalitarian dictator. And this failure helps explain why the elusive phenomenon baffled the theorists' persistent effort to identify the driving force of the "it." They did not grasp that the actions of the "it" must be traced to their source inside a "him."

III

One of the most important contributors to our thinking about the elusive phenomenon wrote the following:

Totalitarianism has abolished freedom of thought to an extent unheard of in any previous age. And it is important to realize that its control of thought is not only negative but positive. It not only forbids you to express—even to think—certain thoughts, but it dictates what you *shall* think, it creates an ideology for you, it tries to govern your emotional life as well as setting up a code of conduct. And as far as possible it isolates you from the outside world, it shuts you up in an artificial universe in which you have no standards of comparison. The totalitarian state tries, at any rate, to control the thoughts and emotions of its subjects at least as completely as it controls their actions.

I count seven uses of "it" here, plus two references to "totalitarianism" and "the totalitarian state."

The passage just quoted was written by George Orwell in an article, "Literature and Totalitarianism," published in *The Listener* on June 19, 1941, three days before Hitler's armies invaded Stalin's Russia, with which Hitler had been joined in an alliance since the accord of 1939. Earlier in the article, Orwell referred to Germany, Russia, and Italy as the three extant totalitarianisms, and said: "I think one must face the risk that this phenomenon is going to be world-wide." To illustrate the effort of the "it" to control its subjects' emotional life, he also said:

> . . . every German up to September, 1939, had to regard Russian Bolshevism with horror and aversion, and since September, 1939, he has had to regard it with admiration and affection. If Russia and Germany go to war, as they may well do within the next few years, another equally violent change will have to take place. The German's emotional life, his loves and hatreds, are expected, when necessary, to reverse themselves overnight. I hardly need to point out the effect of this kind of thing upon literature.[13]

From this it is clear why Orwell, though no theoretician, was, nevertheless, a significant contributor to thinking about totalitarianism. As a writer he was concerned about emotions, and although he kept speaking of the "it," he was interested in the thing's effect upon people's emotional life. Very likely this was the impulse that led him to imagine the phenomenon of totalitarianism in a vividly concrete way and to portray it in his novel, *1984,* published in 1949. Orwell accepted the idea of totalitarianism's impersonality, yet did more than anyone else to dispel its elusiveness. By producing a work of creative litera-

ture rather than a theoretical tract, a picture instead of an
abstract description, he achieved something that none of the
theoreticians did: he made his imagined world real for us,
whereas very much of the scholarly literature made the real
seem remote.

IV

1984 is about a society, Oceania, or one part of it, Airstrip One,
whose name in 1948 had been England. Oceania is ruled by an
Inner Party with the help of a larger Outer Party of which the
hero, Winston Smith, and his illicit lover Julia are working
members. Their love is illicit, and hence secret, because, in
Oceania's ideology of anti-sex, all erotic emotion is to be fixated
on the figure of the leader, Big Brother.

Winston and Julia are employed in the Ministry of Truth,
whose function is to falsify the past in accordance with the
needs of present policy. Thus, when Oceania suddenly shifts
alliances, becoming the ally of Eurasia and the enemy of Eastasia, with which it had been in alliance against Eurasia, the
Ministry of Truth falsifies all past records to show that Oceania
never had been an ally of Eastasia and never an enemy of
Eurasia.

This helps the citizens respond appropriately to the philippics against Eastasia that they now see and hear over their
telescreens, and the friendly references to Eurasia. And if they
fail to think the proper new political thoughts as commanded,
these telescreens, which are two-way affairs, enabling unseen
authorities to spy on their doings and feelings inside their apart-
ments, may detect them in such "thoughtcrime." Then they
will be taken to the torture chambers of the Ministry of Love,
from which, if they emerge at all, they will emerge mentally
transformed into robot-like receivers of telescreen's signals.
Those who do not reemerge have their names eliminated from
all past records by the Ministry of Truth, so as to make it appear
that they never did exist; they become unpersons.

In an essay of the 1950s, Isaac Deutscher argued that Orwell borrowed "the plot, the chief characters, the symbols, and the whole climate of his story" from an earlier book, *We*, written in 1920 by the Russian, Yevgeny Zamyatin.[14] But that judgment is too sharp. For *1984* quite clearly reflects the deep impact on Orwell of the contemporary political pageants of Stalinist Russia and Nazi Germany, especially the former.

Thus the sudden switch of alliances by Oceania resembles the switch by Stalin in 1939 to his accord with Hitler. The object of the Two Minutes Hate sessions on public squares and on everybody's home telescreens, Emmanuel Goldstein and "Goldsteinism," is Trotsky (whose original name was Bronstein) and Trotskyism. Above all, the Big Brother who is both omnipresent and invisible, who never makes a personal appearance but whose portrait looks down on you everywhere, in public and in private, with his moustache and his enigmatic smile, is certainly the reclusive Stalin. Hitler had a moustache, but no enigmatic smile.

If I may insert here a personal memory, when I first read *1984* soon after its publication, I was living in Moscow as a member of the American Embassy, and the story seemed very real to me. It portrayed things I had seen happening, like individuals disappearing overnight and nobody daring even to try to find out from that kidnapping organization, Stalin's NKVD, what was happening to them. Everybody was terrorized, unlike today when, however revolting in many of its manifestations, the repressiveness of Russia can best be represented by Arendt's concept of "dictatorial terror." Today's Russia is an authoritarian police state of one particular kind. It is not the Russia of *1984* that actually existed in 1949.

The question then arises whether terror in an extreme form is in fact the "very essence," in Arendt's words, of the nightmare state. There are two issues here. First, her distinction between "dictatorial" and "total" terror, although important, is not easy to apply in practice because it is not clearcut; the difference is one of degree. Dictatorial terror spreads fear among a far greater circle of people in a society than those actually victimized and their relatives and associates. The spread effect is deliberate. Indeed, it is in the nature of state terror, which aims, by victimizing the relatively few, to paralyze the many by showing them that they too are in deadly danger of being victimized if they speak out or resist the government in any way. Hence "total" terror is but an extreme form of "dictatorial" terror. The distinction is nevertheless of huge significance to the people of a society, as evident in the difference between today's Russia and Stalin's. For example, anti-Brezhnev anecdotes have been rife in present-day Russia and could be repeated orally with impunity, whereas people were sentenced to ten years in a concentration camp if overheard telling an anti-Stalin anecdote in 1938 or 1948. Why it was so very dangerous to take Stalin lightly will be indicated presently.

The second issue is whether extreme or "total" terror is in fact the very essence of the totalitarian phenomenon. It belongs to the essence, but is not the whole of it, and perhaps the greatest merit of *1984* is that it shows what else belongs there. People are ruled by fear in Oceania, as in any authoritarian police state where terror is practiced by the government. But this fear is not the peculiar reality, the distinctive feature, of life in the nightmare state. Orwell depicts two other emotions as salient in the public and, to a great extent, the private life of Oceania: love and hate. Boundless love and adoration of Big Brother and, by association, anyone or anything closely linked with him; and fierce, sadistic hatred of those declared to be Big Brother's and hence everyone's enemies.

The implicit message is that in order to decide whether the phenomenon of the nightmare state exists, we have to ask: What are the role and significance of the erotic theme and the hate theme in the controlled public life of the state in question? If it is simply a land where people live in fear of the authorities because one can be made to disappear unaccountably and torture is practiced, it is not the full-fledged nightmare state, however nightmarish for those who fall victims to the dictatorial terror and those closely associated with them. But if, in addition, it is a society where you must be in love with the leader and convulsed with hate for those identified as his (and hence your) enemies, then you are in the presence of the elusive phenomenon.

Applying this criterion, we can see that the two indubitable historical cases are not the only ones on the record. Another was Mao Zedong's China of the so-called Cultural Revolution, begun in 1966, when Chairman Mao appeared on Tien An Men Square at dawn, like the sun with which he was compared in the song constantly heard then, from a show called *The East Is Red:*

> From the Red East rises the sun,
> There appears in China a Mao Zedong.

This dawn appearance was the first of eight occasions when Mao reviewed a total of 11 million Red Guards whom he launched into the "Cultural Revolution" (an Orwellism for what might better be called the revolution against culture). When he appeared, a hundred thousand Red Guard throats opened to greet him in frenzied adulation. "Teenage girls became hysterical, their faces contorted; they wept uncontrollably and, half-fainting, had to be supported by those next them."

The account just cited comes from a Chinese-speaking Englishman, Roger Garside, who later became first secretary of the British Embassy in Peking. In 1966 he was stationed in Hong Kong. As this rally was being broadcast from Peking over a station heard in Hong Kong, Garside walked into the living room of Chinese friends and found them "listening in silent horror as a high-pitched voice whipped a crowd to a delirium of fury." The voice was that of Lin Biao, then a close companion of Chairman Mao (later an unperson). Mao was beside him as he spoke, "glancing over his shoulder at the text and smiling approvingly." Garside recalls: "The savage frenzy made me think of Hitler's Nuremberg rallies," and when Lin Biao shouted: "All our victories are victories of the Thoughts of Mao

Zedong," Garside was struck by the thought that he was "unconsciously echoing the propaganda for Big Brother in George Orwell's *1984*."[15]

He notes that little children were being taught to sing a song that said:

> Father is dear, mother is dear
> But Chairman Mao is dearest of all.

And during this time of exaltation, when people were exclaiming "Chairman Mao has come among us!", hundreds of thousands of people, old and young, were killed, maimed, and tortured as enemies of Chairman Mao, or "freaks and monsters," as they were called. Mao saw them as ghosts from the past, and called the Ministry of Culture the "Ministry of Ghosts" because it allowed figures from history and legend to crowd the theatrical stage and the pages of books. To give some idea of the scale of the repression that accompanied the adulation, according to figures that have now been released by the present leader of China, Deng Xiaoping, 2.9 million people purged or imprisoned during the Cultural Revolution had been rehabilitated, of course in many cases posthumously, by 1979.[16] The numbers of those done to death alone are estimated by usually reliable sources at 400,000.

Like Russia after Stalin, China after Mao remains an authoritarian state with a tightly controlled population; but it is not the nightmare state of Mao's last period. The elusive phenomenon dissipated when Big Brother died. No more frenzied eroticism, no more paroxysms of hatred, and no more extremes of paralyzing fear.

This phenomenon can exist in small forms as well as large, in little assemblages as well as great states. And it can come into existence among us. This is shown by accounts of the People's Temple Colony of Americans transplanted to Guyana and ruled by a Big Brother named Reverend Jim Jones, whose megalomaniacal feelings drove him, finally, to ask the last sacrifice of his little flock of 900 men, women, and children, their collective suicide when his cause was lost. It was an act reminiscent of Hitler's effort to bring Germany down to destruction when he saw his cause was lost. In his limitlessly egocentric mind, the Fatherland, not having proved worthy of its *Fuehrer*, deserved to be destroyed.

V

In *1984*, Winston Smith is obsessed by an overwhelming question. As a functionary of the Ministry of Truth, he knows how the system works, but he can't puzzle out why it does the things that it does. He says: "I understand *How;* I do not understand *Why.*" This is Orwell's question, I think, expressed through his hero.

Winston suspects that the mystery of the *why* is bound up with the answer to a further question: Does Big Brother really exist?

Reading Emmanuel Goldstein's forbidden book, *The Theory and Practice of Oligarchical Collectivism,* he finds a negative answer: "Big Brother," writes Goldstein, "is the guise in which the Party chooses to exhibit itself to the world. His function is to act as a focusing point for love, fear and reverence, emotions which are more easily felt towards an individual than towards an organization."

Winston wasn't satisfied: "He had still, he reflected, not learned the ultimate secret. He understood *how;* he did not understand *why.*"

Then, when he and Julia are found to be engaged in a love affair and to be secret followers of Goldsteinism, and are taken to the Ministry of Love for interrogation under torture, he takes the opportunity to ask the interrogator, O'Brien: "Does Big Brother exist?" O'Brien replies: "Of course he exists. The Party exists. Big Brother is the embodiment of the Party."

Winston: "Does he exist in the same way as I exist?"

"You do not exist," said O'Brien.

As for the secret *why* of it all, O'Brien says to Winston: "The object of persecution is persecution. The object of torture is torture. The object of power is power."

O'Brien was either misinformed or lying. For the truth that history has revealed about the *why* is that *Big Brother really existed*. He exists in every instance of the nightmare state, and it is his needs—above all the colossal grandiosity, the need to be adored, worshipped by millions of subjects, and to gain never-ending vindictive triumphs over hated enemies—that motivate, under his near-total domination, the life of the society and the workings of the state. They motivate its repression of every fact that contradicts a Big Brother's monstrously inflated image of himself as one who could never err; its insistence on some form of a culture of anti-sex so that all erotic emotion can focus on the single object at the center of it all; its projection of violent hatred upon the collective and individual enemy figure; and its twisting of historical reality to conform with the demands of Big Brother's demented self. Understandably, the fulfillment of such a set of needs necessitates virtual totality of control by the state over the inner as well as outer lives of its subjects. It has to be a total state, or something very close to it.

Orwell did not see the "him" at the source of the "it." Yet his genius broke through the obstacle of abstract sociopolitical reasoning at the end of the book, where Winston Smith, having been utterly broken by unbearable torture,

> gazed up at the enormous face. Forty years it had taken him to learn what kind of smile was hidden beneath the dark moustache. O cruel, needless misunderstanding! O stubborn, self-willed exile from the loving breast! Two gin-scented tears trickled down the sides of his nose. But it was all right, everything was all right, the struggle was finished. He had won the victory over himself. He loved Big Brother.

In the person of his creation, Winston Smith, Orwell showed that the real purpose was not power for power's sake or torture for torture's sake or persecution for persecution's sake; it was to get everybody who counted to love Big Brother and to hate everyone Big Brother hated.

But that understanding was in Orwell's artist mind; it was not in his intellectual mind. There he failed to comprehend the *why*. His failure was manifestly not his own alone; it was the failure of a generation of powerful, uncomprehending theorists who influenced his thinking about the elusive phenomenon.

Had not the real-life Goldstein, Trotsky, written in his book *The Revolution Betrayed* in 1937: "Stalin is the personification of the bureaucracy. That is the substance of his intellectual personality."[17] Orwell certainly read that book.

Had not Franz Neumann written in his *Behemoth* in 1942 that the totalitarian state must *not* be seen as a *Fuehrerstaat*, despite its proclamation of the *Fuehrerprinzip* and its ruler cult? For the doctrine of one-man rule was, he wrote, "merely a device to prevent insight into the operation of the social-economic mechanism," in which "The decisions of the Leader are merely the result of the compromises among the four leaderships."[18] Orwell very likely read this book too.

These and other brilliant minds resisted the thought that Big Brother as a person might be "the very essence," "the linch-pin," or "the nerve" of the phenomenon with which they were dealing, although acceptance of that thought would in no way absolve the Eichmanns, the Berias, and thousands of other executors of Big Brother's will of their full share of responsibility for the misdeeds they committed in the leader's name.

But all credit still goes to Orwell for what he did do in his book: he showed us this infinitely evil thing in action. He gave us the *how*, without which the answer to the *why* wouldn't really take us very far. In his own way he told us the truth about the nightmare state, where, by virtue of various techniques of control and manipulation, the inner workings of a dictatorial leader's mind are institutionalized in outer political life. The fantasies of a Big Brother—fantasies of being loved by the multitude of people, of being the savior, the hero, of being omnipotent, and of wreaking a terrible vengeance upon those he has come to hate as enemies—are enacted for him by servile functionaries and masses of often deluded men, women, and children.

Perhaps a better name for it would be Big Brother's "fantasy state." The fantasies are enacted for him in the most diverse settings and forms: in courtrooms where purge trials take place and the victims, after confessing their crimes, abase themselves by paying a final public tribute to him, their murderer, upon pronouncement of the death sentence; in theaters where idealized versions of his fantasied hero's life are performed for him by talented artists; in mass rallies where people by the tens of thousands enact their adoration of him; in schools where children are taught to thank him for their happy lives and, if need be, to denounce even their parents as his enemies; in concentration camps where hated ones are destroyed in awful ways for whatever he fancies their crimes have been; and perhaps on battlefields where soldiers go into battle for his greater glory.

It is his fantasies that are being enacted by contrivance of the organs of the state; and he, in whose mind the fantasies arose, is not only the author but also the appreciative spectator of the performance, because he believes it. When he dies or is displaced, the show is over. What's left behind is death and misery, guilt and the denial of guilt, wasted lives, memories of horror, another authoritarianism with its army, police, and other institutions—the ruins of the fantasy state.

This, it seems to me, is the message to us of psychological understanding and history, including the now no longer so mysterious history of those two indubitable cases—Hitler's Germany and Stalin's Russia.

7 On "Failed Totalitarianism"

I

George Orwell's *1984* was first published in 1949. By then, many of its major themes had been anticipated, both in conservative literature and in the internal debates of the democratic left (and in earlier anti-utopian novels, like Zamyatin's *We* and Huxley's *Brave New World*). Yet, in another sense, Orwell was a forerunner: the major theoretical works on totalitarianism as a political regime—on its origins, history, and internal character—all appeared in the early and middle fifties. It is as if *1984* released the flood, and writers of all sorts (many of them, unlike Orwell, refugees from totalitarian states) hurried forward to complete or revise Emmanuel Goldstein's *Theory and Practice of Oligarchical Collectivism.* Hannah Arendt's *Origins of Totalitarianism* appeared in 1951, Jacob Talmon's *Origins of Totalitarian Democracy* in the same year; Czeslaw Milosz's *Captive Mind* came out in 1953; C. J. Friedrich's *Totalitarianism,* an important collection of essays, appeared in 1954 and marked the academic arrival of the new theory; Zbigniew Brzezinski published his *Permanent Purge* in 1956, and Friedrich and Brzezinski's *Totalitarian Dictatorship and Autocracy* came out in the same year.

These books are often treated as if they were so many volleys in the developing cold war—efforts to draw the line between the

---

Author's note: Some paragraphs of this paper are drawn from my essay on J. L. Talmon and the theory of totalitarianism, prepared for a colloquium in Talmon's memory held in Jerusalem in June 1982, under the sponsorship of the Israel Academy of Sciences and Humanities.

free world and Communist tyranny and to define the Russian enemy as the very embodiment of evil. Perhaps they played that role; certainly their arguments, in vulgarized form, made useful propaganda. But the collective effort to understand what had happened in Germany and Russia was immensely serious, and the level of analysis in the books I have listed was very high. Nor was the distinction between freedom and tyranny their central point. The major theoretical argument of Orwell's book and of all the books that followed is the startling novelty of totalitarian politics. Totalitarianism is a new kind of regime, different not only from liberal democracy but also and more importantly from every previous form of tyranny. "By comparison with that existing today, all the tyrannies of the past were half hearted and inefficient"—thus Orwell's Goldstein.[1] "Modern totalitarian democracy," Talmon wrote a few years later, ". . . is completely different from the absolutism wielded by a divine-right king or by a usurping tyrant."[2] *Completely different,* something new under the sun, the terrible creation of our own contemporaries.

The argument that totalitarianism represents a radical break even within the long history of unfreedom has recently been revived by a group of conservative intellectuals.[3] They are right, it seems to me, to stress the importance of the argument. But the distinction they go on to draw between totalitarian and "authoritarian" regimes plays a part in their work that the theorists of the fifties never intended: it functions very much like and often simply replaces the cold war distinction between communism and the free world. Indeed, it is one of the purposes of conservative intellectuals to revive the spirit of the cold war. The shift in terminology suggests a certain loss of confidence in the idea of a *free* world—a loss that helps to explain, perhaps, the increasing stridency with which we are called upon to defend not only free but also tyrannical regimes, so long as they are not totalitarian. Still, the argument for novelty is interesting and deep, and I mean to consider it here at some length. I shall adopt the conservatives' terms, using "authoritarian" to refer to all the forms of unfreedom—tyrannies, oligarchies, military dictatorships, colonial regimes, and so on—save for those that resemble Nazism and Stalinism.

II

Three factors above all mark the novelty of totalitarian regimes as they are described in the theories of the 1950s. The first is the political mobilization of the masses. Totalitarianism, we are told, is incompatible with passivity; it draws its special power from a disciplined, active, engaged population; it requires people who *march*. [4] In a sense, then, totalitarianism is the heir of all those democratic and Socialist movements that first brought the people into the political arena. But it is a strange heir who disowns his heritage, and it might more easily be said that totalitarianism represents the demobilization of democratic parties, movements, and unions—the transformation of political action into ritual performance and of arguments into slogans. What is necessary is that the people be present and accounted for, available for demonstrations and mass meetings. But discipline, action, and engagement are required only from the members of the new elite, the totalitarian party. Orwell saw this clearly, more clearly, I think, than theorists transfixed by the idea of totality. The collectivism of the Ingsoc regime of *1984* derives indeed from English socialism, but the institutional structures that the Socialists built have been dismantled, and the "proles" they organized have been returned to a state of apolitical quiescence. Popular mobilization consists only in this: that insofar as the people have any public life at all, it is planned and run by party officials.

The second mark of totalitarianism is its extraordinary sense of purpose. Authoritarian rulers aim only to stay in power; but the totalitarian party aims at the creation of a new humanity and a perfect regime. Talmon called this commitment "political messianism" because it suggested the possibility of reaching the end of days through sheer political willfulness. If the people are to march, they must march somewhere, and where else but to the promised land, the messianic kingdom? No other goal could possibly sustain the spirit of the marchers. Here again, totalitarianism appears as the heir of the left, building upon revolutionary aspiration as church officials once built upon eschatological hope. But others can build here too. *Novus ordo seclorum,* a new cycle of the ages: these words are engraved on the Great Seal of the United States and suggest that a non-totalitarian and a secular politics can also be founded upon revolutionary aspiration. The theorists of the fifties must have thought that the special mark of totalitarianism was to take revolutionary aspiration seriously and to use state power to enforce its ends. But we might follow Orwell and describe this use of power as an example of *doublethink,* simultaneously genuine and deeply cynical. It only intermittently determines the policies of the totalitarian party; most often it serves purely hortatory and legitimizing purposes, like other and older ideologies. Power is actually used with other ends in mind.

The third mark is the decisive one. Totalitarianism involves a systematic effort to control every aspect of social and intellectual life. Thus the Nazi *Gleichschaltung,* the top-down coordination of economy, politics, education, religion, culture, and family.[5] Radical control, control in detail: perhaps earlier rulers dreamed of such a thing, but it became technically feasible—this is one of the central themes of *1984*—only in the twentieth century.

Orwell suggests that control has two forms, negative and positive. The proles are merely pacified, like a colonial population; it is enough if they neither think nor act in an oppositionist way. But Party members are conceived to have made a profound commitment to political life (again, the model derives from the revolutionary movement) and to have accepted the discipline of the collective. So their lives are carefully shaped and directed; their every movement is watched; they are allowed no private thoughts or feelings, no respite from political enthusiasm. They are expected to live, writes Orwell's Goldstein, "in a continuous frenzy of hatred of foreign enemies and internal traitors, triumph over victories, and self-abasement before the power and wisdom of the Party."[6] One might think that this intense and pervasive discipline is somehow functional to the stated purposes of the Party, much as worker solidarity is functional to the purposes of trade unionism. But the only purpose of Party discipline, Orwell argues, is greater discipline. Totalitarianism is the exercise of power for its own sake. Hannah Arendt makes a similar point when she writes that the totalitarian regime finds its perfect form not in the messianic kingdom but in the death camp.[7] We never control a man so totally as when we kill him. Orwell had already taken the argument one step further: Winston Smith is alive at the end of *1984* and ready at last to acknowledge that he loves the leader of the Party. We never control a man so totally as when we seize his soul.

Totalitarianism can be described as the absolute reversal of radical politics: popular movements are demobilized and replaced by a disciplined elite party; revolutionary hope is turned into an ideology of domination; social control is intensified to the point where commitment and self-discipline lose all meaning. To a significant degree, obviously, the reversal is self-inflicted—at least in the sense that revolutionary movements destroyed or fatally weakened the old authority structures and then were unable to replace them with democratic institutions. (Whenever the replacement was successful—even when, as in France, it was precariously successful—totalitarian politics had little appeal.) Totalitarianism is parasitic on failed revolutions; this is so when its agents are themselves revolutionaries, like Stalin, and when they are counterrevolutionaries, like Hitler. Ingsoc is parasitic on English socialism, which it defeats and replaces. And the novelty of totalitarianism is tied, backhandedly, to the novelty of radical politics—to the hopes it engendered, the discipline it taught, and the people it organized.

III

But I don't want to concede that novelty, for the argument looks rather different today from the way it did in 1949 and the years immediately following. What struck Orwell, Arendt, Talmon, Milosz, and the others was the sheer success of totalitarian politics. Nazism had been defeated only by overwhelming external force. Inside Germany it seemed to have overcome all opposition, and its officials had actually carried through the systematic murder of millions of people. Stalinism was triumphant not only in Russia but in eastern Europe, and then in China, too. Milosz's captive minds were really captive. If *1984* was a piece of political science fiction, it hardly required any great imaginative leap. The speeches of Stalinist officials were already written in something very much like Newspeak, and I don't think Orwell doubted that the two-way television set would actually be in use by 1984, if not sooner.

Compared with all this, merely authoritarian regimes can indeed be made to look like a kind of small-time thuggery: amateurish, corrupt, inefficient. Perhaps, as Orwell's Goldstein says, "the ruling groups were always infected to some extent by liberal ideas" (though it's not hard to list authoritarian rulers of whom that can't plausibly be said); in any case, they "were content to leave loose ends everywhere."[8] They were not ambitious, or they did not have the resources to realize their ambitions. Most of their subjects lived, as they had always lived, more or less at peace.

It was never the intention of the theorists of the fifties to celebrate authoritarianism, but perhaps the celebration is a natural step once the contrast has been drawn in this way. Contemporary conservatives have taken the step with calculated ease. Since authoritarian rulers aren't even touched by messianism, since they neither seek nor pretend to seek social transformation, since all they want is to hold on to their power and prerogatives, not to exercise greater and greater power, they don't produce the terrible upheavals of totalitarian politics. They don't attack the traditional social structure, or turn millions of their subjects into refugees, or systematically murder men, women, and children because of their ethnic identity or their class standing: so we are told. The human costs of their rule are hardly worth noticing.

But this is to make both politics and political theory a great deal easier than they are. The contrast between totalitarianism and authoritarianism makes sense if we imagine Hitler's and Stalin's regimes as permanent political systems (or as theoretical ideal types). But the contrast makes less sense if we focus on the regimes that are today called totalitarian, that is, if we query the permanence of the totalitarianism described by the theorists of the fifties. The query is appropriate because it is one of the points of the contrast—emphasized heavily by contemporary conservatives—that totalitarianism is stable in a way that authoritarianism is not. The brutality of old-fashioned tyrants is temporary, a brief eruption; authoritarian regimes come and go. But the totalitarian state, because of the deep transformations it brings about and the intense control it exercises over its subjects, is something entirely different; totalitarianism is a long dark night.[9] Is this an accurate account of contemporary politics?

Is it, for that matter, an accurate account of the history of authoritarianism? The easy contrast surely misconstrues the impact of old-fashioned tyranny on its subjects and victims. Consider the tyranny of conquest and imperial rule: the Spanish destruction of Aztec civilization, for example, or the terrible cruelty of the early years of Belgian rule in the Congo. Hannah Arendt begins her own account of the origins of totalitarian politics with the last of these (and with European imperialism generally), though the three features that make for the novelty of totalitarianism are none of them present. Or consider the history of religious repression: Louis XIV's destruction of French Protestantism, for example. The Massacre of St. Bartholomew's Night may represent a brief eruption of brutality, but Louis's campaign was sustained over many years, and it was largely successful, a triumph of authoritarian rule. Or consider the history of ethnic persecution: the slaughter of Armenians by Turks in the early 1900s or the killings of Bengalis in what was then East Pakistan in 1971. In both these cases, there is considerable evidence of planning and coordination. Or consider the history of political terror: the proscriptions of the late Roman republic and the early empire, when the political elites of the city were systematically slaughtered, first by one military faction, then by another, and finally by the early emperors and their henchmen, seeking not total but absolute power; or the more far-reaching terror of the Zulu emperor Shaka, which has been powerfully evoked in Victor Walter's well-known study and which sounds indeed like a primitive totalitarianism—except, again, that none of the special features of totalitarian politics are present.[10]

I don't mean to compare any of these examples of authoritarian brutality with the Holocaust or the Gulag. But the list makes an important point. Old-fashioned authoritarianism is neither petty nor benign. It was the peace that tyrants brought, after all, that was once called the peace of the grave.

> Mark! where his carnage and his
> conquests cease!
> He makes a solitude and calls it—peace![11]

Seizing power and staying in power can both be a brutal business. Aristotle certainly understood this when he advised the tyrants of his own time on how to maintain their position: break up traditional patterns of association, cut off the natural leaders of the people, sow distrust and mutual suspicion.[12] It is not an unambitious program, and it doesn't support the radical distinction between authoritarianism and totalitarianism. Even the least efficient of authoritarian rulers makes some gesture toward a program of this sort. And what is totalitarianism as an ideal type but a superbly successful Aristotelian tyranny?

IV

Hitler and Stalin briefly approached the "ideal," and so they encouraged theoretical idealization. But I shall attend more closely to the epigones of Hitler and Stalin, the men who come after, the heirs and imitators. Mass mobilization, political messianism, and intense social control are supposed to produce a new age and a new human being. Totalitarianism does not build upon an existing social base; it creates the material and moral foundations of its own existence. But is there any evidence that any totalitarian regime has accomplished anything like this anywhere in the world?

The place to begin is with the elite movement or party that replaces all the demobilized movements, parties, unions, cooperative associations, sects, factions, and so on. Totalitarianism in the theory of the fifties is more clearly a kind of movement than a kind of state. It requires agitation, disturbance, crisis—the "continuous frenzy" that Orwell describes. Political (as distinct from religious) messianism is an impossible creed without a lively sense of motion, the constant overcoming of material obstacles and, what is probably more important because more dangerous and stirring, of human enemies. The movement must move, the members must march, toward the end of days. In the course of the struggle for power, the movement cultivates this sense of motion, and can't relinquish it afterwards. In power, too, the movement requires permanent revolution, permanent war, or what Brzezinski called "permanent purge," else enthusiasm flags and the new regime, committed in principle to total transformation, is itself transformed into something less than total. When things slow down, when patterns emerge and institutions and relationships take on some sort of stability, totalitarian rule becomes impossible.

Social control, too, at least in the heightened form that Orwell gives it, is dependent upon continuous upheaval, crisis, struggle, and instability. All those together breed uncertainty and distrust among the people or among the members of the Party, and mutual distrust (as Aristotle said) is the key to all the forms of tyrannical rule. The greater the distrust, the more total the tyranny. The totalitarian movement-state strives to break up every sort of loyalty among individuals, from class solidarity to friendship and family love, and then to focus undifferentiated loyalty on the Party or the leader of the Party: thus Orwell's Big Brother, whom no one really knows. Every more specific brotherhood is systematically attacked.

The attack on the family is the most important of totalitarianism's internal wars; it has a characteristic form that we know from Russian history. Orwell provides a literal portrait in his account of the Parsons family, which concludes: "It was almost normal for people over thirty to be frightened of their own children. And with good reason, for hardly a week passed in which the *Times* did not carry a paragraph describing how some eavesdropping little sneak—'child hero' was the phrase generally used—had overheard some compromising remark and denounced his parents to the Thought Police."[13]

The reference here is to a specific historical incident. In 1932, Pavlik Morozov, a Russian boy in his early teens and a member of the Young Pioneers, denounced his father to Stalin's secret police. Pavlik was killed by angry relatives and subsequently made into a martyr and "hero" by the Soviet press: the model of a child who put party and state above "old-fashioned" loyalties. But who could live with such a child? Home would become an unendurable place. And what is unendurable won't be endured, not for long at any rate; parents and children will find their way back to some more stable and trusting pattern of family relations. Recently, a Russian newspaper reviewed the brief history of "child heroes" and concluded: "There is something fundamentally unnatural in having a child . . . assailing the holy of holies—respect and love for father and mother."[14] A society in which this "holy of holies" is recognized in the official press may be an awful society in many ways, but it is, again, something less than totalitarian.

Something less: the problems with the ideal type can be seen with special clarity in all those countries to which totalitarianism was exported by force of arms. It is as hard to reproduce as to sustain the sense of perpetual motion on which totalitarian politics depends. The "frenzy" of party members will seem especially peculiar and artificial if there hasn't been a local struggle for power. Political messianism doesn't follow the sword. Totalitarian states can acquire an empire, as the Russians have done in eastern Europe, and they can insist upon the supremacy of the party in the lands they conquer. But whereas in its own country the party is simultaneously the heir and the annihilator of revolutionary aspiration, in the countries of the empire, it is an annihilator simply—and then an agent of foreign rule. It doesn't generate any sort of enthusiasm; its captive minds are prisoners of necessity, not converts to a messianic faith. Among the demobilized people, it produces sullen resentment and sporadic resistance. The governments of eastern Europe, especially after the East German rising of 1953, the Hungarian Revolution of 1956, the Czech spring of 1968, the rise and fall of Poland's Solidarity Union in 1980–81, all look like authoritarian regimes, dressed up, as it were, in the ideology of totalitarianism. They rule by brute force—not even their own brute force—and they are concerned above all with holding on. But this is what the leaders of the totalitarian homeland look like too, once the struggle for power has receded into the past; it is as hard to sustain as to export and reproduce the crucial sense of permanent crisis.

V

Stalin's epigones in Russia (and now Mao's in China) rule their own country like imperial bureaucrats; they resemble the puppets they have installed in neighboring states, and they share the same devitalized purpose. Stalinism might have endured had Stalin lived forever, a figure embodying and evoking terror, personalizing the seizure of power . . . and then the seizure of more and more power. In another of the essays in this book, Robert Tucker explores the importance of personality and of the "cult of personality" in totalitarian politics. For reasons he helps us understand, the most intense social control has been achieved under the most heightened form of personal rule.[15] Orwell recognized this fact earlier than anyone else (except, perhaps, the totalitarian leaders themselves), and he proposed to solve the succession problem by making Big Brother immortal: in *1984*, the faceless Party rules permanently behind the mask of an eternal Stalin.

Only an extraordinary lack of ambition among the epigones, however, would make this a plausible solution. In fact, would-be leaders are always waiting for the Leader to die (and he does die). Conceivably, the first succession crisis is functional to the movement-state; it makes for struggles, denunciations, and purges. But the results are so frightening that the survivors are likely to decide, as Stalin's survivors decided, to do things differently next time. And then the charisma doesn't pass on. The installation of a totalitarian leader is unimpressive without the sacrament of blood. In the regime of the epigones, the frenzy ceases, enthusiasm fades. The end of days becomes nothing more than a rhetorical flourish. Ideological zeal is a sign only of conformity and not of conviction. Corruption and cynicism are common at every level of society. About China's rulers we know very little, but the leaders of Russia today are very much like old-fashioned oligarchs: heavy, suspicious, uninspired, brutal—and, like their counterparts in the empire, holding on.

Is Russia today usefully described as a totalitarian regime? One way to answer this question is to talk in terms of a Weberian routinization: the end of days has been postponed, not forgotten; the party has settled in for the long haul; working for the cause has been transformed from a calling into a career. But I think that an argument of this sort misses the main point. When Weber talked about the routinization of charisma, he did not mean to describe the death of charisma. Christianity after its routinization was still a vibrant faith. For all the weight of its new institutions and the frequent corruption of their person- nel, its leaders still inspired awe; its central theological doc- trines were still capable of evoking passionate belief, disinter- ested conduct, artistic and intellectual creativity. No one can say that of Soviet Marxism today. I suppose it isn't inconceiv- able that there could be a political messianist revival or even a Communist Reformation. But neither of these seems likely. The truth is that none of the totalitarian creeds was rich enough or resonant enough to sustain popular enthusiasm or official recti- tude for long. Perhaps no this-worldly creed can survive the survival of this world. Totalitarianism is far more dependent than religious messianism upon a quick success. The revolu- tions, wars, purges, crises must have a visible end—and then they must have an end. And this suggests that the movement- state may not be capable of routinization but only of decay. Russia today is a dictatorship resting on popular apathy, the hollow shell of a totalitarian regime.

The oligarchs are still brutal, and political opposition is still a dangerous and most often a lonely business. There is no space for dissent or debate, no space for a free intellectual or cultural life. Bureaucratic and police control are probably more strict than in most historical and contemporary authoritarian states. But whether the strictness is an aftereffect of the Stalinist terror or some more lasting feature of the post-Stalinist regime re- mains unclear. The officials of the regime believe, and they are probably right, that their power can be maintained only by upholding the apparatus of the movement-state—*Gleichshalt- ung,* parallel hierarchies, party discipline, secret police, and so on—even if none of these serves any "higher" purpose, even if the movement-state doesn't move. Hence no political or cul- tural thaw can ever be allowed to usher in a genuine spring. Still, in describing the regime of the oligarchs, it is hard to strike the apocalyptic note so easily struck in the 1950s. One can imagine struggles for power, large-scale proscriptions, great cruelties still to come. But the ideological frenzy and the idealized savagery of the Stalin years look now like a moment in history and not like an historical era. The moment can be repeated in new places, as it has recently been repeated in Cambodia, but it can't be sustained.

I suspect that this conclusion is implicit in the literature of the 1950s, just as it is inherent in the phenomenon that literature attempted to explain. If totalitarianism finds its perfection in the death camps, then it can only be a temporary society. A regime that systematically murders its own people is in one respect at least like a utopian community whose members are pledged to celibacy: neither one of them can last indefinitely. Nor is there any such thing in human life as "continuous frenzy." Nor is there an imaginable political elite that will accept and live with the reality of a "permanent purge." Nor, finally, is it possible to conceive of an ongoing social system in which every participant radically distrusts every other (even if all of them love Big Brother). Totalitarianism as an ideal type cannot be realized in fact, or it cannot endure. That is true, of course, of all ideal types, but here the common truth has a special pointedness. For totalitarianism *is* the idealization of authoritarian rule. It is Weber's "typological simplification" ruthlessly put into practice: Aristotle's advice to tyrants brought to its logical conclusion, Shaka's terror turned systematic, the Roman proscriptions universalized, and so on. If the idealization doesn't work in the real world, then the theory of totalitarianism needs to be revised.

Orwell makes the most heroic and perhaps the most original attempt to defend the long dark night thesis. The crucial means of totalitarian endurance, he argues in his novel and more explicitly in the Appendix to the novel, is Newspeak, a language actively fostered by the Ingsoc regime, designed to replace conventional English. Totalitarian endurance is usually seen as an institutional problem; Orwell sees it as an epistemological problem. The solution lies in creating a language that serves "as a medium of expression for the . . . mental habits proper to the devotees of Ingsoc" and that "makes all other modes of thought impossible."[16] Not only explicitly oppositionist thought; every form of irony, sarcasm, doubt, hesitation must be eliminated from the minds of the people, and this is to be achieved in the most direct and simple way: words simply won't be available to formulate, let alone express, ironic, sarcastic, doubtful, or hesitant thoughts. Were Newspeak established, Orwell writes, "ideas inimical to Ingsoc could only be entertained in a vague wordless form. . . ." This probably means that inimical "ideas" could not be entertained at all. Even vague feelings of unease about the regime, of the sort that "can't be put into words," probably require words before they can be felt—for otherwise they would be nothing more than sensations, and the connection to the regime could not consciously be grasped. Success here means that every inner thought and feeling, even vague thoughts and feelings, would be ideologically controlled. Moreover, to someone who knew only Newspeak, every past utterance would be literally incomprehensible. The break with the past would be definitive, and the projection of the present into the future would be permanent.

But Orwell's argument confuses vocabulary with language, and it confuses the writing of a dictionary with the establishment of a vocabulary. Indeed, the regime can control the dictionary, and it can control the teaching of language in the schools and the use of language in all published materials. There is no reason to think, however, that it can control ordinary conversations or that it can bar slang usages or dominate entirely the rhythms, intonations, juxtapositions, and so on that constitute what we can think of as the linguistic resources of any people who can speak at all. At least, it can't do these things through linguistic means, but only through social and political means: by listening in on every conversation and punishing anyone who speaks (or pauses in speech, or shrugs while speaking) inappropriately. The regime can't rest on Newspeak, then, because the success of Newspeak depends on the success of the regime. Social control is the precondition of linguistic control, and if social control is anything less than total, "ideas inimical to Ingsoc" will find expression.

These won't necessarily be oppositionist ideas. What is more likely than opposition, as I have already suggested, is cynicism and corruption. The decay of the totalitarian regime will leave its mark in the language, as in the conduct, of the people—in the sardonic aside, the muttered reproach, the derisive joke, and at the same time, in the obsequious greeting and the overemphasized slogan. Here is the likely form of doublethink. It won't be a matter of simultaneously knowing and not-knowing, as Orwell thought, but rather of performing in a certain way while deriding the performance: a co-existence of opportunism and contempt. This is not a mental set consistent with the kind of political mobilization or messianic zeal described by the early theorists of totalitarianism, and while it represents an accommodation to social control, it is also an evasion of anything that can plausibly be called total control. Terror, wrote the Jacobin St. Just in his private journal, makes the heart grow cold.[17] There is no merely linguistic remedy for this coldness, no way in which words alone, however rigorously they are defined, can heat the heart.

VI

What are we to call this regime of coldness, this government of opportunists and cynics? I suggest that we call it "failed totalitarianism." It is the living tomb of a utopian—or better, of an anti-utopian—project. One might think of it as an authoritarian state with a peculiar (and a peculiarly brutal) history. In fact, however, failed totalitarianism is one of the more common forms of the modern state, and it isn't necessary to go through a Nazi or Stalinist terror in order to achieve it. One can also achieve it by imitation. Proclaim the messianist creed and establish the disciplined elite. Failure is instantaneous: no one believes the creed; everyone evades the discipline. But the result can be repressive enough, for the imitation commonly extends to torture, censorship, prison camps, secret police, and so on. Hence the single-party states of the Third World, with their faked ideologies and their ideologically justified brutality. These regimes are the work of political leaders who have, perhaps, the ambition but not the resources necessary for totalitarian rule; they can't quite manage the required upheaval, nor can they achieve a genuine *Gleichshaltung* of social spheres. Instead, they and their subjects enjoy what Veblen called the advantages of coming second: they escape the trauma of creation, the revolutionary crisis out of which totalitarian politics was born, and they inherit the most advanced, which in this case means the most decayed, form of the politics they imitate. The result is one or another variety of authoritarian rule, dressed up to look "total," in which this or that aspect of Communist or Fascist ideology is haphazardly acted out. A mixed regime, new but not importantly new—and that outcome may well suggest the future of those totalitarian states whose failure is more authentic.

We ought to distinguish, I think, between the moment of totalitarian terror and the regime that makes that moment possible. In our minds and memories the moment is (and should be) eternal: we can never forget it or give up trying to explain how it happened. But the regime has a short life, and we won't succeed in understanding it if we assign it a permanent place in the typologies of political science. That would be like sneaking the Apocalypse into a standard chronology. The end of days is not a date, and totalitarianism is not a regime. We might better think of totalitarianism as the name we give to the most frightening form of authoritarian rule. It is a form continuous with the other forms, but marked by a sense of secular willfulness that is immediately recognizable as a general feature of modern culture. Against a background of urbanization, economic development, nation-building, and large-scale warfare, tyrannical ambition is transformed: it reaches farther than ever before. But except in the matter of murder, it isn't notably successful. It doesn't produce a new man and a new woman; it doesn't produce a new language; it can't sustain the enthusiasm of its subjects or transform their primary loyalties. The thrust toward totality is so extravagant a version of willfulness that it is doomed to failure.

And failure brings with it what we can immediately recognize as a central feature of pre-modern culture: the rulers aim above all at maintaining themselves and serve no "higher" purpose. They repress their enemies, control their subjects, and look only for some marginal improvement in their domestic or international position. They make their peace with the family; their language is a bureaucratic version of Oldspeak; they make only the most routine ideological gestures. In a certain sense, they live off the memory of the totalitarian moment, but they have no intention of repeating that moment. They are the authoritarian autocrats and oligarchs of our own time, doing what autocrats and oligarchs have always done.

Failed totalitarianism, both in its authentic and in its exported and imitated versions, may well be one of the relatively stable forms of authoritarian politics. For its leaders, like the absolutist monarchs of the early modern period, have managed to create a fairly cohesive elite. The members of this elite are bound together more by place and privilege than by doctrinal commitment, more by personal than by ideological ambition, but they are bound together nonetheless; they don't break under pressure; they have too much to lose. It is not quite what Orwell imagined, though his juxtaposition of Party and proles does capture something of the class structure of failed totalitarianism. Djilas's *New Class,* which appeared just after the spate of books on totalitarian politics and which provides a useful corrective to their (anti-) utopianism, suggests what is probably a more accurate, and certainly a more conventional, sociology.[18]

Yet however cohesive the new class is, the regime it constitutes is not exempt from internal and unplanned transformations. That popular resistance is still possible has been demonstrated repeatedly in eastern Europe. "The proletarians will never revolt," O'Brien tells Winston Smith in *1984,* "not in a thousand years or a million. . . . There is no way in which the Party can be overthrown."[19]

As an account of the internal politics of the movement-state, this is surely wrong, for we have seen both the decay of the

Party and the power of the proles. Recent events in Poland suggest that one way of dealing with these phenomena, one response to the ultimate failure of failed totalitarianism, is a military takeover and an overt return to authoritarian rule. The situation isn't very different in pre-totalitarian tyrannies, which are also open to unplanned transformations—one of which, of course, is the totalitarian seizure of power itself. Indeed, the routine repressiveness of authoritarian regimes helps to account for the secretive, disciplined, and elitist character of the party that seizes power—and also for its (shortlived) mass appeal. Totalitarian ambition is bred by authoritarian politics, and terror on the Stalinist or Nazi model seems more likely to figure in the future of old-fashioned tyrannies than in the future of failed totalitarianisms.

The line that marks off these two is hard to draw, and to insist upon its central importance doesn't serve any useful political or moral purpose. More accurately, that insistence serves a repugnant purpose: it provides an apologia for authoritarian politics. That apologia was no part of the original theory, whose terms were fixed by the Holocaust and the Gulag. Orwell and those who followed him were driven to explain what looked indeed, though not in the sense of the messianic faith, like the end of days. But we must come to grips with the return of tyranny after the failures of messianism, with the sheer persistence of regimes that are ugly enough, though neither utopian nor anti-utopian—with *non-ideal brutality*.

This is the real world of 1984. The dominant fact about politics today is the dominance of repression, censorship, torture, and murder, all of a largely traditional kind, though the traditionalism is sometimes masked by ideological pretension. Authoritarian rule has turned out to be the true legacy of totalitarian movements and parties. I suspect it is also their nursing mother. Those who defend authoritarianism because it isn't "total" have failed to grasp the historical connection between what they defend and what they decry.

Leszek Kolakowski

8 Totalitarianism and the Virtue of the Lie

I

The validity of "totalitarianism" as a concept is occasionally questioned on the ground that a perfect model of a totalitarian society is nowhere to be found and that in no country among those which used to be cited as its best examples (the Soviet Union, especially under Stalin, Mao's China, Hitler's Germany) has the ideal of the absolute unity of leadership and of unlimited power ever been achieved.

This is not a serious obstacle. It is generally acknowledged that most of the concepts we employ in describing large-scale social phenomena have no perfect empirical equivalents. There has never been an absolutely pure capitalist society, which does not prevent us from making a distinction between a capitalist and pre-capitalist economy, and the distinction is very useful. The fact that there is no such thing as total freedom does not make the distinction between free and despotic regimes any less cogent or intelligible. Indeed, the best examples of totalitarian societies were arguably closer to their conceptual ideal than any capitalist society was to its abstractly perfect description. (Among arguments purporting to do away with the concept of "totalitarianism," the most absurd says that the Soviet Union, for instance, is in fact a "pluralist" system since there are always in the establishment some cliques or particular groups vying for power and influence. If this is a symptom of pluralism, then the concept is simply useless and meaningless, since all political regimes throughout history have been "pluralist" in this sense.)

There is no single cause on which we may place the responsibility for the emergence of a system that tries to give the state total power over all areas of human life, to destroy civil society entirely, and to extend state ownership over all things and all people. To be sure, power has always been sought by people as a value in itself, and not only as a means to gain wealth or other goods; this does not mean, however, that the phenomenon of totalitarianism may be casually explained by the thirst for domination inherent in human nature. The ambition for power and the struggle for it is quasi-universal, whereas the inner drive toward totalitarianism is not. Most of the despotic regimes we know in history were not totalitarian; they had no built-in tendency to regulate all realms of human activity, to expropriate people totally—physically and mentally—and to convert them into state property. Whether or not the term is properly used to describe some historical epochs in ancient China, Czarist Russia, or in certain theocratic societies and religious groups, or some primitive communities, modern totalitarianism is inseparably linked with the history of socialist ideas and movements. This does not mean that all the varieties of socialism are totalitarian by definition. European versions of totalitarianism—Russian Bolshevism, German Nazism, Italian fascism—were bastard offshoots of the socialist tradition; yet in bastard children a similarity to parents is preserved, too, and can be unmistakably perceived.

The socialist idea emerged in the early nineteenth century as the moral response of a few intellectuals to social misfortunes brought about by industrialization—the misery and hopelessness of working-class lives, marked by crises, unemployment, glaring inequalities as greed governed human motivations, dissolving traditional communities. In many respects these characteristics of post-revolutionary societies clearly converged with the attacks coming from reactionary romanticism and from emerging nationalist ideologies. Socialism was essentially about "social justice," even though there has never been an agreement about the meaning of this vague term. All versions of socialism implied a belief in social control of production and distribution of material goods (not necessarily the abolition of private property or a controlled economy run by the state). All predicted that social control would secure the welfare of all, prevent waste, increase efficiency, and eradicate "unearned income" (another concept for which there has never been a satisfactory definition). Most of them were not explicitly or intentionally totalitarian and some strongly stressed the value of cultural freedom.

Yet in those versions of socialism that relied upon the power of the state to achieve a just and efficient economy, intimations of a totalitarian philosophy can be found, at least in hindsight. Marxism was repeatedly attacked in the nineteenth century, especially by anarchist writers, as a program for unabashed state tyranny. Historical developments perfectly bore out this assessment. Paradoxically, however, the despotic nature of Marxian socialism was to some extent limited by that component of the doctrine which was prominent in its late nineteenth-century version, and eventually entirely discredited (rightly so) as superstitious wishful thinking: the notion of historical determinism, some of whose elements Marx had taken up from Hegel and the Saint-Simenians. For the Marxists of the Second International, the determinist faith acted, on the one hand, as a source of their ideological confidence and, on the other, as a warning that history cannot be violated. This was a natural basis for an evolutionary concept of socialism, and it played this role in "centrist" Social Democratic orthodoxy. The crisis of the socialist idea that revealed itself at the very beginning of the twentieth century was expressed, among other signs, in the (not quite unjustified) contention that if Socialists were to rely upon "historical laws" and expect the "economic maturity" of capitalism to nurture the revolutionary, they might just as well bid farewell to all socialist hopes. There were those for whom revolutionary will and the political opportunity to seize power were all that counted, and they produced two totalitarian versions of socialism: fascism and Bolshevism (Domenic Settembrini emphasizes the essential similarity of Lenin's and Mussolini's ideological approach very convincingly).

In both forms of totalitarian socialism—nationalist and internationalist—social control of production for the common good was stressed as essential. The model developed in the Soviet Union, China, and other Communist countries proved to be more consistent and more resilient than the fascist or Nazi varieties. It carried out the total nationalization of the means of production, distribution, and information, pretending to have created thereby the foundation of the Great Impossible—all-encompassing universal planning. It is clear, indeed, that a fully consistent totalitarian system implies complete state control of economic activity; therefore, it is conceivable only within a socialist regime. Fascism and Nazism did not attempt wholesale nationalization (their tenure was relatively short; the Soviet Union waited twelve years before incorporating agricultural production and the peasants themselves into state property). To this extent they were less totalitarian, insofar as they left segments of the society economically less dependent on state power. However, this does not at all imply that they were any "better" in human terms; indeed, in various ways Nazism was more barbarous than Bolshevism.

In both cases the overriding ideology stressed the idea of social justice and proclaimed that some chosen parts of mankind (a superior race or nation, a progressive class or vanguard party) had the natural right to establish uncontrolled rule by virtue of historical destiny. And, in both, the seizure of power was carried out under slogans that appealed to and incited envy as the driving revolutionary force. As in many (but not all) revolutionary movements, what was justice in doctrinal terms was, psychologically and practically, the pragmatism of envy. The immediate aim was to destroy the existing elites—whether aristocratic or meritocratic, plutocratic or intellectual—and to replace them with a parvenu political class. Needless to say, egalitarian ideologic ingredients, insofar as they played any role at all, could not long survive the seizure of power.

II

There is no need to prove that no modern society can dispense with a principle of legitimacy and that in a totalitarian society this legitimacy can only be ideological. Total power and total ideology embrace each other. The ideology is total in a much stronger sense, at least in its claims, than any religious faith has ever achieved. Not only does it have all-embracing pretensions, not only is it supposed to be infallible and obligatory; its aim (unattainable, fortunately) goes beyond dominating and regulating the personal life of every subject to the point where it actually replaces personal life altogether, reducing human beings into replicas of ideological slogans. In other words, it annihilates the personal form of life. This is much more than any religion has ever prescribed.

Such an ideology explains the specific function and specific meaning of the *lie* in a perfect totalitarian society, a function so peculiar and creative that even the word itself, "lie," sounds inadequate.

The crucial importance of the lie in the Communist totalitarian system was noticed long ago by Anton Ciliga, in his *Au pays du grand mensonge,* published in 1930; it took the genius of Orwell to reveal, as it were, the philosophical side of the issue.

What are the staff of the Ministry of Truth, where Orwell's hero is working in 1984, doing? They thoroughly destroy the records of the past; they print new, up-to-date editions of old newspapers and books; and they know that the corrected version will soon be replaced by another, re-corrected one. Their goal is to make people forget everything—facts, words, dead people, the names of places. How far they succeed in obliterating the past is not fully established in Orwell's description; clearly they try hard and they score impressive results. The ideal of complete oblivion may not have been reached, yet further progress is to be expected.

Let us consider what happens when the ideal has been effectively achieved. People remember only what they are taught to remember today and the content of their memory changes overnight, if needed. They really believe that something that happened a day before yesterday and which they stored in their memories yesterday, did not happen at all and that something else happened instead. In effect, they are not human beings any longer. Consciousness *is* memory, as Bergson would have put it. Creatures whose memory is effectively manipulated, programmed, and controlled from outside are no longer persons in any recognizable sense and therefore no longer human.

This is what totalitarian regimes keep unceasingly trying to achieve. People whose memory—personal or collective—has been nationalized, become state-owned and perfectly malleable, totally controllable, are entirely at the mercy of their rulers; they have been deprived of their identity; they are helpless and incapable of questioning anything they are told to believe. They will never revolt, never think, never create. They have been transformed into dead objects. They may even, conceivably, be happy and love Big Brother, which is Winston Smith's supreme performance.

This use of the lie is interesting not only politically but epistemologically as well. The point is that if physical records of some events and their recollection in human minds are utterly eradicated, and if consequently there is absolutely no way anybody can establish what is "true" in the normal sense of the word, nothing remains but the generally imposed beliefs, which, of course, can be again canceled the next day. There is no applicable criterion of truth except for what is proclaimed true at any given moment. And so, the lie really becomes truth or, at least, the distinction between true and false in their usual meaning has disappeared. This is the great cognitive triumph of totalitarianism: it cannot be accused of lying any longer since it has succeeded in abrogating the very idea of truth.

We can thus see the difference between the common political lie and its totalitarian apotheosis. The lie has always been employed for political purposes. Yet trivial lies and distortions used by politicians, governments, parties, kings, or leaders are far removed from the lie that is the very core of a political system, the heart of a new civilization. The former are used as a rule for specific purposes, as an instrument to achieve specific gains. The normal political lie leaves the distinction between truth and falsity intact. From the history of the Church we know a number of falsifications, distortions, and legends fabricated for well-defined goals. Constantine's contribution was a forgery that legitimated the Church's claims to political supremacy. It was exposed by a great ecclesiastical scholar and eventually recognized for what it was; so were many other legends that Catholic and Protestant historians examined and dismissed. The commemoration of the Three Kings was a contrivance to bolster the doctrine whereby the Church claimed supremacy over the secular powers. Yet the Church has not rewritten the Gospel of St. Matthew in order to justify the legend, and anybody can look into the text and see that there is no hint that the three wise men who visited the infant Jesus were actually monarchs. The story remains alive as an innocent, folkloristic event. Nobody knows who inserted "comma Johanneum" into the text of the Apostle's letter; this was an unpleasant problem, to be sure, but eventually Catholic editors of the New Testament came to recognize the insertion.

During the last few centuries Catholic and Protestant cultures have produced a large number of outstanding historians who, far from employing various sorts of *pia fraus* to embellish the annals of the Church, have pioneered in subjecting Church documents to critical examination. They have produced many works of everlasting value (and where are the Communist historians who are worthy of this respect?). The Church purified itself of forgeries and gained. The forgeries were, in fact, aimed at specific targets, unlike the modern totalitarian lie, of which the ultimate goal is the total mental and moral expropriation of people.

The destructive action of totalitarian machinery, no matter

whether or not the word is used,* is usually supported by a special kind of primitive social philosophy. It proclaims not only that the common good of the "society" has priority over the interest of individuals but that the very existence of individuals, as persons, is reducible to the existence of the social "whole"; in other words, personal existence is, in a strange sense, unreal. This is a convenient foundation for any ideology of slavery.

III

I have been talking, of course, of an ideal totalitarian society, of which the existing ones are (or were) only more or less successful approximations. Later Stalinism (and Marxism) was a reasonably fair approximation. Its triumph consisted not simply in that virtually everything was either falsified or suppressed —statistics, historical events, current events, names, maps, books (occasionally Lenin's texts)—but that the inhabitants of the country were trained to know what is politically "correct." In the functionaries' minds, the borderline between what is "correct" and what is "true," as we normally understand this, seems really to have become blurred; by repeating the same absurdities time and again, they began to believe or half-believe in them themselves. The massive and profound corruption of the language eventually produced people who were incapable of perceiving their own mendacity.

To a large extent this form of perception seems to survive, in spite of the fact that the omnipresence of ideology has been somewhat restricted recently. When the Soviet leaders maintain that they "liberated Afghanistan," or that there are no political prisoners in the Soviet Union, it is quite plausible to believe that they mean what they say: they have confounded linguistic ability to such an extent that they are incapable of using any other

---

*The adjective "totalitarian" was used in a positive sense by Mussolini and Gramsci but never by Soviet ideologists or, to my knowledge, by the Nazis.

word than "liberation" for a Soviet invasion and have no sense at all of the grotesque distance between language and reality. It takes a lot of courage, after all, to be entirely cynical; those who lie to themselves appear among us much more frequently than perfect cynics.

A very small and innocent anecdote. In 1950, in Leningrad, I visited the Hermitage in the company of a few Polish friends and we had a guide (a deputy director of the museum, so far as I remember) who was obviously a knowledgeable art historian. At a certain moment—no opportunity for ideological teaching dare be lost—he told us: "We have in our cellars, comrades, a lot of corrupted, degenerated bourgeois paintings. You know, all those Matisses, Cézannes, Braques, and so on. We have never displayed them in the museum but perhaps one day we will show them so that Soviet people can see for themselves how deeply bourgeois art has sunk. Indeed, Comrade Stalin teaches us that we should not embellish history." I was again in the Hermitage with other friends in 1957, at a time of a relative "thaw," and the same man was assigned to guide us. We were led to rooms full of modern French paintings. Our guide told us: "Here you see the masterpieces of great French painters—Matisse, Cézanne, Braque, and others. And," he added (no opportunity may be lost), "do you know that the bourgeois press accused us of refusing to display these paintings in the Hermitage? This was because at a certain moment some rooms in the museum were redecorated and temporarily closed and a bourgeois journalist happened to be here at that moment and then made this ridiculous accusation. Ha, ha!"

Did he lie? I am not sure. If I had reminded him of his earlier statement, which I failed to do, he would have simply denied everything with genuine indignation and he probably would have believed that what he told us was "right" and therefore true. Truth is, in this world, what reinforces the "right cause." The psychological mechanism operating in minds that were properly trained and twisted in a totalitarian mincer is a matter for Professor Festinger to analyze.

Lying as a matter of political expediency is itself not a particularly interesting phenomenon or worth investigation, so long as it is a lie pure and simple, devised for a special purpose. A minister said that he had not slept with this girl, but in fact he had; a president stated that he was not aware of what his subordinates had been doing, but in fact he was. Nothing mysterious and nothing exciting in such facts; they are ordinary by-products of political affairs. Lying becomes interesting in totalitarian systems not because of its extent and frequency but because of its social, psychological, and cognitive functions. For example, it would be very superficial to imagine that the lie as it appears in the Soviet press is a simple amplification and intensification of the normal political lie. Certainly, if one wishes to collect political lies, any issue of *Pravda (Truth)* or *Literaturnaya Gazeta* will do. Each issue is full of outright lies, suppressions, and omissions; and in each case the purpose they serve is obvious. They become remarkable only when seen within the grand machinery of education designed to build the New Civilization.

The cognitive aspect of this machinery consists in that it effaces the very distinction between truth and political "rightness." Its psychological function is important in that, by training people in this confusion and by inoculating them to believe that nothing is true in itself and that anything can be made true by the decree of authority, it produces a new "socialist man," devoid of will and of moral resistance, stripped of social and historical identity. The art of forgetting history is crucial: people ought to know that the past can be changed overnight—from truth to truth. In this manner they are cut off from what would be a source of strength in identifying and asserting themselves by recalling their collective past. The point is not that there is no teaching of history (though apparently there was hardly any in Mao's China; no books were available except for Mao's works and technical manuals) but that people know that what they are taught today is both "objectively" true and true for today only, and that the rulers are masters of the past. If

they get accustomed to that, they become people without historical consciousness, thus without the ability to define themselves except in relation to the state; they are non-persons,
perduta gente.

This mental and moral sterilization of society is, however,
blistered with dangers. It works so long as the totalitarian
regime, in dealing with its subject, needs only normal passive
obedience. If, in a moment of crisis, it needs personal motivations, the machinery fails. Stalinism was brought to such a crisis
during the war with Germany, when the only way to mobilize
the mass of Russians for defense was virtually to forget Marx-
ism-Leninism and to use specifically Russian historical symbols
and national feelings as an ideological weapon. An ideal totalitarian society consisting of malleable objects is strong in relatively stable conditions but very vulnerable in unstable ones.
This is one of the reasons why a perfect totalitarian regime (or
"the higher stage of socialism") can never be built.

No matter how much has been done to realize the great
ambition of totalitarianism—the total possession and control of
human memory—the goal is unattainable, and not only because human memory is strongly intractable. Nor is it because
the human being is an ontological reality. To be sure, it can be
immobilized by coercion, but it always strives to regain its
rights at the first opportunity. Even in the best of conditions the
massive process of forgery cannot be completed: it requires a
large number of forgers who necessarily have to understand the
distinction between what is genuine and what is faked (the
crudest example would be an officer in the military cartographic
office who has to have unfalsified maps at his disposal in order
to falsify the maps). The power of words over reality cannot be
unlimited since, fortunately, the reality imposes its own unal-
terable conditions. The rulers of totalitarian countries wish, of
course, to be truthfully informed, but time and again they fall
prey, inevitably, to their own lies and suffer unexpected defeats.
Entangled in a trap of their own making, they try awkward
compromises between the need of truth for themselves and the

quasi-automatic operations of a system that produces lies for everyone, including the producers.

Briefly: Since totalitarianism implies the complete control by the state of all areas of life and the unlimited power of an artificial state ideology over minds, it can achieve excellence only if it succeeds in eliminating the resistance of both natural and mental reality, in other words, in canceling the reality altogether. Therefore, when we talk about totalitarian regimes, we do not have in mind systems that have reached perfection, but rather those that are driven by a never-ending effort to reach it, to swallow all channels of human communication, and to eradicate all spontaneously emerging social life forms.

In this sense all Soviet-type regimes have been totalitarian, yet they have differed from each other in the degree of achievement—in the distance separating their real conditions from the inaccessible ideal.

It is fair to say, first, that in Central and East European Communist countries, the distance has always been larger than in the Soviet metropolis, the totalitarianism has never achieved the Soviet degree of efficiency, and, second, that in the Soviet Union itself, we have been observing the growth of distance, a movement backward from totalitarian perfection. We cannot pretend, however, to know the exact meaning of this process or to foretell its future course.

The slow but real retrogressive movement of Sovietism has nothing to do either with the lack of totalitarian will within the system and its ruling class or with the "democratization" of the regime. It consists in some reluctantly given, or rather, extorted concessions to irresistible reality. (Incredibly enough, Soviet ideologists in the early fifties managed to hamper the development of military technology by their obscurantist attacks upon "cybernetics.") For obvious reasons, totalitarian states—fortunately for the fate of mankind, unfortunately for the generations who live out their lives in this darkness—are inescapably and irreparably inefficient in economic management. All economic reforms in Communist countries, to the extent they yield any results, go in the same direction: partial liberation of the market mechanisms; in other words, partial restoration of "capitalism." The omnipotence of ideology proved to be disastrous in many areas subjected to its rule, and so its power had to be restricted. The crisis of legitimacy is patent as well as the desperate quest for a reshaped ideological foundation. As a result, the state ideology becomes more and more incoherent, meaningless, and elusive.

This does not imply that we may expect a gradual corrosion, which step by step will lead to a miraculous mutation and transform the totalitarian society into an "open" one. At least, no historical analogies are helpful in making this sort of prediction. As long as the built-in totalitarian drive, supported by the powerful vested interests of privileged classes, operates in the Sovietized territories, there is little hope for a progress that one day would imperceptibly cross the line separating despotism from democracy. The examples of Spain and Portugal are not very useful either, both because of the different international environment of those countries in the moment of their transition and because they had never been very close to totalitarian perfection. Let us give rein to our fantasy and imagine a day when the Soviet political system is roughly similar to that of Spain in the last ten years of Franco's rule. This would be hailed by enlightened and liberal opinion of the West as the greatest triumph of democracy since Pericles and would ultimately prove the infinite superiority of the "Socialist democracy" over the bourgeois order.

Still, a relatively nonviolent collapse of totalitarianism is imaginable and the frail hope for such a development was supported most strongly so far by the example of Poland in 1980–81. Among Soviet dependencies, Poland has notoriously been less consistent than others in totalitarian progress, all the monstrosities of Stalinism notwithstanding. My strong impression is that in the first postwar years the committed Communists (they were still in existence, unlike the sixties and later) were less corrupt mentally but more cynical than in other countries

—cynical not in the sense of not believing in the Communist idea but in that they had little "false consciousness." They knew that what the party tried to convey to "the masses" was a pure lie, and they approved it for the sake of the future blessings of the socialist community.

On the other hand, despite all the efforts of the rulers, despite the overwhelming burden of organized mendacity, Poland's cultural continuity has not been broken. Throughout the post-war decades any relaxation of political conditions, whatever historical accidents might have brought it about, immediately pushed the suppressed historical identity to the surface and displayed the glaring and incurable incompatibility of Communism with the deeply rooted traditional, national, religious, and political patterns. Historical books, whether printed in Poland or smuggled from abroad, if they were not tainted with official mendacity, have always enjoyed an enormous popularity, not only among the intelligentsia but—especially in the last years —among workers and young people.

The months of "Solidarity" seemed to have opened a new unexplored avenue whereby an inefficient and clumsy totalitarian system could conceivably be propelled toward a hybrid form that would include genuine elements of pluralism. The military dictatorship has temporarily crushed the organizational form of this movement, yet it has failed to destroy the hope. Indeed, the fact that the Communist tyranny does not even try to assert the principle of its legitimacy any longer and that it was compelled to appear without ideological disguise as a naked violence is itself a spectacular symptom of the decay of a totalitarian power system.

Milovan Djilas

Translated by Michael Petrovich

9 The Disintegration of Leninist Totalitarianism

I

What is totalitarianism? An ancient tyranny under new conditions, or a new phenomenon?

The totalitarianism of which we speak—that is, Leninist totalitarianism as established in Soviet Russia and imposed on the other East European lands—is beyond doubt the most complete, and most successful, tyranny of the industrial epoch. It was that very epoch, with its "scientific philosophies" and scientific production, that endowed Leninist totalitarianism with new, essential qualities that distinguish it from earlier tyrannies.

Though I believe that the critical investigation of a reality that actually exists brings us closer to the truth than any schematic formulations, I nevertheless think it useful to list those qualities of Leninist totalitarianism that seem essential:

1. The formation and entrenchment of the party bureaucracy ("vanguard of the proletariat," "the new class," "bureaucratic caste," "partocracy," "political class") as a privileged stratum.

2. The absolute authority of the party bureaucracy as an instrument of social change governing the life of the nation.

3. The monopoly of the party bureaucracy in manipulating key sectors of the economy, or, in the language of the bureaucrats, "Socialist property."

These characteristics are quintessential to the "Leninist" states, including that in Yugoslavia. They are also the characteristics that make these states different from past tyrannies. Even personal tyrannies such as Stalin's differ from classical tyrannies: the tyrant in the "Leninist" states is not only a tyrant but the leader of a mass movement and commander of a ruling social stratum. Yet it is also true that with the passage of time these characteristics have ceased to be absolute; they are no longer the *only* essential aspects of "Leninist" states. New forms of spiritual striving and social aspiration have penetrated all of these societies—in various ways, with different degrees of intensity. Not one East European state is any longer *purely* a Leninist totalitarianism, though none has ceased having strong totalitarian elements.

That holds for the Soviet Union as well, though among the Communist countries it comes closest to the "pure form" of totalitarianism. It also continues its efforts to impose totalitarianism on other nations, at least those that it has pressed into its military-imperial sphere. Yet even in the Soviet Union, concentration camps of the Stalinist (Gulag) type have diminished in number; the secret police no longer carries out summary punishment of "enemies" according to its own dictates. The courts, it is true, are controlled by the secret police and party agencies, but they do follow some formal procedures (such as they are) and are open to the public in a limited way. True, the number of political transgressors can be counted in the tens of thousands, and conditions in the "correctional" labor camps do not remotely resemble those in Western prisons. Yet things are considerably different from the Stalinist days when millions of camp prisoners were abandoned to the bullets of arbitrary officials or to death from starvation and exhaustion.

Nor does ideology reign supreme any more except in the sphere of "pure" politics. Deviations in art from ideological stereotypes and party "resolutions" are by now quite numerous, even in that "most sensitive" and popular branch, the cinema. Belittling their significance would simply lead to perverted, stereotyped anti-Communist conclusions. And, finally, though not least significant: side by side with the "Socialist" state economy there has developed in the Soviet Union an alternate economy (the free market for part of agricultural production, personal services by tradespeople, massive speculation and corruption, and all kinds of petty personal enterprise). According to Academician Sakharov's appraisal, that alternate economy reaches up to 15 percent of the value of Soviet production. It is also significant that the "Socialist" sector of the Soviet economy is actually forced to make use of the services of private craftsmen and middlemen in ever greater proportions. But most significant and most characteristic of the Soviet economy are tendencies—tendencies irresistibly emerging from time to time despite the thickheaded conservatism of the bureaucracy— toward reforming the "Socialist" sector, and thereby the economy as a whole, in the direction of profitability, that is, a free market.

It would be erroneous, and dangerous, to conclude from these phenomena that a change in the Soviet system is imminent or even in sight. Far from it! These phenomena only demonstrate that this system is not "perfect"—no longer a totalitarian tyranny in the full sense. In other words, these phenomena reveal that even the Soviet system is subject to its own inner crises. It would, however, be erroneous and dangerous to conclude that the reigning party bureaucracy in the Soviet Union will become more broadminded or pacific as the tendencies toward reforming the system multiply. The disintegration of totalitarianism in the Soviet Union is, in fact, only the "flip" side of the Soviet Union's transformation into a military empire, accomplished by Soviet expansionism over the entire globe.

True, the decisive steps in the transformation of a revolutionary Soviet Union into a military empire had already been accomplished under Stalin—closely tied with industrialization, the codification of ideology, and total terror. The military-imperial transformation is not the consequence of Stalin's reign but its very essence, lasting and immutable. The triumph of the party bureaucracy occurs simultaneously with the transformation of the state into an ideological military empire. Stalin understood that the "new class"—the party bureaucracy, and with it the revolution itself—would perish if it did not move toward monopolistic rule and expansionist policies. He acted accordingly, and the most "upwardly mobile" strata followed him, while he destroyed or suppressed the rest.

Unlike the Stalinist terror, which in time became intolerable to the bureaucracy, military imperialism continued to be the essential condition of the regime's survival. As Stalin's tyranny became transformed into a dictatorship of the party oligarchy, military imperialism became stronger, both relatively and absolutely.

The disintegration of totalitarianism—whose causes in the Soviet Union must be sought primarily in the requirements of that same party bureaucracy for a richer, less coercive and more secure existence—had as its consequence the strengthening of military imperial tendencies and "theory." The harsh Stalinist methods hampered the imperial aspirations of the party bureaucracy. All the more so because the party bureaucracy had to strengthen its empire in a period during which other Western empires were collapsing and when it found itself in a severe ideological and political confrontation with another dynamic world power, the United States of America. Accordingly, one should see in the disintegration of totalitarianism in the Soviet Union not only the weaknesses of the system but also a conscious, organized adaptation by the party oligarchy.

The disintegration of totalitarianism in the Soviet Union is a twofold process: the spontaneous emergence of new forms out of the decay of the system, and the imperatives of adaptation, given the expansionism of the ruling strata. And precisely because this is a twofold process, the oligarchic "conscious Socialist forces" not only do not wish but are not able to tolerate spontaneous opposition forces, let alone conscious, creative ones. By its very system, the Soviet Union is condemned to decay or to change, insofar as life allows, or at least insofar as this meets with the calculations of the ruling oligarchy. One should not soon expect fundamental or imminent changes in the Soviet system or a collapse of Soviet military imperialism, let alone the "dissolution" of the empire.

Ideology, too, has reflected the changes in the Soviet system. The nature of these changes is best illustrated in the fact that after the short-lived Khrushchevian ideological confusion—a confusion that was one of Khrushchev's merits—Communist ideology is beset by sclerosis, by total uncreativity. With the disintegration of totalitarianism and the reinforcement of its military imperialist aspirations, the ideology of the Soviet Union has become transformed into a ritualistic code. No one believes in this ideology any more; all are sick of it, but nobody —except for a mere handful of dissident intellectuals—has, or has yet, the strength to stand up against it.

Life itself, in all of its aspects, has made the ideology senseless. Who can speak of a classless society when even the most unscrupulous capitalists can envy the privileges of the bureaucracy? What kind of brotherhood of peoples and what kind of internationalism is it that is achieved by military occupations and by strangling the Communist parties of other peoples?

Soviet ideology, though formally adhering to Marx and Lenin, has long since abandoned not only the humanist side of Marx's teachings but also the revolutionary internationalism of Lenin. In the Soviet Union there are no more Marxists or Leninists. What remains in the Soviet Union are either officials who preach Marxism as a substitute religion, or rulers for whom Marxism is simply a reflex of their power. Side by side with a false ideology, great power nationalism flourishes in the form of "Soviet patriotism" and an idealization of the "Soviet state." Soviet authorities are most tolerant toward expressions of Great Russian nationalism, which means that the ruling class can, if it finds itself threatened, resort to that most obscurantist and chauvinistic of "values."

The disintegration of totalitarianism as an ideology reveals itself in the fact that the state leader is no longer the ineffable ideologue, the "hallowed" seer, such as Stalin was and Khrushchev pretended to be. Brezhnev was "only" a "faithful" and "foremost" Leninist: the dictatorship of the oligarchy does not brook a dictator, nor can a dictator stand above the plenum.

All these structural and ideological changes in the Soviet Union have progressed from a way of thinking into merely a mode of expression. Expressions such as "changed relation of forces," "the interests of the Soviet state," "near the Soviet border," "the leading Russian nation," "parity of forces," and the like have become the everyday language of the Soviet media, where once they had been the "inside" language of a narrow Stalinist circle.

II

The disintegration of totalitarianism in the subject states of eastern Europe has taken different forms. All of them still preserve certain totalitarian forms similar to or even identical with those in the Soviet Union, but every one of these states has also established its own individuality. Even the tempo of the disintegration of totalitarianism differs from country to country: not only are the national traits of these countries finding ever greater expression but also the national aspirations of their party bureaucracies. And the Soviet leadership has accommodated itself, against its will, to the national traits and pretensions of these national bureaucracies—at least to the point where they do not threaten Soviet imperial interests.

These interests focus, first of all, on the preservation of the "Socialist order," that is, the total power of the party bureaucracy in these countries. For, unlike financial and commerical empires, the Soviet empire, being a military-ideological one, can ensure its domination over other lands only through related social groups, namely, "sister parties." This mutual relationship has its resemblances to that in the Middle Ages between the monarch and local feudal lords.

In the subject East European countries, the disintegration of totalitarianism began, so to speak, at the very moment of Soviet domination at the end of the war. The two exceptions are Yugoslavia and Albania, countries in which relatively independent party bureaucracies achieved dictatorial power through revolution. From the beginning, totalitarianism of the Soviet type was simply contrary to the most vital currents of the East European nations. Nor was this totalitarianism embraced even by the entire national Communist parties of these countries; it was taken over only by those elements within the parties that were blinded by dogma or corrupted by absolute power. Resistance to Soviet dictation and economic plunder appeared even in the first months after the war—at first quietly, under the illusion that the Soviet leaders would "recognize" reality and injustice, and then openly, after the Soviet attack on Yugoslavia in 1948.

Because of its conflict with the Soviet Union, the Yugoslav party oligarchy undertook a revision of Leninist totalitarianism, as much out of a need for self-preservation as for the sake of national independence. True, this revision did not go in a straight line, nor was it synchronized in all its aspects. Nor could it be, in view of the differences in ideological prejudice and the power-seeking aspiration among the Yugoslav leaders. Moreover, the process of democratic reform and liberation came to a halt after Stalin's death and Tito's reconciliation with the Soviet Union. Yet the final result is this: after thirty years of meandering by the top leaders, purges in the party, and a predominantly ideologized economy, it would be extremely simplistic and doctrinaire to regard Yugoslavia—particularly the present, post-Tito Yugoslavia—as a totalitarian state.

Yugoslavia is no longer oppressed, nor is it inspired, by its leadership, if only because in Yugoslavia there is no longer a united and effective leadership or a single dominating ideology. Indeed, ideology no longer plays an essential, unifying role. The republican national parties are increasingly permeated by a *sui generis* bureaucratic nationalism, while still other ideological views are gaining ground—religious, rational democratic, nationalist, and others. Yugoslavia has fallen into a structural economic crisis, and the top leaders, blocked by dogma and mutual discord, have no idea of how to get out of the crisis even as they remain bent on preserving naked power. The absolutist authority of the party, and the predilection of the leaders for that kind of power, continue to form the basic residue of Leninist totalitarianism in Yugoslavia.

Albania's development was different from, and opposite to, Yugoslavia's. The aspirations of the party bureaucracy for independence, and the cultist power of Enver Hoxha, largely motivated by the long enslavement and backwardness of the country, fortified revolutionary dogmatism and a party-police totalitarianism. Albania is today the most totalitarian state in eastern Europe. In some of its forms, this totalitarianism is even more "total" than that of the Soviet Union under Stalin. It is hardly credible that such a totalitarianism will long survive Enver Hoxha, especially if it does not continue to inspire national aspirations. Even though Albania is the first state to succeed in banning religious communities, it is probable that underground religions, as elsewhere in eastern Europe, are gaining a mystical power and will flare into the open with a change in political conditions. Men can be held in bondage for a time, but it is not possible to do away with their longing for what they perceive as good and for immortality. The "perfecting" of totalitarianism, of which Albania is the most obvious example, demonstrates the organic weaknesses more than the strength of totalitarianism. Its disintegration has not yet begun in Albania, but it too will be unable to withstand the urge toward a full life.

In Rumania, totalitarianism has held on though somewhat differently and more "inconsistently" than in Albania. Rumania lacked the strength to take itself out of the "Socialist community" dominated by the Soviet Union. But Ceausescu has, by strengthening his own personal power, succeeded in gaining greater autonomy than that enjoyed by the other governments in the Soviet camp. This autonomy is little more than the autonomy of total power for Ceausescu and his clan; yet it is also an example of how nations, even when "accepting" conditions of slavery, can pull themselves out of the more bla- tant kinds of national subjection. Internally, however, Rumania is in many ways more totalitarian than the Soviet Union. That is the price the Rumanians are forced to pay for crumbs of national autonomy, while for the Soviet leadership it is also the guarantee that Rumania cannot leave their camp.

Although Bulgaria has most "faithfully" followed the Soviet model, the disintegration of totalitarianism in that country has lagged behind the Soviet Union. The only apparent "indepen- dence" Bulgaria has expressed has been in its expansionist de- mands regarding its neighbors, notably the Yugoslav Republic of Macedonia. Bulgaria has been assigned, though only ostensi- bly so, the role of a sub-imperialist in the Balkans, similar to the role of Vietnam in Southeast Asia. But the Bulgarian leader- ship is not as independent as the Vietnamese: it can only serve as a vassal. The illusion of the Bulgarian leaders that the Soviet "Big Brother" will support them in their expansionist megalo- mania has undoubtedly influenced segments of the Bulgarian nation as well; it helps to stifle local tendencies toward the disintegration of totalitarianism. Yet the first symptoms of disintegration are obvious there too—in the stupid and hysteri- cal official "patriotism," in the alienation of the creative intelli- gentsia, in the lack of quality and efficiency in the economy.

The disorders of 1956, particularly the uprising in Hungary, had, in my judgment, an exceptionally crucial significance for the crisis of totalitarianism. They pointed beyond its mere disin- tegration and toward an ultimate destruction, revealing not only inner weaknesses but also the fact that it maintains itself largely through the military presence of the Soviet Union. Yet the 1956 uprising made it possible for Kádár gradually to re- form the Hungarian economy by practical measures. This was also accompanied by a certain kind of tolerance and culture. Today, Hungary is not only the most prosperous state in east- ern Europe; it is seen even in the Soviet Union as a possible model for economic reform. I myself do not believe in that model. It seems more probable that Hungary will, in the fore-seeable future, fall into a structural crisis similar to the one in Yugoslavia. The reforms that prolong cannot cure the system. Hungary is no longer a totalitarian state, in the same sense that Yugoslavia is not: The party holds a monopoly of power, but the remaining forms of social life enjoy a certain autonomy—an autonomy limited, of course, by Soviet control and the party monopoly of power.

The disintegration of totalitarianism in Czechoslovakia had acquired, by the year 1968, final shattering dimensions, espe-cially in culture and political philosophy. Moreover, even the political structure was undergoing radical changes, which did not acquire a more definite form only because of the vacillation of the leaders and the fear of Soviet intervention. Soviet inter-vention put a stop to that process, but it could not suppress the memory of bitter experience with totalitarianism. Totalitarian-ism in Czechoslovakia is spiritually dead; it rests on nothing but a domestic police and an alien military force. In all of Czecho-slovakia there is not a single creative force, hardly a single creative individual that would support totalitarian forms. Ideol-ogy in Czechoslovakia is the business of the police and paid hacks. The Czechs and Slovaks endure; their creative intellectu-als protest and fill dungeons. All are biding their time.

It would not be incorrect to conclude that Poland was never a totalitarian state, if only because some form of spiritual life —in the first place the Catholic Church—preserved a measure of autonomy. Also, peasant holdings remained largely private property. On top of that, thanks to the Warsaw uprising in 1944 and armed and other resistance immediately after the war, the vast majority of Poles received both the new regime and Soviet control without any illusions about Soviet "liberators." Poland has been, in fact, largely a police state.

The 1956 revolt in Poznań had a crucial significance for Poland's internal autonomy. If Poland did not proceed more rapidly in this respect, it is Gomulka, with his dogmatic "So-cialist" narrowness, who in large measure bears the historical responsibility. He retarded but did not stop the anti-totalitarian movement in Poland; it is there that the totalitarian idea has been most decisively rejected.

The military junta has, in the name of the party, dissolved Solidarity with its 10 million members, and visited the darkness of "martial law" on the land. Formally, the party still exists, and some still speak of its renewal. But both the party and its ideology are in disarray, while the junta justifies itself with the argument that it is the only alternative to brute Soviet intervention.

In *The New Class,* a book published in 1957, I asserted that a military dictatorship would be an improvement in comparison with a party monopoly of power. But in Poland, the installation of the junta has in fact had the opposite significance. Even if we set aside the change in conditions from 1957 till today, the rule of the junta in Poland does not resemble the kind of military dictatorship on which I based my assertion in *The New Class.* For the junta in Poland has not replaced the party bureaucracy: it has merely replaced a civilian party bureaucracy with a military party bureaucracy in order to rescue the party. The sanctity of "the leading role of the party" has been compromised, and the military party leaders will hang on to their decisive role even if there should occur a temporary "consolidation" of the situation and a renewal of the "civilian" party. In Poland, an illegal pluralistic society has arisen beneath a legal government totalitarian in tendency but not quite in actuality.

The disintegration of Leninist totalitarianism is expressed most profoundly and obviously within the West European Communist parties that in recent years have been moving away from Moscow through a shifting politics that has come to be known as Eurocommunism. Similar processes are taking place in parties on other continents, mainly in Asia. However, I shall consider only the European parties, both because the ideological disintegration of Leninism has progressed the farthest among them and because they typify best the movement of Communist parties in a direction that strengthens national, as opposed to pro-Soviet, tendencies.

Of the three most significant parties in western Europe—the Italian, Spanish, and French—that process has, in effect, taken over the first two, while in the third there have appeared, and will continue to appear, "reformist" non-Leninist and anti-Leninist currents. The leading bodies of the first two parties have rejected, in declaration and often in practice, the basic propositions of Leninism. They have declared their adherence to parliamentary and other democratic forms. They have repudiated Leninism by turning away from revolution as an instrument for the transformation of society and by abandoning "the dictatorship of the proletariat" and party monopoly of power in a Communist-governed state. The disintegration of Leninism in the "Eurocommunist" parties continues; and apart from some "Stalinist" resistance, it has also encountered misunderstanding and suspicion not only from reactionary analysts but also from democratic observers who do not see that something deep and permanent is taking shape.

Put another way, the disintegration of Leninism among West European parties is not caused solely by the transformation of the Soviet party into a monopolistic caste and its expansionist interventions in other countries. A greater impetus may be traced to the inner democratic transformation of Western societies and to what is becoming ever more obvious: Leninist ideology is utterly inapplicable in developed countries and democratic societies. What is most significant in these parties by way of proving that their position is neither a "maneuver" nor a "demagogic" trick can be seen in the fact that the "separation from Moscow" is developing gradually and is attaining its own positive, creative forms—its own kind of movement, both philosophical and practical, toward democratic socialism.

III

What are the further prospects for Leninist totalitarianism? The following outcome seems probable, though not, of course, certain:

1. *The weakening of ideology as an inspirational and cognitive factor, even though the ruling party stratum will insist ever more stubbornly on its ideology.* No dictatorship, and especially not a party one, can maintain itself without the deception and self-deception of ideology. The Soviet bureaucracy will try to supplement "classical" Leninism, and even supplant it, with a "more democratic," primarily "patriotic," nationalist ideology; that is, it will attempt to redesign its own bureaucratic cause into a national cause.

2. *The emergence of new, free economic forms, not only side by side with the bureaucratic form of property but within its framework ("self-management," "group property").* Ceaseless, quite unsuccessful, efforts at inconsequential reforms in an effort to patch up the system by improving the quality of "Socialist" production. Even if the present crises in the "capitalist" economies go away, the crises in the "Socialist" economies will continue because the most important and most numerous causes originate in their very structure.

3. *A stronger military component in the party's bureaucratic system while ideology becomes petrified and loses its rationale, as "Socialist property" is seen as the source of bureaucratic monopoly and inefficiency.* This will affect both the outside world and internal opposition forces. The most important factor will continue to be Soviet military imperialism, which will further stimulate resistance not only from nationalist and social dissidents but from the military-party structures in the subject lands.

The crises in Leninist totalitarianism will be linked with crises in other systems and the threat of war. The disintegration of Leninist totalitarianism is more likely to bring about new storms and bloodshed than peace and tranquillity—not only because of the party bureaucracy's mortal fear but because that disintegration can be erroneously perceived by the "other side" as "a good opportunity" for imposing its own kind of domination and wealth. For Leninist totalitarianism is not a world in itself; it is a component of Europe and of the world.

Johanno Strasser

Translated by John E. Woods

10 *1984:* Decade of the Experts?

When in 1949 George Orwell published his gloomy vision of the future, *1984,* Europe had just begun to clear away the rubble of the most horrible war it had yet known. Two world wars, Stalin's purges, the Nazi reign of terror, atom bombs dropped on Hiroshima and Nagasaki—all this had profoundly shaken the enlightened, humanist creed of man's progress toward a more reasonable and humane world. This was no bull market for utopias. People had their hands full dealing with the present. Whoever bothered to glance at the future generally did so with radical skepticism. 1984? Those who had lived through Stalinism and fascism had no doubts that among humankind anything was possible.

Meanwhile life went on. From America, the most resplendent and powerful of the nations that had defeated Nazi Germany, tidings of unbelievable prosperity, of sheer unlimited technological possibilities broke in upon a ravaged Europe. The glittering marvels arriving from across the Atlantic in great number fired men's imaginations, became the stuff of dreams. In America, cars were bigger, buildings taller, the rich richer. These were patent proofs of the triumph of progress. The terrible past seemed to be some remote, barbaric antiquity. Modernity, the future—that was America. Emulation appeared to offer the best guarantee that the horrors of the past would not be repeated.

The slogan was Progress without Ideology. Its advance was marked by new records that were constantly being broken both in technology and the economy. Soon the Germans, too, had set

records, the so-called *Wirtschaftswunder* (economic miracle).
The severely damaged self-confidence of the Germans revived
with the pride taken in economic success. We were somebody
again. The "deferred nation" had finally, or so it appeared,
shaken off the crippling ballast of its unmastered past and—at
least in its Western half—captured a position in the front ranks.

During the sixties, who would have predicted anything other
than new economic and technological achievements, still more
prosperity, power, security and freedom? Nevertheless, in the
fifties and sixties Orwell's book was a best-seller in Germany,
too. Apparently people were not quite so certain that the radi-
ant promises of technological and economic progress would be
fulfilled. But there was a proven medicine for preventing Orwellian nightmares by tacit agreement: we transplanted these pessi-
mistic visions of the future to the East, across the border separating the two "systems." There was hardly anyone who
seriously believed that something of the sort could develop here
in the West.

It is amazing how quickly the belief in progress recovered
from the heavy blows dealt it in the first half of this century.
The Nazi reign of terror was now interpreted as a relapse into
ancient barbarism. This was all the easier since the German
version of inhumanity had draped itself in pseudo-Teutonic
trumpery that quite obviously had nothing more to do with a
modern (American) style of life. Fascism and Stalinism were
regarded as thoroughly antiquated. When one spoke out against
"totalitarianism," one meant the old demons: dogmatism, the
desire to redeem the world, intolerance, lust for power. A society that had renounced all ideology, it seemed, was immune to
any relapse into barbarism.

Today, we are not so sure of all this. Since the early seventies,
we have become increasingly conscious that we cannot progress
much longer down our present path without destroying the
natural basis of our lives. The enormous apparatus that produces and administers our prosperity has proved to be more
susceptible to disruption than we had thought. The introduc-

tion of new and dangerous technologies has raised the question of whether we have not become slaves to our own products. Anxiety and skepticism once again characterize our vision of the future. According to a January 1980 poll, only 33 percent of the citizens of the Federal Republic of Germany still believe that technological development will lead to greater freedom; 56 percent think that it is more likely to make us less free.

Whoever reads Orwell's book again nowadays cannot comfort himself so easily any more with the thought that all this has nothing to do with the reality in which we live. "The ideal set up by the Party was something huge, terrible, glittering—a world of steel and concrete, of monstrous machines and terrifying weapons."[1] Is this not the world that is planned and developed in the head offices of large corporations and in governmental bureaucracies? And do not metropolises like New York with its endless slums, unmanageable mountains of garbage, rampant crime, overburdened logistical systems, oppressive poverty, and ever-increasing psychological stress show that Orwell was also correct in his description of the shabby underside of this world of technological miracles? Granted, the framework of political conditions is clearly different. But who can guarantee us that this will continue to be the case? Is the German practice of interrogating conscientious objectors and candidates for civil service positions about their political views not already a first step toward Orwell's Thought Police? Are not coinages like "restoring strategic balance" and "disposal parks for nuclear waste" already the start of that perfidious Newspeak that could turn a torture chamber into the Ministry of Love?

Careless analogies to Orwell's *1984* could certainly prove disastrous if they helped revive the fatal "fascism theory" of a part of the new left. To label the Federal Republic of Germany or the other Western democracies fascist or quasi-fascist tyrannies shows a dangerous blindness to reality and to what fascism is really about. But the worry remains. The refinement of surveillance systems using spies and data processing, the almost limitless possibilities for manipulating the mind with psychopharmaceuticals and brainwashing, and finally the new technologies allowing for planned genetic modification that are being perfected at a feverish pace by molecular biologists—do not these all make Orwell's negative utopia appear feasible? And do we not have reason to assume that what is feasible will at some point in time really be done?

There are places where human rights are daily ridden roughshod, where people do not even have the freedom to offer political resistance to their own disfranchisement and dehumanization. But that should not lead us to conclude that apart from a few small defects everything is in order with us. This warning is above all relevant for the Federal Republic of Germany, where a glance over into the other German state almost of necessity evokes a sigh of "Well, we're still doing all right!" And indeed, all the acts of intimidation and deliberalization that accompanied the hunt for radicals, all the anti-terrorist hysteria on this side hardly seem worth mentioning in comparison to conditions in the German Democratic Republic. 1984? Here? If someone is really looking for a contemporary stage on which to play out Orwell's scenario of oppression, then it would appear that the state whose propaganda turns the Berlin Wall into an "anti-imperialist wall of peace" would be the place.

Our ability to repress our own fears of the future still functions astonishingly well. In Germany, the enemies of freedom are found almost always on the other side of the border—both the border that runs between the two German states and the one that divides the vast majority of citizens from the small band of "extremists." There are dangers to our freedom and our humanity within our own lifestyle, in the social structures of a world whose distinguishing features are science and technology, but these are dangers that are overlooked more often than not. The debate inspired by Robert Jungk's *Atomic Nation* was centered on precisely this point. Is it perhaps that the old demons are not what threaten our freedom any more? Have we possibly let a herd of Trojan horses into our democracy along with new technologies, ones that may very well prove disastrous to us, and soon?

If this is so, we must indeed read Orwell quite differently nowadays. The menace hovering over the eighties is not total dominance by some fanatical party elite, but rather the progressive undermining of democracy by the silent dictatorship of forces inherent in our reality. The greatest danger does not threaten us from reactionaries, from unenlightened powers of the past, but from the most modern achievements of our technological and economic lifestyle. *1984* does not mean the possibility of *relapsing* into barbarism. It means the possibility of perverting progress—because progress has lost the gauge by which to measure what is both feasible and humane.

For some time now cracks have been visible in the worlds of technology and economics, but we have usually interpreted them to be the result of difficulties of adaptation. And here, too, America offered solutions, solutions arising out of the same intellectual climate that had created the problems: "operations research," "technology assessment"—technological mastery of technological problems. In the first half of the seventies, German Social Democrats called this "improvement of capability for prognosis, planning, and direction." What differentiated the Social Democrats from the conservatives was their conviction that "every advance in technology and science could and must resolutely be tied to advances in democracy and social justice."[2] That the course of technological and economic development might itself assail democracy and social justice did not even enter the mind of the left.

It first took the social conflicts centering on nuclear energy to direct attention toward technology and its inherent dynamic. What surfaced at Wyhl, Brokdorf, Grohnde, and elsewhere, manifesting itself in an ever-growing tide of literature critical of technology, what caused new political forces to arise and alter the agenda and the alignments of old ones, particularly among Social Democrats, was no less than an anxiety gradually developing into a clear certainty that the technological, economic model for progress which has moved out from Europe to conquer the world contains an element inimical to human life, to all life—one that cannot be checked by all our efforts to bring

about more democracy and social justice. We must now deal
critically with the dynamics of our technologies and economies,
even more radically than has traditionally been the case when
dealing with capitalism per se, where the conditions of production are criticized while the powers of productivity—technology, machines as such, the immense administrative apparatus
—are declared innocent.

What Horkheimer and Adorno have called the "dialectic of
the Enlightenment" does not have its basis in some deplorable
inadequacy of mankind, but in the onesidedness and distortions
found in a rationalistic, enlightened world view. This is what
the technofanatics, who with their faith in computers beguile us
with a science-fiction future as the hope of mankind, cannot
comprehend. "Tell me what happiness is, and I will build a
computer that can be happy." Who can still chuckle at a statement like that? Is not the triumph of technocratic rationality
built upon the notion of eliminating whatever is undefinable or
non-quantifiable, of treating life itself, subjectivity, the individual as no more than some troublesome, peripheral bit of data?

For the unfortunate Karl Steinbuch, there is not the least
doubt that "perfect technology is the terminus toward which
technology is moving." If this "ideal" is perhaps never totally
achievable, it is because of the irrationality, the inadequate
adaptability of man. "The individual, with his unpredictability
and an egotism that is only seemingly tamed," Steinbuch warns,
"simply ought not be allowed sole responsibility for pulling the
lever of a perfect technology."[3] The only solution is: *object-
ization* (= de*human*ization) of social structures and processes. Eliminate the human factor, and I will construct an ideal
society for you! But what if such vestiges, considered here as
vestigial risks, are the essentials that make life worth living? Is
there a path to follow other than the one we've already started
down? Do we even have a choice?

Both the fervent apologists and the sworn opponents of our
technological civilization are generally convinced of the inevitability of this development toward a "perfect technology." What

for Steinbuch is an irresistible decree of reason, is for Spengler a gloomy "spiritual necessity." Spengler denounces the evil but sees no escape from it:

> In reality, however, it is out of the power of heads or of hands to alter the destiny of machine-technics, for this has developed out of inward, spiritual necessities and is now correspondingly matured towards its fulfillment and end. . . . The creature is rising up against its creator. As once the microcosm Man against nature, so now the microcosm Machine is revolting against . . . Man. The lord of this world is becoming the slave of the machine, which is forcing him —forcing us all, whether we are aware of it or not—to follow its course. The victor, thrown, is dragged to his death by the team.[4]

That was written in 1932, and Spengler was a conservative, which makes it easy to distance oneself in the name of progress from his critique of technology. The few leftists, above all Ernst Bloch, who share this skepticism about technology have not prevailed. The left, the Marxist left at least, has as a rule been unshakably convinced of the inevitability of technological and economic development. What concerned them almost exclusively was the political and social framework, the problems of distribution, the class basis of social relationships, the political nature of authority. The scientific, technological paradigm of our civilization was left untouched. Only in recent years has it dawned upon many people that in raising the question about an alternative to capitalism, one could not exclude calling into question the scientific, technological civilization created by capitalism. Herbert Marcuse's *One Dimensional Man* made a substantial contribution here.

Many people have still not comprehended the problem. This is true for by far the largest part of organized labor and for large segments of the Social Democratic Party (SDP). But at least something has been set in motion. Nowhere are ecological problems and the dangers of new technologies discussed with more passion than in the SDP—in contrast to the dogmatists in the German Communist Party (DKP). "In the issue of the peaceful use of nuclear energy," the DKP executive committee states in a press release,

> We see ourselves confronted—and this is the decisive point—with the issue of class. The question is: Under what social conditions is nuclear energy used? The technological principles by which nuclear reactors are operated in the Soviet Union or in the Federal Republic of Germany are essentially the same. And those technological principles make a safe use of nuclear reactors possible. Whether or not such a safe operation does in fact occur or not, however, depends above all else on social conditions.[5]

In comments such as this, technology is only superficially made a political question. The insistence that it is a class issue only says: in the Soviet Union the same technology is applied with greater perfection and a greater sense of responsibility—not exactly a convincing claim when one sees how these poor, repudiated cousins of Henry Ford have been trying in vain for decades to attain the living standard of the United States. The topic "technology and political power" is taboo under so-called realized socialism. Whole automobile factories—and that includes the way the work done is organized, the assembly line, the hierarchies of command, the extreme division of labor, and so on—have been taken over from the class enemy, and then comes the happy proclamation that in the Soviet Union, "work has more and more become the primary need in people's lives."[6] A contradiction whose very bleakness is based on the fact that the attempt here is to raise the dialectic of progress to the level of propaganda.

The problem is obvious: wherever only *one* technology is allowed, wherever the *actual* development of technological means of production are considered the *only possible* or, better, the *only reasonable ones,* there is no alternative between desperation and uncritical affirmation. There is no room left for a critical engagement with our technology and its effect on society's life. "The technology we have known till now," Bloch writes in *The Hope Principle,* "stands in nature like an army of occupation in enemy territory."[7] He envisions another technology, a "technology of alliances." That makes an ally of nature, both extrinsic and intrinsic to man, allowing man to be himself in the implementation of technological processes—to be an individual, a social and natural creature.

Until recently, the left, to the extent that it has taken note of Bloch, has read over such passages without remarking how timely these ideas are. Only now are we gradually becoming aware of the meaning of the issue "technology." Freedom, equality, brotherhood—that great hope of the bourgeois revolution, first betrayed by capitalism and then revitalized by the workers' movement—can that hope ever be realized if we continue the present course of technological and economic development? Or do we have reason to assume that the modest portion of humanity and freedom that could be wrested from capitalist conditions of production will in time be destroyed if that course remains unchanged?

Those who cling to both democracy and socialism, because the one without the other is a denial of the meaning of being human, cannot dodge these questions. They must put not only the conditions of production but also the forces of production to the proofstone of criticism, and they will then of necessity be led back to the ideological foundations of our scientific, technological civilization.

From the beginning modern technology has been characterized by the same spirit of abstraction, calculation, and exploitation that are the hallmarks of capitalism. At first there was the modern struggle against the obscurantism of "occult qualities." Without doubt, this was an act of emancipation, of liberation from the spiritual paralysis and shallow charlantanism that, even in our own time, is content for example to see human want as a result of self-caused poverty. But the struggle against the "occult qualities" of medieval philosophy ended quite unintentionally in a discrediting of "quality" in general. The rationalists wanted to explain the world *more geometrico,* and whatever did not conform to their new "geometrical" method was declared to be irrational. For Galileo and Newton the true and the real are countable, measurable, quantifiable. And their bias for what could be converted to mathematics has been retained until today. Wherever modern technology has got a foothold, people have likewise been subjected to the tyranny of numbers. In East and West, technology reduces men and women to units of work, measurable in hours and piecework.

Friedrich Engels saw the despotism of modern production methods, but considered it unavoidable, its basis being material rather than a matter of social relationships: "The mechanical apparatus of a large factory is much more tyrannical than any petty capitalist employing workers ever was. And though man has subdued the powers of nature with the aid of science and the genius of invention, they nevertheless have their revenge, for to the same extent that he puts them at his service, they subject him to a veritable despotism independent of all social organization."[8] Engels argues against the anarchists, who were not ready to accept the "despotism" of modern technology as a force inherent in reality. For him they are romantic madmen, who demand freedom and self-determination, where the only reasonable choice is submission to the laws of reality.

What becomes then of liberation from work, of the overcoming of alienation? According to Engels, the abolition of capitalist exploitation and a just distribution of society's wealth, even if it were to succeed completely, would not in fact abolish the despotism of the modern means of production. All hope must therefore be directed toward an ever-increasing freedom from work. Reduction of hours worked by means of technological progress, rationalization and automation—that is the sober view of the leap into the "realm of freedom" to which Marx as well, under Engels's influence, finally had to pay his tribute.

In the third volume of *Capital,* he writes: "The realm of freedom first begins in fact where labor determined by necessity and external expediency ceases; by the very nature of things, then, it lies beyond the sphere of actual material production."[9] There is not much left here of the critique of the division of labor. Nowadays the visions orthodox Marxists have of the future are hardly different from those of a Herman Kahn on this crucial point. There as here, the dreams center on the goal of an automated economy whose immense productivity will at last allow people to free themselves from the forces inherent in the technological apparatus and so develop the fullness of their personalities during their free time. We now know that fully automated production on a grand scale is an ecological monster. When, at the end of the sixties, Herman Kahn and Anthony J. Wiener published their bold predictions for the year 2000, they silently passed over their presupposition of a four-hundredfold increase in world energy use.[10] This fact alone is enough to wrench us from our technological daydreams. But let us for a moment assume that the goal of an automated economy were in fact achievable. Would that truly be a "realm of freedom"?

In no way! There is no greater dependence imaginable than the dependence upon the highly vulnerable, centralized logistical structures of a fully automated economy. All social life would depend to the tiniest detail upon the smooth functioning of a single, gigantic, highly complex apparatus. Each individual would have to adapt the course of his life to the tempo set by the automata. Zones of freedom, islands of self-determined activity would have to be abolished, anomalies prevented whenever possible. "As far as the possibility of creating a fully automated world goes," writes Lewis Mumford quite correctly, "only naive people could regard such a goal as the apex of human development. It would be the final solution for humanity's problems only in the sense that Hitler's program of annihilation was a final solution for the 'Jewish question.' "[11]

The dream of a "realm of freedom" cannot be fulfilled if we stick to the path of technological and economic development we are now on. On the contrary, at the end of this path is a "realm of necessity" more relentless and inhuman than anyone can imagine. It is not the ineradicable old Adam, the unpredictability of the "human factor" that is the problem, but the grip of an ever more perfect technological apparatus on the life of humankind. Orwell's book can serve us today as a warning if we comprehend that the further we advance along the road to "perfect technology," approaching the technocracy of a world of production and consumerism controlled by computers, the closer we are to his horrible vision. The menace is all the greater because it is presented with all the marks of well-intentioned reason and dispassionate fulfillment of duty. It is not easy to argue "objectively" against it. Each step taken is the logical answer to a given problem. It may well be that here too the devil is in the details; but he only becomes visible when one regards the whole.

Now we are of course nowhere near that merciless state of "perfect technology" of which Steinbuch dreams, and presumably we never will arrive at it. But only when it is regarded from its logical end point does the process of technological and economic progress we are currently pursuing reveal its inherent destructiveness and inhumanity. Can that course continue to mean everything to us when its final goal is the destruction of humanity? Today, to question progress is above all to question the meaning and goal of the technocratic project that promises freedom from work rather than the liberation of work.

Once the magic spell cast over that final goal is broken, we can enter more freely into discussion about our course. Why should we agree to new and increasingly risky adventures of a technology removed both from nature and mankind, when the end of that dangerous road is not the promised land of freedom and abundance? Should we not then seriously ponder other, more humane and ecologically more reasonable possibilities? It is not a question of storming the machines, nor of a vain attempt to turn back the wheel of history; it is a matter of searching for alternative paths of technological and economic development that are in accord with nature as it exists both without and within mankind.

It is first and foremost the question of a technology policy that is more than public financing of what a technocratic elite of scientists contrive and what the head offices of giant corporations plan. Do we have criteria by which we can measure what progress truly is? Do we have means by which to carry out a truly human progress as well? The final question touches upon the classic Socialist theme of economic power. Nor is it in any way out of date. Without democratization of the economy, the attempt to bring reasonable order to the "metabolism of man and nature" cannot succeed. But democratization of the control of the means of production through co-determination and socialization are not sufficient in themselves. The method of production itself must be changed.

Which brings us to the topic of a different, a gentle, emancipatory technology. Is that possible? What might it look like? We are still hardly beyond the first groping attempts in that direction. A few outsiders among scientists and engineers have thus far done the pioneer work; individual politicians have taken up their suggestions. They are still derided by the great majority of those inside institutionalized science and politics. But that can change very quickly. For the more clearly we recognize that the main highway is more likely to lead us backward than forward, the more interesting the byways and detours become. When straight ahead means straight ahead to ruin, muddleheads are in demand.

But were not the development of our modern technology and the growth of heavy industry in Europe accompanied by the birth of democracy? And is there not a connection between these two movements? Certainly. The rise of a rationalist, scientific world view loosened the ties to old authorities and finally destroyed them; heavy industry socialized production and the people working in it, and so made a democratic citizenry possible. A wealth of technological inventions and their application by heavy industry have abolished material want, for the most part at least, in our portion of the globe. To that extent our technological and economic development has indeed built the actual historical basis of modern democracy.

That is the one side. But over against it there is also the other, the menacing side, and it becomes more and more obvious with time:

- The development of our technology inevitably has led, apart from the specific capitalist tendencies toward concentration and centralization, to an ever greater accumulation of power in a few centers, thereby increasing the chances of the use of that power to thwart democratic decisions.

- The same process furthers and accelerates centralization in political systems that are increasingly distant from the citizenry, since executives strive to adapt their sphere of action to economic realities.

- The increasing size of technological and economic projects, their gigantic financial requirements, and a whole series of "external effects" and coincidental costs create immense demands that dramatically narrow the room for democratic decision making. Thus, the actual development tends to exclude other alternatives.

- The hierarchical structure of the technological apparatus, the radical separation of labor between planners and executors and the division within the labor process, lead to onesidedness and atrophy, and demand subordinate behavior.

- To the extent that new segments of life are constantly being opened up by the marketing strategies of large corporations and taken into the grip of the technological apparatus, and to the extent that new occupations become professionalized, the dependence of people on external services grows, while their ability to help themselves diminishes.

- The questions that are added to the political agenda become ever more complicated, the scope of relevant data ever more overpowering, the process of shaping popular will and decision ever more inscrutable. Despite all education efforts in this area, the political competence of the layman, one of the buttresses of democracy, is undermined. We are moving toward an expertocracy.

- The more complicated the technical world becomes, the less information the citizen can glean from his own experience and perceptions. For the most part he experiences what his world looks like and what goes on in it through the media. Whoever controls the media has, then, not only a means of influencing public opinion but also an instrument for comprehensive control of the sphere of human experience.

- Because of a rapidly increasing use of raw materials and energy sources, the dependence on foreign supplies of countries like the Federal Republic of Germany that lack such raw materials grows ever greater.
- The vulnerability of our technological and economic systems and the danger of ecological catastrophe is constantly increasing. At any time breakdowns can lead to ecological emergencies or a serious crisis of supply. The scarcity and rising prices of raw materials increases the danger of disputes that can lead to war. The probability of a general emergency increases; and emergencies are the hour of executive decisions, not of democracy. To prevent these growing risks, we defend ourselves with ever more comprehensive security measures. The danger that we will defend democracy to death is self-evident.
- New technological possibilities for securing control over mankind or manipulating it—of which the most horrifying is genetic engineering—threaten freedom and humanity more radically than all other forms of control man has known before.
- The unbridled use of raw materials and energy sources and the increasingly bitter competition for access to sources of raw materials make a military confrontation between the superpowers (USA and USSR) probable in the near future. Each side is preparing itself for a showdown by increasing its armament efforts. But the faster "progress" in armament technology moves forward, the more precise weapons of destruction become in targeting and the shorter the reaction time becomes, a third world war "by mistake" becomes just that much more probable (see Carl Friedrich von Weizsaecker). The suicidal absurdity of the system is nowhere clearer than in the case of armaments: the apparatus designed to defend us becomes the greatest threat to us.

Conclusions of this sort are not the products of a morbid propensity toward apocalyptic visions. One cannot simply cast them aside as the expressions of an intellectual incapacity to deal with the hard facts of life. They name the real dangers in a world where science and technology have already taken control of society.

What we are now experiencing is that steady increments can indeed convert quantitative factors into qualitative ones. The dialectic of progress makes it possible for prosperity to become a plague. Productivity pushed to ever greater increases, concentration of ever more gigantic technological and economic potential, an ever more comprehensive apparatus for controlling risks, the progressive technologicalization of all segments of life —all this adorns the banner of progress. Is that really progress?

Our sense of vulnerability sits deeper than most people want to admit. For a long time it was never expressed politically. Irrational eruptions of violence, "flipping out," self-destructive flight into drugs and alcohol are widespread reactions. Where the revolt becomes a conscious one, becomes political, it comes up against the grand coalition of "reason." Naturally, what represents itself as pure reason is in large measure naked, egoistic self-interest; it is a matter of profits, positions, power. But that is not the entire truth. Many of those who defend the path we have taken toward technological and economic development do so with the honest intention of wanting to achieve the best for the majority, for the people as a whole. And, for them, the best is quite self-evidently the biggest, the tallest, the fastest, the latest item on the market of technological vanities.

But optimization and maximization are in no way the same thing. The greatest danger comes from immoderation, from those who can promise themselves rising profits and growing power on the short term. That is a classical theme. From Aristotle to de Tocqueville it forms the basis of the conservative complaint about the hubris of progress. Today the roles have been interchanged to some extent. In the Federal Republic of Germany, it is the conservatives who are the most ruthless advocates of industrial expansion, while the left discusses the limits of growth, demanding a technology and an economy cut to human measurements. Erhard Eppler has tried to clarify this change of roles by differentiating between "conservators of structures" and "conservators of values." But the concepts are tricky. It is correct, however, that in the view of the technological elite who believe in progress, the insistence of democratic Socialists upon values like freedom, solidarity, and human dignity must appear old-fashioned.

Of course not everyone is at the forefront of progress who thinks he is; and where a change in direction becomes necessary, the vanguard may become the rearguard. In our society, the forces are growing that might prepare the way for such a development. There has seldom been a change in consciousness so rapid as that which has occurred on the issue of ecology. The fascination with technocratic models and the messianic effect of their prophets have noticeably decreased. The number of citizens who resist their future being "obstructed" has grown by leaps and bounds in recent years. Have we Germans finally understood that one cannot take ownership of democracy in the same way one does of a new house; that the state, the political parties, the unions are not service agencies from which we can expect, for an appropriate fee, our prosperity, freedom, and happiness? Whatever those who discovered a "change of mood" (to conservatism in the late seventies) may have thought they saw, things have not turned out that way. That democracy lives or dies in the way it is lived each day, that it depends upon civil courage, commitment, and, when no other alternative is possible, upon the resistance of the individual—these simple truths appear to be winning ground again after years of resignation.

"Where danger grows, the means of salvation grow as well?" One can never be sure. But the democratic Socialist, who, unlike the orthodox Marxist, has not made a pact with ostensible objective laws of history, is duty-bound to hope. *1984* cannot be allowed to become reality, not in 1994 or in 2004. In the eighties, the switches will be thrown that lead us in one direction or another. We have the possibility to correct misguided developments, to test out new approaches. Let's meddle!

James B. Rule

11 *1984—The Ingredients of Totalitarianism*

I

Surely no fictional work—perhaps no work of any kind—has so shaped our view of the future as *1984*. Consider only how our political vocabulary has been transformed by terms like Newspeak, doublethink, and Big Brother. These are not just words but critical ideas that fortify us against menacing political realities.

It is now almost a reflex to condemn any ugly intrusion into private affairs as smacking of *1984*. Even Richard Nixon, in a frantic effort to stave off his political demise in 1974, established a high-level "privacy protection" effort, solemnly declaring: "When personal information is given or obtained for one purpose . . . it should not be secretly used . . . for any other purpose." When respect for privacy receives this kind of support, one knows that appreciation of these values does not go very deep. Orwell's book deserves a better fate.

Strictly as prophecy, *1984* remains happily unfulfilled. Contrary to Orwell's gloomy anticipations, the Western democracies have not abandoned their institutions to imitate Nazi Germany or Stalin's U.S.S.R. Opposition forces and dissident tendencies remained viable and resilient, even in de Gaulle's France and Nixon's America. For this much, we have a right to be grateful, though hardly complacent.

But the deepest significance of *1984* lies in its analysis of tendencies in our own world, rather than simply in anticipation of evils to come. What frightens us is its view of a coalescence of unholy social and political elements, many of which we can already see all around us. The most obvious is sheer political repression—physical destruction of all opposition. Less terrifying but alarming enough is the vision of the penetration of state monitoring, and hence state power, into every recess of private life.

Notwithstanding a few hysterical commentators like Herbert Marcuse, opposition is not dead in the West. We have avoided both systematic, brutal physical repression and the exhaustion of oppositional ideas. Yet, at the same time, the ability of the state and other powerful organizations to monitor ordinary people's private lives has grown enormously. Since Orwell wrote, most of the technologies that figure as science fiction fantasy in his work have become reality—though not necessarily employed quite as Orwell envisaged.[1] Even in the democracies, unprecedented amounts of personal information have become available to centralized bureaucracies in ways Orwell could hardly have imagined. The result has been an enormous potential of power in the hands of these organizations.

Seldom are these developments due to any deliberate scheme for repression. They occur as state and private organizations seek to perform accepted tasks more efficiently and widely. Throughout this century, bureaucracies dealing with the public have increasingly found it feasible to collect and use more and more detailed data on ordinary private persons. Often the immediate purposes of such innovation have been strictly benevolent, as in the provision of social insurance or delivery of health care. In other cases—for example, crime control or taxation—the purposes are more coercive. The result in either case enhances the power of centralized bureaucracies over ordinary people. And within the last twenty years, these tendencies have accelerated with the advent of computing.

II

In an inflationary world, computing is perhaps the one major activity of organizations whose cost is dropping. Thus the enormous attraction of substituting electronic processes for both human labor and the movement of things and people. Bureaucracies are now finding ways of substituting the movement of computerized information for the movement of data in its archaic, paper-based form: And much of this computerized information concerns people. As more and more American families come to have home computers or terminals, perhaps using their TV screens as display units, the nature of information exchange between private citizens and public and private organizations changes profoundly.

Electronic Payments

All but the smallest organizations now maintain financial accounts by computer. Large financial institutions make payments and debits to and from one another's accounts through electronic media—using paper, if at all, merely to confirm the electronic fact. Thus private individuals' reliance on checks represents a costly archaism. The processing of paper-based instruments is, relatively, energy- and labor-intensive; as a result, many banks are investing vast amounts in "electronic funds transfer systems."

If these changes come about—and they are already being tested on a large scale—electronic terminals linked to banks and other account-holding institutions could be placed everywhere, making it possible to enter deposits or debits without going near the bank. Some supermarkets have already initiated "electronic tellers," which make deposits to and withdrawals from customers' accounts through a special cashier. An interlocking net of computer lines could potentially link every terminal with every account-holding organization.

But who is going to control the personal information generated by systems like these? After all, any electronic payment system will generate electronic "logs" of transactions made through it. Such logs will have to show the dates and amounts of transactions, the establishment in which they take place, and perhaps also the goods or services purchased. These account records could amount to a financial diary of the consumer, perhaps even more than do one's accumulated checks. Obviously, access to such records will be much sought after by investigative agencies.

Today in the United States copies of *all* personal checks are retained for at least five years. This is the result of federal requirements aimed at making persons' financial affairs accessible to investigative agencies. Not only the Internal Revenue Service but also a wide variety of other federal, state, and local agencies enjoy access to these personal records, often without subpoena or the individual's knowledge. The total number of these inquiries is not known, but in one survey twenty-two banks reported responding to an average of five hundred requests per year. The great majority of such investigations arise from routine law-enforcement concerns, including tax evasion and other crimes. But under oppressive political conditions, as during the Nixon years, such investigations can and do serve as instruments of political harassment.

The main check on such investigations today is that they are extremely labor-intensive. Going through microfilm records of a person's financial affairs can tie up an agent for days or weeks. If such records become computerized, however, the job will be much easier. The "log" of a person's financial transactions may be located by searching the computerized net and examined simply by printing out the record of a particular account. By making access to private persons' account data cheaper and more efficient, financial institutions will also have made monitoring of individuals' lives easier for state agencies. If precedent is any guide, these opportunities will not be neglected.

Mail

Moving letters and packages is a labor- and energy-intensive business, much like the processing of personal checks. Hence the impetus to electronic mail. Mailgram service, in which messages are electronically relayed to the recipient's nearest post office and delivered in the next day's regular mail, is only a start of this trend. With home terminals, the proper electronic "net" could make it possible to tap out a letter in one's own study and have it transmitted instantly to any address served by another terminal, as on any present Telex system. Some multinational corporations are already using such systems, which can also transmit copies of documentary materials. Mass production will probably bring big reductions in the costs of these technologies, while ordinary mail becomes costlier and slower all the time. Unions representing postal workers have already begun to register alarm at the massive displacements of labor that could result.

But the prospect of replacing conventional mail with a computerized electronic net should raise deep political concerns. Ever since colonial times, authoritarian political climates have led to state monitoring of the mail.[2] Even when not actually opened, it has been subjected to "mail covers," in which the frequency and origins of correspondence are systematically recorded. During a two-year period in the 1960s, some 24,000 Americans were subjected to such surveillance—a practice, incidentally, that is not illegal.

Like in-person investigation of microfilmed checks, mail openings and mail covers are labor-intensive. Electronic mail would make such activities much cheaper—and probably also easier to conceal. Indeed, the new technologies would threaten to erase the distinction between "mail covers" and actual opening of communications, since access to the "inside" of an electronic letter would presumably be no more difficult than access to the address.

News and Home Data Services

As Tony Smith has shown in his fascinating book *Goodbye Gutenberg,* modern newspapers have thrived by becoming large, heterogeneous "bundles" of information. When we "consume" a hefty *New York Times* or *Washington Post,* we rummage through these bundles, discarding most of their contents and using only a few nuggets of information. But with the costs of newsprint and transport rising, publishers are feeling pressure to break up the "bundles" and eliminate waste by sending readers only the information they are most likely to read.

This process has already begun. Special editions are set up for special groups of readers: suburban editions of newspapers or "businessman's editions" of national magazines. These changes are minor compared to what could be done if paper were dispensed with altogether, and informational "products" delivered directly to a person's living room via computer. Subscribers could then indicate in advance what news, features, and ads they were prepared to read, and the material so selected could be displayed on their TV screens. Some cable TV providers have already instituted systems allowing considerable flexibility in program selection. As people's informational requirements are identified with more and more exactitude, the "waste" of untargeted journalism and broadcasting would decrease in favor of what some have called "narrowcasting."

But who will be able to monitor the use of services like these? Patterns of personal information use tell a great deal about political attitudes and interests. It is difficult to imagine any home information system that could avoid creating a "log" of the informational choices of the users—if only as a by-product of the billing process. There would certainly be no technological barrier to direct state monitoring of the choices of each user. And if state authorities are willing to go to the trouble of harassing subscribers to periodicals of a particular slant—as they have done in recent history—will they resist the more tempting possibilities presented by the new systems?

Electronic Dossiers

The growth of systematic record keeping on individuals has been a feature of "advanced" social systems for much longer than have the new electronic technologies. Since the turn of this century, large organizations—both governmental and private—have increasingly developed written dossiers on members of the general public, and used the records as bases for organizational action toward these individuals.[3] Now, these record systems are more and more computerized. Computerization does no more than intensify a central fact of life in the modern world: that one's records *matter* enormously in dealings with all sorts of powerful institutions.

Computerization, however, is now greatly streamlining the collection, storage, and, above all, transmission and use of personal dossiers. A key feature of the new computerized systems is their ability to produce very rapid responses to requests for information and to make what would otherwise be enormously laborious cross-checks at minimal delay and cost.

Thus it is now possible for federal officials to check anyone entering the country from abroad against elaborate computerized records. At present, roughly two thirds of all incoming travelers have their identities checked against this central file, known as TECS; further improvement should raise this level. The computerized inquiry, in effect, determines whether the traveler—who may be foreign or a U.S. national—is of interest to any of a variety of federal agencies. Such interest may run from that of an agency only wanting to be kept informed of someone's movements to that of a local, state, or federal law-enforcement body seeking that person's arrest. Where no action is taken at the time of entry, a record of the traveler's name and date and place of arrival is retained in the computer memory for an extended period.

Most of the arrests made through TECS are of persons listed in the National Crime Information Center, the FBI's computerized roster of persons wanted for arrest throughout the United States. A quick check of names against this list makes it possible to identify all sorts of persons who would otherwise pass through the net of law enforcement attention. There are now plans to computerize the daily reports written by every FBI investigator, including those about the reported *associates* of persons under investigation. The names of these persons could then be checked against the computerized listing of wanted individuals or monitored by FBI staff for any other purpose they saw fit.

We see evidence of imaginative use of similar capacities all the time, for example, in the cross-checking of welfare rolls against computerized payrolls. Often the applications in question are for purposes hardly anyone could dispute. But in the long run, dare we assume that these sophisticated capabilities will not be used for tracking political enemies? Remember only the Nixon era, with its use of federal data files to harass political opponents.

III

One could cite many other new technologies which, though conceived as solutions for mundane bureaucratic problems, clearly have authoritarian potentialities. And this poses a ticklish problem: How shall we respond?

The simplest response—and much the least convincing—is that typically given by sponsors of new data systems. For public consumption, they often insist that the larger social or political significance of their activities is nil. Innovations in Social Security accounting, police record keeping, mail delivery, consumer credit reporting, or the like simply enable organizations to improve what they have really been doing all along. Since they enhance efficiency in providing desired services, they can only make the world more productive and humane. Or so the argument goes.

This line has little or nothing to recommend it. Incremental developments over long periods are bound to bring about qualitative change. These changes will amount to *new kinds of social relations* between central institutions and "private" citizens. The question is, what political tendency is apt to dominate these relations? What social interests are the new systems most apt to serve?

A gloomier approach to these developments is to assume that

technologies that seem merely to permit manipulation and re-pression actually demand these things.[4] The obvious conclusion is that technologies for monitoring human lives can never be simply neutral instruments in human hands. But this argument, suggestive in many contexts, seems weakest when applied to information technologies. The same technologies which could sustain totalitarianism and intrusive surveillance could also support new democratic forms. New applications of computing, for example, perhaps in conjunction with closed-circuit TV, could make possible exchanges of views and information on public issues through "town meetings" in which participants need never leave home. Other applications of home computing could enable people to inform themselves, at minimal cost, about activities of governments and other institutions. The pos-sibilities of new technologies are endless; which possibilities will be realized can hardly be understood by considering technology alone.

Thus one analysis based on a priori pessimism and another on blindered optimism. The trouble with these otherwise anti-thetical positions is that both ignore *power*. What concrete social interests are apt to direct the development of these sys-tems, and to shape the uses of the personal information gener-ated by them?

A writer who has begun to confront this question is Daniel Bell, whose recent works have stressed the role of information in shaping the world of the future. Given this bent, one would expect Bell to have much to say about the interests most likely to be served in the developments of these technologies.

Yet, strangely enough, he does not. He acknowledges the totalitarian potential of the new technologies: "The new revolu-tion in communications makes possible both an intense degree of centralization of power, if the society decides to use it in that way, and large decentralization because of the multiplicity, diversity and cheapness of the modes of communications." But he declines to take the logical step of exploring which of these possibilities are most likely to be served: "Real as these issues are for liberty . . . they are not the true locus of the problem.

It is not in the technology *per se* but in the social and political system in which that technology is embedded."[5]

True enough. But it seems perverse to let matters go with this sort of intellectual shrug. The political forces apt to shape the future development of these systems are neither mysterious nor inaccessible to study. They are the same forces that have been shaping similar systems in the past.

And the historical record gives no grounds for complacency. In America, politically repressive climates recur with sad regularity—above all during war or the fear of it, and during times when people are obsessed with domestic subversion. At such times, pressures to appropriate personal information for political purpose become intense. The precedents extend from the opening of private persons' mail in colonial America, to Lincoln's attempt to gain access to private telegraphic communications during the Civil War, to Nixon's use of IRS information to harass political opponents in the 1970s.

Social Security was established with elaborate assurances that personal information stored within it would be used only for internal purposes. Today this information is made available for a variety of outside purposes, some of them by no means friendly to the individual. These range from verifying eligibility for welfare payments to tracking of parents who abscond on child support. Such erosions of the original integrity of the system appear to have been dictated by forces outside Social Security, notably Congress. Professional administrators within Social Security appear to have resisted these pressures as far as they could. The same seems to have been true of Treasury and IRS career officials in response to Nixon's efforts to use tax records for political purposes.

IV

During the 1940s and 1950s Western intellectuals came increasingly to view the future in terms of "mass society." In this view, the world's most "advanced" societies were increasingly characterized by highly influential, impersonal directives from autocratic elites to atomized, disorganized, and manipulable populations. The origins of this vision can be traced to early twentieth-century anti-populist thinkers, notably Ortega y Gasset and Gustave Le Bon. Such ideas gained momentum, of course, from the examples of Nazi Germany and Stalinist U.S.S.R. By the 1940s, many feared that all modern societies were on the way to domination through the bombardment of docile populations with carefully orchestrated mass propaganda; the result, it was felt, would be manufacture of popular consent, a parody of authentic democracy. Orwell shared this fear at least in part.

Since the forties, however, we have found some reasons to qualify this view. By no means do people always uncritically accept even the most persuasive messages over the mass media; face-to-face associations and community influences play a big role in the assimilation of such mass messages. Yet much of the insight contained in theories of mass society retains validity. A key feature of "advanced" societies in the twentieth century is the ability of elites to influence entire populations through command of mass communications. No one can expect to retain power in any modern society without considerable mastery over these media.

In the information processes described in this essay, one detects a trend comparable to the rise of mass communications. I call these new information processes "mass surveillance"— the monitoring by large organizations of large numbers of ordinary people. Obviously mass communications and mass surveillance have much in common; both involve direct relations between central powers and large numbers of individual citizens. But in some ways the two are also diametrically opposite. For mass surveillance enables organizations to respond to the fine detail of each individual's situation. Where mass communications entail bombarding individuals with identical and undifferentiated stimuli, mass surveillance involves attending to the peculiarities of the individual with tailor-made organizational action.

Mass communications and mass surveillance can both be seen as part of a still broader development: the "mobilization" of populations within the modern state. As many writers have noted, the modern state has intensified the direct ties between central institutions and ordinary individuals. Thus the increasingly broad participation of modern populations in warfare, welfare systems, electoral processes, and the like. These new ties involve both claims by the state on individuals—for military service, taxation, and so on—and claims by individuals for state services, such as insurance and medical care. Plainly this process has brought its share of advantages to ordinary people. But it has also brought vast concentration of power in agencies capable of "reaching out" to mobilize the actions or resources of large numbers of persons.

Among certain conservative theorists, there is a tradition of opposition to "progress" based on skepticism about the long-term effects of such mobilization. The modern state, such thinkers have argued, destroys traditional restraints on political behavior and political power. Instead of a large number of power centers, the modern state becomes a single focus of power, unchecked by any other. Even the archaisms of traditional social systems are seen as preferable to the centralized power imprudently concentrated in the modern state.

Those of us on the democratic left have ordinarily felt no such sweeping opposition to modernization. We tend to see abuses of central power in modern societies as stemming from the particular interests dominating the state apparatus, rather than from the structure of that apparatus. Leftists have most often sought political salvation in converting state institutions to more humane and egalitarian uses, rather than in attacking bureaucracy on principle. Enhancing the efficiency of such institutions has appeared as a contribution to progress.

But I believe we must be uncomfortable with the growth of technological and bureaucratic powers which could so readily serve the requirements of totalitarianism, even when such use not immediately intended. Their sheer existence poses risks that cannot be allayed in purely political terms. For democrats, totalitarianism represents the ultimate political disaster.

The response to these problems in the Western democracies has been to seek "due process" checks. Thus both the United States and other countries have enacted legislation mandating individuals' access to their own records, correction of erroneous information in files or computer records, and so on. As far as they go, such measures are useful; but they do not really address the broader historical concerns at issue here.

Mortals will never know in advance the future political conditions shaping the application of due process guarantees. Even rather moderate changes can bring abuses of IRS files and other government data by a Nixon. A more sweeping shift in political fortunes can bring actions like those of the Nazis in Holland during the occupation, when they appropriated Dutch population registries to locate Jews. The only *absolute* safety lies in avoiding the development of systems that concentrate potentially volatile information.

True, we do have some room for maneuver. It is feasible, I would argue, to reduce risks involved in systems like those discussed here by adopting less "information-intensive" practices. This means seeking to deliver services while using and retaining less information on the persons concerned.[6] The result would be reduced bureaucratic control: less accurate discrimination between those worthy of credit and those unlikely to pay their bills, less discrimination between the acutely needy and the not-so-needy in welfare payments, less effective monitoring of the movements of criminals and suspects, and so on. These changes may often be desirable in themselves. But they are bound to be opposed by powerful bureaucratic interests.

Sometimes, however, less "information-intensive" alternatives are just not available. In computerized mail communications, for example, the dangers of abuse seem inherent in the logic of the system itself. As long as letters and other personal communications are carried through an electronic net, such communications are more easily monitored than those written with old-fashioned paper and pen. A regime willing to ignore statutory limitations could, for example, scan communications in which a particular name appears, or all those to a particular address, or even all those with a particular theme. Similar reservations apply to home information services, electronic payments, and many other personalized data management systems. One might, within limits, minimize the duration in which personal information accumulates in these systems. But their very existence will always present risks.

Orwell foresaw—and made unforgettable—a world in which ruthless political interests mobilized intrusive technologies for totalitarian ends. What he did not consider was the possibility that the development of the intrusive technologies would occur *on its own, without the spur of totalitarian intent*. This, in fact, is what is now happening.

I believe we have a great deal to worry about in the growth of new personal information systems. The recipient of mass communications can at least ignore a propagandistic media event or thumb his nose at the President's televised news conference. But in the new computerized communications, the recipient will leave an electronic record of his interactions with the system. That record provides central powers with opportunities for deeper and more powerful penetrations into private life. The accumulation of such records represents a blank check to the political intentions of those who can control the systems. Surely we would be better off not to write that check, even if this means renouncing some of the benefits of the new technologies.

And how one wishes, finally, that Orwell, the "inventor" of the telescreen, were still here with us, to comment on this development in democratic countries. Imagine Hate Week with electronic devices, a memory hole with up-to-date technologies. What would Orwell say if he were to see that some of the frightful things he imagined as a result of totalitarian evil could also occur during the ordinary course of democratic benevolence? Or as the "neutral" result of technological development?

12 *1984* and the Conservative Imagination

I

George Orwell was no conservative; liberal democratic socialist —albeit salted with skepticism—probably comes closest to describing his political views. All the same, one is struck by the presence in his novel of certain themes or vistas that go back to not liberal or radical sources in modern thought but conservative. There is the use he makes of the past, deemed an indispensable foundation of freedom, its distortion and erasure equally indispensable to the totalitarian despotism in Oceania; it is only memory of the past, however dim, that makes possible the occasional eruption of dissidence. The intellectual class, represented by O'Brien, is depicted as both Edmund Burke and Alexis de Tocqueville depicted this class in the Enlightenment and the Revolution in France: as a new aristocracy rooted not in the land but in word and symbol, its primary mission that of generating new and bizarre conceptions of past and present —or as Orwell puts it, Newspeak and doublethink. The early nineteenth century premonition of the masses—of those in but not of the social order, uprooted from tradition and moral code, mute until played upon by their masters—is of course highly luminous in Orwell's treatment of the proles. The iron relationship Burke saw between revolution and the militarization of a country, each a side of the same coin, is highlighted by Orwell's treatment of Oceania's wars, real or imaginary at any given moment, and of the reinforcing effects of military propaganda and terror. Finally, the theory of history implicit in *1984*, one in which the present reality of a totalitarian state is made a more or less continuous outcome, not a reversal, of an increasingly socialized mass democracy in the recent past, is quintessentially conservative.

These are, I believe, perspicuous themes and emphases in Orwell's classic. They are also, in striking degree, the essential themes and emphases of Edmund Burke's response in 1790 to the French Revolution, which may fairly be called the West's first experience with the image, if not the reality, of totalitarianism; one based upon republican virtue and disposed to any extreme of violence, terror, and propaganda as a means of remaking human nature. So are they the essential themes of the conservative tradition of thought in the nineteenth and early twentieth century that flowed directly from Burke's *Reflections on the Revolution in France*. All of the early conservatives— Bonald, Haller, Savigny, Southey, Balmes, among others—expressed their indebtedness to Burke's work. In the twentieth century we have but to scan the writings of Ortega y Gasset, C. S. Lewis, Mallock, More, Dawson, and Eliot to see instantly how intact the Burkean conservative writ remains. From Burke's *Reflections* down to Oakeshott and Muggeridge in our time, the conservative vision is made distinctive by premonition that out of mass democracy and boundless social and moral liberalism would come not greater freedom and justice, but a new and terrible form of society characterized on the one hand by the kind of absolute and ubiquitous political power that Burke saw as the chief contribution of the French Revolution and on the other by the incessant generating of what Burke called an "unsocial, uncivil, unconnected chaos of elementary principles . . . one homogeneous mass." And from Burke through Burckhardt to Christopher Dawson, and, yes, George Orwell, it was never doubted that the sole basis of rule in such a political aggregate must be by what Burckhardt called "military commandoes."

Burke thought the French Revolution "the most astonishing that has hitherto happened in the world. . . . Many parts of Europe are in open disorder. In many others there is a hollow murmuring underground; a confused movement is felt, that threatens a general earthquake in the world."[1] Earlier revolutions such as that of 1688 in England and the American uprising against the British crown had been, Burke thought, limited revolutions, with freedom the animating objective. But what was beginning to take shape across the Channel by 1790 was, Burke declared, unlimited, boundless, and insatiable in its political millennialism. In the name of reason and virtue, nothing less than the remaking of human personality as well as society everywhere was the objective, Burke saw, of Jacobin leaders.

Millennialism was old in the history of mankind, as were uses of terror, slaughter, and pillage, but always before its roots were religious—from the Middle Ages on, the expectation of Christ's return to the earth. For the Jacobins, however, the millennium was to be inaugurated solely by the state on which the Jacobins were already hard at work in the name of perfect virtue when Burke was writing his *Reflections* for publication in 1791. The Jacobin political order—never to be realized in full but luminescent all the same in political theology thereafter—was not the less millenarian in design for its repudiation of Christianity and Judaism. Nor was it the less religious in most respects. Burke, early in the *Reflections,* stresses the elements of zeal and passion in Jacobin works which had hitherto been reserved for religions. Tocqueville, a half a century later, in his study of the Revolution, echoed Burke:

> The French Revolution's approach to the problems of man's existence here on earth was exactly similar to that of the religious revolutions as regards his afterlife . . . for the ideal the French Revolution set before it was not merely a change in the French social system but nothing short of a regeneration of the whole human race. It created an atmosphere of missionary fervor and, indeed, assumed all the aspects of a religious revival.[2]

It was the calculated instilling of what had been strictly religious forms and roles into the Revolution that led in a short time to totalitarian aspirations. If man was to be truly liberated from errors of the past and thence saved for all humanity, he must be spared the ambiance of traditional institutions. Thus the systematic obliteration, in the name of freedom and justice, of patriarchal family, of the sacrament of marriage, of primogeniture and entail, the craft guilds, the aristocracy, the monarchy, even the ancient communes and provinces, and, well above all, the Church and all its component entities—monasteries, schools, universities, asylums, and ecclesiastical courts.

But it is never sufficient to raze, jettison, or obliterate when the work at hand is the remaking of human personality. And the more fervent Jacobins, taking their inspiration from Rousseau's thrilling chapter on "The Legislator" in *The Social Contract,* proposed nothing less than that: the reconstruction of man in the image and likeness of Virtue. Such reconstruction would take time, but what could be established overnight, it was believed by the revolutionary millennialists, was a new political and social order within which the children of the present generation could be nourished psychologically and morally.

Hence, early in the Revolution, the totalitarian use of political power to achieve and create as well as destroy. The map of France was thoroughly redesigned in its political subdivisions, departments replacing the ancient provinces, cantons the traditional communes. Everything was oriented toward the absoluteness and primacy of Paris where all of the new leaders of France would cluster. All education was deemed to be the prerogative of the state; private schooling was banned. There would be one curriculum for all of France, its administration centralized in Paris, the University of Paris to be the capstone of the system. A new monetary system was devised, a new calendar, one in which a mere daily glance would quickly succeed in blotting out of the French mind memory of old chronology and old symbols of association.

The important role of individual identity in society was not overlooked, and "citizen," as a term of address, rapidly succeeded older ones, even those derived from kinship. After all, Rousseau had assured his readers in his third discourse that the

father speaking in the name of citizen would be not the less
obeyed. With extraordinary shrewdness the leaders of the Revolution sought also to minimize the difference between army
and citizenry, indeed between peace and war. It was the Revolution that instituted, for the first time in Western history, the
levée en masse, the forced conscription of all able-bodied males.
Subtly but powerfully the army was made into a microcosm of
the whole political and social Revolution, while at the same
time the nation—"the armed nation"—was celebrated in rites
and symbols that stressed the affinity between revolution and
war.

I am not suggesting that every idea of the Revolution-intox-
icated Convention, Committee on Public Safety, and other bodies during the Revolution became fulfilled in policy and practice. Far from it. But the real historical influence of the
Revolution lies in the language of its varied decrees, in the
rhetoric that clothed the ideas of Danton, Robespierre, Saint-
Just, and others. There is, as I want to emphasize, a straight and
continuous line from this language and rhetoric from Robespierre to Lenin—and Orwell's *1984.*

Religion was not forgotten. Rousseau—whose *Social Contract* attained a popularity among revolutionary leaders, indeed
among a substantial number of citizens, it had not had before
the Revolution—had declared religion indispensable to man
and recommended the establishment of a purely civil religion
by the sovereign state, its articles of faith few and simple, aimed
at full devotion to the nation-state. "While it can compel no one
to believe them," Rousseau wrote, "it can banish from the State
whoever does not believe them. . . . If anyone after publicly
recognizing these dogmas, behaves as if he does not believe
them, let him be punished by death: he has committed the worst
of crimes, that of lying before the law."[3]

In 1794 Robespierre drew up a civil religion for all France,
one that he preferred to call the Religion of the Supreme Being
and Nature; the Supreme Being was of course the Revolution
itself. In article after article of the new religion, the essence of

the constructed religion was veneration forever of the great personages and events of the Revolution. "The French people," Robespierre wrote, "appear to have outstripped the rest of the human race by two thousand years."[4] Once sacred France had become wholly consolidated and unified by its new beliefs, then France would become the vanguard of the revolution that will not stop until the entire world has been transformed. The drawing up and diffusion of the principles of the new religion of France, *une et indivisible*, corresponded perfectly with the instigation and regularization of the Terror, of the ritual beheadings of so many of the revolutionists themselves who had been found guilty of hypocrisy. Hannah Arendt has written illuminatingly on hypocrisy as the crime of crimes in the Revolution:

> The momentous role that hypocrisy and the passion for its unmasking came to play in the later stages of the French Revolution, though it may never cease to astound the historian, is a matter of historical record. The Revolution, before it proceeded to devour its own children, had unmasked them, and French historiography in more than a hundred and fifty years has reproduced and documented all of these exposures until no one is left among the chief actors who does not stand accused, or at least suspected of corruption, duplicity and mendacity.
>
> It was the war upon hypocrisy that transformed Robespierre's dictatorship into the Reign of Terror, and the outstanding characteristic of this period was the self-purging of the rulers.[5]

II

This is essentially the French Revolution that Burke saw or foresaw in his *Reflections*. For him there was no relation whatsoever, logical or historical, between the American and the French revolutions. The former had been the work of liberation of a people and their customs from the increasingly harsh and exploitative government of Great Britain, the struggle, in sum,

of Englishmen abroad against those Englishmen at home who
would take from them their birthright in the principles of the
Glorious Revolution of 1688. It was Burke's dedication to that
Revolution and its heritage that made him the champion of the
American colonists and also of those in India and Ireland who
suffered under the British government and its agencies.

Far different, thought Burke, was the French Revolution: the
very obverse of the American indeed. It was not, by Burke's
reckoning, freedom of individual French that the Revolution's
leaders were seeking but instead the power to yoke the French
people to a system of government vastly more powerful than
any known under the monarchy. In the name of Virtue and
Reason, or of whatever ideal, the French leaders were seeking
precisely that total transformation of French culture and character that Rousseau had called for. And their means were inescapably military. "It is impossible," Burke wrote, "not to
observe that in the spirit of this geometrical distribution and
arithmetical arrangement, these pretended citizens treat France
exactly like a country of conquest. Acting as conquerers, they
have imitated the policy of the harshest of that harsh race."[6]

How accurate Burke's highly polemical envisagement of the
French was need not concern us here—beyond observing with
amusement that had the leaders of the Revolution at its height
been asked to compare Burke's rendering with that of, say,
Richard Price, they would have doubtless rejected the latter's
as naive and credulous. They may not have liked Burke's values
any more than he liked theirs, but they could not have quar-
reled with Burke's prophecy that the French Revolution would
go well beyond freedom and justice to the very nature of government, society, and the human mind.

What is alone important here is the fact that Burke's particular view of the French Revolution became that essentially of
nearly all conservatives in the nineteenth century—Bonald, de
Maistre, Savigny and Hegel, Southey and Coleridge, Haller,
Taine, and others—and that this view is also a foundation of
twentieth-century conservatism's contemplation of totalitarian-

ism. Although the word was not in Burke's vocabulary, "totalitarian" expresses almost perfectly his epitomization of the French Revolution. When we examine the writings on revolution and politics of the reigning conservatives in the twentieth century—Irving Babbitt, Paul Elmer More, A. J. Nock, Russell Kirk, Christopher Dawson, Michael Oakeshott, Jacques Maritain, Bertrand de Jouvenel, and Hans Barth, among others—we find that their own assessments of the totalitarian phenomenon come very close to Burke's assessment of the French Revolution.

III

It is important to begin with the philosophy of history that contains the conservative view of totalitarianism. This philosophy stresses the continuity of the rise of totalitarianism in Europe after World War I so far as antecedent conditions and changes in political and social life were concerned. Far from being some inexplicable mutant, the totalitarian order is a pathological development of certain reigning forces in the nineteenth century: nationalism, mass democracy, plebiscitary government, individual alienation from traditional dogmas on ever-widening scale, and so on. Burke and Tocqueville had both specifically related the French Revolution to pre-revolutionary patterns of thought and action. If we read the major conservatives of the nineteenth century, Taine, Burckhardt, Le Play, and Maine, there is always to be seen the specter of a political power of the future that is more despotic for its claimed roots in the masses. The same perspective is found in the writings of such twentieth-century conservatives as Babbitt, More, Brooks Adams, and Ortega y Gasset. The phenomenon of total political power, first seen in practice in Russia and Italy after World War I, is, for the conservative, spectacularly *modern:* rooted in or otherwise positively connected with such modern forces as mass democracy, socialism, and a general secularization of culture.

In this respect, conservative analysis largely flies in the teeth
of the liberal and radical diagnoses that were so popular in the
1930s after Hitler came to power. Nazism for one was declared
an atavism, the recrudescence of ancient forms and passions.
For the liberal *progressiste*, nothing evil could be modern, much
less a harbinger of the future, for by definition history moved
from the generally bad to the generally good. Given the democratic trends of two whole centuries in the West, anything
politically repugnant had to be some mutant throwback, an
eruption of the still unconquered past. "Irrational," "archaic,"
"reactionary," and "primitive" are a few of the popular charac-
terizations from the liberal sector of the totalitarian behemoth.
Stalinism was a reversion to primal Russian despotism, not the
inevitable outcome of a society dedicated to militant, mass
collectivism. Similarly, Nazism was, in one especially fatuous
ascription, "the return of the Middle Ages."

In all truth, the totalitarian order is as rational and as modern as any other large-scale structure of the twentieth century,
its inherent, unbanishable evil notwithstanding. In terms of
aspiration and indeed organization, it is as modern as the huge
corporation, the massive bureaucracy, the large political party,
or any other structure that comes to mind. Michels saw what
was coming in this respect at the beginning of the century, in
the Socialist parties of Europe: in their ever greater centralization of power and singlemindedness of dreams of use of this
power. James Burnham made this fact central in his prescient
and largely unappreciated *Managerial Revolution*, written in
the 1930s. So did Walter Lippmann in his book of the same
decade, *The Good Society*.

Though we are loath to admit it, the first twentieth-century
preview of the totalitarian state was provided by the United
States in 1917–18 after we joined the Allies in the war against
Germany. Not even the Kaiser's military-political order, much
less that of either England or France, reached the totality of the
war-state that America did in extraordinarily short order once
war on Germany was declared. The relentless forces of centrali-

zation, nationalization, and collectivization of political power reached literally every significant area of American life: the economy and the government in the first instance, but hardly less the communications system, education at all levels, entertainment and recreation, even and especially religion, where the spectacle of preachers presenting arms became overnight a common one.

To this day, few Americans have any genuine awareness of the sheer totalitarianism of the American war venture in 1917–18. Industry-labor councils with absolute powers over wages and prices, 175,000 Four-Minute Men with orders to invade any assemblage whatever for propagandist purposes, sedition laws, systematic mobilization of teachers, clergy, artists, writers, actors, and the like, arrests, with heavy fines or imprisonments, in the name of "Pro-Germanism," and above all the infectious spirit of a centralized collectivism fighting for a great moral objective—all of this and more offered a preview to what would become grim reality in Russia, Italy, and Germany. It is a tribute to the native conservatism of the American people of 1918 that virtually all the machinery of totalitarianism was dismantled once the war was ended. But the impact of President Wilson's transformation of America within two short years would not be forgotten, either at home or abroad.

The essentiality of modernity in the totalitarian mystique is clear in most conservative writings on politics in this century. Ortega y Gasset, in *The Revolt of the Masses,* called specific attention to the markedly *un*totalitarian character of the earlier European despotisms, writing: "It would be worthwhile insisting on this point and making clear that the epoch of absolute monarchies has coincided with very weak states." Why is this? Because, Ortega answers, of a lack of technological and organizational means of making them strong, and, "besides that, it also happened that the absolute State and the aristocracies *did not want to aggrandize the State at the expense of society in general.*"[7] On the other hand, Ortega continues, "Mussolini found a state admirably built up—not by him, but precisely by

the ideas and forces he is combating: by liberal democracy."[8]
Christopher Dawson, also writing in the 1930s, thought the
Russian, Italian, and German experiences so deeply connected
with major strands of modern Western history that he had no
hesitation in declaring the strong probability of like experiences
occurring in other Western countries, England and America
included. These, he wrote, "will result in the formation of a type
of totalitarian state which bears the same relation to Anglo-
Saxon political and social traditions as the Nazi state bears to
the traditions of Prussia and Central Europe."[9]

In his *Old Regime and the French Revolution,* Tocqueville
demonstrated the almost perfect continuity of the Revolution
in modern French history. "Chance," he wrote, "played no part
whatever in the outbreak of the French Revolution. . . . It was
the inevitable outcome of a long period of gestation."[10] There
are a great many conservative writers of the last sixty years
who have said essentially the same thing about the totalitarian
state.

IV

Of all aspects of modernity that conservatism tends to see as
seedbeds of the totalitarian order, the political-democratic
comes first. The total state is not in the first instance anti-
Semitism, capitalist exploitation, individual dictatorship, oligarchy, or military seizure, much less renascence of ancient
forms of tyranny. It is, so the conservative argument largely
goes, a direct emanation of the rage to politicize, to nationalize,
and to centralize, which has been growing in the West, with
only occasional lulls, ever since the French Revolution. The
democratic mystique that diffused in exponential degree
throughout the nineteenth century led to a kind of sanctifica-
tion of political power, grounded of course in the sacred general
will of the people. Who, after all, could properly cavil at the
spread of power in the whole society that was of, by, and for
the People?

Totalitarianism is at bottom the elevation to the nth degree of this democratic-nationalist view of political power. The expansion of the state's sovereign authority to all areas of society and culture is at the heart of the phenomenon. It is really of little philosophic importance what the nature of the actual government is; it may be monocratic, oligarchic, even democratic in the sense of diffusion of permitted participation, of plebiscitary consultation with the electorate from time to time. What is alone of importance in the totalitarian, in contrast to, say, the authoritarian state is the never-ceasing invasion of the traditional social order by the political—through education, persuasion, propaganda, bribery, and other means of thought control including terror. It is in this enterprise that the various forms of doublethink and Newspeak are used in totalitarian orders.

The difference between the authoritarian and totalitarian state lies exactly in this realm of the uses of political power. Such uses may include, as in Argentina, Chile, South Korea, and South Africa, the secret police, imprisonment without charge, torture, and exile—precisely as in the authoritarian states of the Bourbons and Tudors in early modern European history—but rarely if ever does this kind of state seek the obliteration or serious crippling of family, local community, church, social class, and other strata of authority intermediate to individual and state. From the point of view of the hapless individual in an authoritarian state, this may seem a distinction without a difference. But it is not. We are, it is true, dealing here with ideal types; the two kinds of state may occasionally shade into one another in practice. But we miss a great deal of the distinctive—and distinctively modern—character of the totalitarian state if we do not go immediately to its permanent war on society; that is, its nihilistic assault on the whole social sphere that is historically prior to and largely independent of the political state. Jeane Kirkpatrick, in *Dictatorships and Double Standards,* writes to this point: "Totalitarianism obliterates the distinction between state and society and eliminates thereby those interstices of the law in which freedom thrives."[11] Thirty years ago, in my *The Quest for Community,* I argued:

What gives historical identity to the totalitarian state is not the absolutism of one man or of a clique or class; rather, it is the absolute extension of the structure of the State into the social and psychological realm previously occupied by a plurality of associations. Totalitarianism involves the demolishment of autonomous social ties in a population, but it involves, no less, their replacement by new ones, each deriving its meaning and sanction from the central structure of the State.[12]

"Structure," though, is hardly the sufficient word here. The ancient and abiding craving for community by man enters into the appeal of the total state. As Hume pointed out in one of his essays, no despotism, ancient or modern, could survive long if coercion and repression were its only attributes. It must proffer something that can be conceived as benign by its subjects, or at least as useful. Protection from adversaries and marauders, succor in time of need, at least minimal regard for public welfare through military and civil services, all of these and other elements enter into the toleration by large majorities of even the most despotic of states. Highest among these elements is, over and over in history, the feeling of community, of being together in something that is valuable to life and property. The state, like the Church, can offer both spiritual and social and political security.

It is the very essence of the totalitarian state that, unlike the authoritarian state, much less the liberal democracy, it should seek to become the *communitas communitatum* of its members; at once family, neighborhood, church, and guild for its citizens. Rousseau, true father of the totalitarian mystique, said: "He who dares to undertake the making of a people's institutions ought to feel himself capable, so to speak, of changing human nature, of transforming each individual . . . into part of a greater whole from which he in a manner receives his life and being."[12a] O'Brien, in *1984*, puts it more pithily: "We control life, Winston, at all its levels. You are imagining that there is something called human nature which will be outraged by what we do and will turn against us. But we create human nature. Men are infinitely malleable."[13] Thus the sacred status of the New Soviet Man. Thus the hideous acts of genocide of Pol Pot. Thus the carrying of the state's power in China to every neighborhood, to every block, to every family, even, as we have learned, to the menstrual cycle of the wife. Side by side with the booted commando in every totalitarian order is the teacher—missionary, preceptor, expositor, call him what we will. Absolute power without a guiding communal ideal would be fruitless. But any ideal without absolute power at its side would be impotent. In his *Discourse on Political Economy,* written to supply the basic guidelines for the ideal political order, one that was to be established in the reality of the general will, Rousseau argued:

> If it is good to know how to deal with men as they are, it is much better to make them what there is need that they should be. The most absolute authority is that which penetrates into a man's inmost being, and concerns itself no less with his will than with his actions. It is certain that all peoples become in the long run what the government makes them: warriors, citizens, men, when it so pleases; or merely populace and rabble, when it chooses to make them so."[14]

Later, in admiring and sedulous devotion to Rousseau, the Committee on Public Safety declared: "The transition of an oppressed nation to democracy is like the effort by which nature arose from nothingness to existence. You must entirely refashion a people whom you wish to make free, destroy its prejudices, alter its habit, limit its necessities, root up its vices, purify its desire."[15] Gletkin, in *Darkness at Noon,* understood that; so did O'Brien in *1984.* And so have Lenin, Hitler, Mao, and Pol Pot understood it. Anything short of that view of man and history would fail the totalitarian ideal of community and of the self formed in the image and likeness of the total community.

Tocqueville, musing on his ideal type, democracy and its potentialities for despotism, wrote:

The first thing that strikes the observation is an innumerable multitude of men, all equal and alike. . . . Above this race of men stands an immense and tutelary power, which takes upon itself alone to secure their gratifications and to watch over their fate. That power is absolute, minute, regular, provident and mild. . . . After having thus successively taken each member of the community in its powerful grasp, the supreme power then extends its arm over the whole community. It covers the surface of society with a network of small, complicated rules, minute and uniform. . . . The will of man is not shattered, but softened, bent and guided. . . . Such a power does not destroy, but it prevents existence; it does not tyrannize, but it compresses, enervates, extinguishes, and stupefies a people till each nation is reduced to nothing better than a flock of timid and industrious animals of which the government is the shepherd.[16]

Tocqueville did not venture to predict that such a polity was the inevitable outcome of prolonged egalitarian democracy; he merely offered it as one more of the ideal types which in their varied, often intuitive, always abstract, patterns form the mosaic that is Part II of *Democracy in America*. He does not say that democracy must or even will eventuate in the kind of polity he has just described. He is saying that *if* democracy—with its constitutive elements of the mass, equality, and centralization of government always ready in crisis to emerge triumphant— passes into despotism, it will do so very much along the line he has limned.

The merit of Tocqueville's preview of totalitarianism is that it does not go to the manifestly repugnant or horrifying, to terror, murder, torture, and imprisonment without trial; for, vivid though these are in the records of twentieth-century totalitarian states, they do not, even in a Russia or China, apply to the vast majority of subjects, who rarely if ever stray from the path of obedience. They are ruled absolutely but benignly or at least custodially, less by threat of force than through a "network of complicated rules, minute and uniform, through which the most original minds and most energetic characters cannot penetrate, to rise above the crowd."[17]

The aim of the totalitarian government is that of finding every possible remaining persistence of the past, of symbol, act, and memory, that might militate against the reigning structure of power. If the people cannot be transformed in nature through indoctrination, blandishment, circuses, and relentless propaganda, then the assistance of raw terror must be sought: sudden arrests in the night, total loss of identity, absolute solititude, torture, imprisonment as a number, not a name, summary execution, and so on. But, it should be observed, such treatment is reserved almost always for minorities, never majorities, and commonly for those who by ethnic composition, religion, occupation, and long-time history are relatively unassimilated, objects of some dislike by the majority. If dissidents throughout the history of a democracy such as the United States have known all too often the stigma of being "troublemakers" and "rabblerousers," and of inviting commotion where none need exist, we can imagine the ease with which totalitarian governments persuade the great majority of their populations that it is in fact "criminals," "enemies of the people" who are occasionally exiled, committed to a psychiatric institution or prison.

V

The creation of the masses is vital, from the conservative viewpoint, to the origin and perpetuation of totalitarianism. By "masses" I mean essentially what has been meant from Burke to Ortega y Gasset and Hannah Arendt by this word: substantial aggregates of the national population that have become relatively amorphous, rootless, disconnected, and estranged from many of the symbols and values which represent the difference between a society and a crowd. Burke referred to the revolutionary actions that sought to "separate and tear asunder the bands of their subordinate community, and to dissolve it into an unsocial, uncivil, unconnected chaos of elementary principles." The rulers of France, he added,

have attempted to confound all sorts of citizens, as well as they
could, into one homogeneous mass. . . .

The policy of such barbarous victors . . . has ever been, as much
as in them lay, to destroy all vestiges of the ancient country, in
religion, in polity, in laws, and in manners; to confound all territo-
rial limits; to produce a general poverty . . . to lay low everything
which had lifted its head above the level, or which could serve to
combine or rally, in their distresses, the disbanded people, under
the standard of old opinion.[18]

The theme of the masses is a persisting one in nineteenth- and
twentieth-century conservative thought. Tocqueville's depiction of the democratic mass that must emerge, to become the
foundation of "the type of despotism that democratic nations
have most to fear," once pre-democratic walls have eroded
away, is no doubt the most famous. But there were others to
raise the specter of a leveled mass, without inner resources,
without capacity of self-governance, and the easy prey of every
passing doctrine in which the formula was continued loss of
their own responsibility for themselves coupled with a kind of
supervening power that would be providential as well as firm.
In the writings of Mill, Maine, Taine, Maurras, Burckhardt,
Sorel, Nietzsche, and many others in the nineteenth century
there is presentiment of a deculturalized, dehumanized mass of
people whose incapacity for self-governance in the smaller
things of life would evolve easily into incapacity of government
in the larger, and who would eventually become dominated by
merchants of power and force.

Despite the clear continuity of the perspective of the masses
in conservative writing, many Americans were unprepared for
the stress on the masses in analyses of totalitarianism that came
from Europeans in the 1930s. Early in that decade, Ortega y
Gasset's *Revolt of the Masses* appeared in this country but was
rarely understood for what it actually was: a prophetic analysis
of the affinity between the "mass man," whatever his numbers
may be, and absolute political power as refuge from the tor-

ments and traps of self-reliance, of the making of decisions. As Peter Drucker emphasized in 1939 in *The End of Economic Man,* the mass may be a relatively small minority of the total population in a country; but its separation from the norms of culture and the codes of the social order render it fearful and apprehensive. "The despair of the masses," Drucker wrote, "is the key to the understanding of fascism. No 'revolt of the mob,' no 'triumphs of unscrupulous propaganda,' but stark despair caused by the breakdown of the old order and the absence of a new one."[19] Hannah Arendt in *The Origins of Totalitarianism* (1951) made the historical formation of the masses or the calculated creation of the masses fundamental in her treatment of totalitarianism in all its forms. "The term 'masses' applies only where we deal with people who either because of sheer numbers, or indifference, or a combination of both, cannot be integrated into any organization based on common interest, into political parties, or municipal governments, or professional organizations, or trade unions."[20]

Where the masses do not exist in substantial number as the result of the erosive processes of history, they must be created. The largest and most spectacular instance of this was in the Soviet Union. To be sure, the appalling impact of World War I on Russian society, the slaughter of many millions and the reduction to starvation, desolation, and civil war of many more millions, did a good deal to convert peasantry and what there was of industrial working class to masslike status. But between the masses Lenin and Stalin needed for their absolute rule and what historical actuality offered there were a great many ancient ties—family, kindred, village community, cooperative, social class, and so on—that had to be forcefully and relentlessly destroyed. The collectivization of agriculture in the 1920s and the liquidation of the kulaks and others did a great deal to provide Stalin with his necessary masses—in contrast to an historically developed society. The human masses are very much like grains of sand in the wind: when separated, they will blow in every imaginable direction; but when damp and coagu-

lated, the impress of the wind is slight. A genuine society is not
likely to be as compliant to the will of the ruler; there are too
many intermediate groups which coagulate, as it were. Hitler
was aware of this, and in his *Mein Kampf* wrote: "The mass
meeting is necessary if only for the reason that in it the individual who in becoming an adherent of a new movement feels
lonely and is easily seized with the fear of being alone, receives
for the first time the picture of a greater community, something
that has strengthening effect upon most people."

In short, a society must first be atomized, "massified," creating the sense of the void. Next, in the early phases of totalitarian
reorganization, the created masses must be made aware of
themselves, of their common identity. Only then can the work
begin which will lead to new and permanent forms of association, all the appendages of the total, collectivized state. The
total state is monolithic, in aspiration at least. Italian fascism
put the matter perfectly: "All for the State; nothing outside the
State; nothing against the State."

VI

Orwell was particularly concerned to feature the intellectual
class in *1984,* a genus he had largely detested during most of
his literary career. "The new aristocracy," he writes of the
rulers of Oceania, "was made up for the most part of bureaucrats, scientists, technicians, trade union organizers, publicity
experts, sociologists, teachers, journalists, and professional
politicians," in sum, the intelligentsia, masters of the uses of
language in the service of power. "It need hardly be said that
the subtlest practitioners of doublethink are those who invented
doublethink and know that it is a vast system of mental cheat-
ing." And Winston, in his secret diary, writes: *"If there is hope,
it lies in the proles,"* the 85 percent of society that was barely
literate, completely outside the political process, and spared the
innovations of the new totalitarian aristocracy.[21]

Burke was, so far as I am aware, the first to call attention to the revolutionary impact upon society of the new class of largely dislocated, unattached intellectuals in France whose principal figures so largely made up the Enlightenment there. He referred to such minds as Rousseau, Diderot, and Voltaire, and also to the reigning figures of the Revolution, as "literary cabalers," "political theologians," and "political men of letters." These individuals, Burke observes dryly, "are rarely averse to innovation, and to them it was indifferent whether the changes were to be accomplished by the thunderbolt of despotism or by the earthquake of popular commotion." No longer supported by the patronage of the aristocracy, it had become necessary early in the eighteenth century for the intelligentsia to find other sustenance and reinforcement. They found this, Burke says, in two places: the new monied class and the reform or revolution-minded men of politics in France. Beyond these sources of support were some of the so-called enlightened despots of Europe. "Writers, especially when they act in a body, and with one direction, have great influence on the public mind; the allegiance therefore of these writers with the monied interest had no small effect in removing the popular odium and envy which attended this species of wealth."[22]

Later, Tocqueville was equally struck by the role played in the French Revolution by intellectuals. How, he asks in *The Old Regime and the French Revolution,* did "men of letters, without wealth, social eminence, responsibilities, or official status" almost alone "speak with accents of authority?" Tocqueville's answer is threefold. First, the intellectuals in France in the eighteenth century were almost entirely without political experience and were consequently made the bolder in political prescription. Second, this very ignorance of or disdain for experience and history made them welcome to the masses, themselves long separated from any active participation in the social order. "When it came to making themselves heard by the masses and appealing to their emotions, this very ignorance served them in good stead." Simple, elementary axioms concocted by individual reason and broadcast in seductive lan-

guage made the intellectual class popular with the masses as
well as with certain men of money and power. Third, Tocqueville suggests, the corruption and very considerable displace-
ment of the old aristocracy in France left a vacuum—"By the
eighteenth century the French nobility had wholly lost [its]
ascendancy, its prestige had dwindled with its power, and since
the place it had occupied in the direction of public opinion was
vacant, writers could usurp it with the greatest ease and keep
it without fear of being dislodged."

"Never before," Tocqueville concludes, "had the entire political education of a great nation been the work of its men of
letters, and it was this peculiarity that perhaps did the most to
give the French Revolution its exceptional character and the
regime that followed it the form we are familiar with. Our men
of letters did not merely impart their revolutionary ideas to the
French nation; they also shaped the national temperament and
outlook on life."[23]

This had been Rousseau's express counsel in the celebrated
chapter on "The Legislator" in the *Social Contract:* that is, the
lawgiver, in whatever form, must "take away from man his own
resources and give him instead new ones alien to him, and
incapable of being made use of without the help of other men.
The more completely these natural resources are annihilated,
the greater and more lasting are those he acquires. . . ."[24]

As the historian Robert R. Palmer has written of Rousseau:
"He became the great revolutionary of a revolutionary age.
. . . He was the revolutionary *par excellence* because it was
moral revolution that he called for, a revolution in the personality and in the inclination of the will."[25] It is no wonder that most
of the leaders of the Revolution read their *Social Contract*
regularly as Puritan zealots a century earlier in England had
read their Bible. He had a vocabulary and style that could be
infinitely embroidered upon during the Terror. "Man is born
free, and everywhere he is in chains." Splendid. But how does
he regain, without returning to a state of nature, this freedom?
Through the General Will, a will that *may* be co-terminous

with the majority will but often is not and must therefore be sought through other means. In entering the perfect state, Rousseau decrees, man must give over to the state his whole being and all of his rights. But this is not, *cannot* be, coercion, for the conditions are the same for all, "and this being so, no one has any interest in making them burdensome to others." But Rousseau has not finished. Such absolute commitment to the state is a way of becoming free. Whoever "refuses to obey the general will shall be compelled to do so by the whole body. This means nothing less than that *he will be forced to be free....*" (italics added).[26]

With Rousseau as their guide, it was not difficult for the leaders of the Revolution to reach even greater heights of Orwellian doublethink. Thus Robespierre's "the government of the Revolution is the despotism of freedom against tyranny." Rousseau had prescribed execution for any man who after affirming the doctrines of *la religion civile* publicly, "behaves as if he does not believe in them." The work of tracking down people, among them leading revolutionists, who behaved as though they didn't believe truly in what they preached became awesome by 1794. The instigation of the Terror and of public guillotining in Paris and other parts of France was done— predictably we might say—in the names of peace, virtue, and liberty. No one but an intellectual could have conceived Robespierre's words: "If the basis of popular government in time of peace is virtue, the basis of popular government in time of revolution is virtue and terror: virtue without which terror is murderous, terror without which virtue is powerless."[27] Never, prior to the French Revolution, had so many words been given new, often opposite meanings; and never had such words as virtue, peace, freedom, and fraternity been linked indissolubly with so much imprisonment, torture, terror, and killing. The task of hunting down "enemies of the people" was by 1794 endless and to the ever more voracious power of the Revolution joyous and fulfilling. As Palmer has written of the Revolution: "it became a thing in itself, an uncontrollable force . . . which no one could direct and guide."[28]

The place of the revolution-consecrated intellectual in European society became ever greater during the nineteenth century. So did the place of doublethink and Newspeak. Prior to the eighteenth century, language had generally been for purposes of clarification; increasingly now its work was that of obfuscation, in the name of one or other promised form of redemptive freedom. From the intellectual and his rhetoric in the French Revolution it is but a short step to the totalitarian states of the twentieth century. The changes which Lenin and Trotsky, Mussolini, Hitler and Goebbels, Mao, and so many others have rung on the words "freedom," "justice," "democracy," and their like are of course notorious. One and all these men were intellectuals, professionally committed to ideas and their uses. One and all they lived, as have their successors, in a world of consecrated ideas. Lenin while in democratic Switzerland, in exile, could see only repression, exploitation, misery, and despair around him and would no doubt have sought to liberate the Swiss people from their tyrants had not the German High Command sent him back to Russia. But once the work of political rule had begun for Lenin in Russia, it was equally easy for him to see the terror he had ordered as nothing but the manifestation of freedom and justice. Naturally, absolute and dictatorial government became in Lenin's mind and speech "democratic centralism." So it has been in every totalitarian government in our century. Orwell made no mistake in centering his Oceania around the power of those who were the keepers of language and ideas.

VII

The final attribute of totalitarianism that tends to be emphasized in conservative analyses since Burke is the militarization of culture and society. The possession of a military, even a vast one, is not in itself indicative. Czarist Russia and the Kaiser's Germany both had large armies prior to World War I, but it cannot reasonably be said that military values penetrated the containing society of each. The military held a very high place in the social hierarchy of each country, but there was no militarization of social roles and relationships, no large-scale, calculated infusion of military symbols and metaphors into Russian and German culture.

Very different, however, are the Russia and Germany of Lenin and Hitler respectively. Once Trotsky took on the responsibility of transmuting the Czarist into the Red Army, military symbols began to burgeon. The military tunic received a value in society it had never held before; so did military rank in all councils of government. Increasingly in the 1920s in Russia and Italy, and in the 1930s in Germany, the challenges, motivations, incentives, and conflicts of ordinary civil society were acknowledged or projected by the government in terms of the military. A record number of military symbols was doubtless employed by the government and press in Russia while the Moscow subway was being built, with the workers likened to soldiers in the Red Army, and with all setbacks in construction charged to "bourgeois," "imperialist," or other recalcitrant and evil representations of the subsoil. Above all, it is the military, including naturally the secret police and counterrevolutionary forces, that ultimately governs the totalitarian social order. Under Mao in China, every one of the multitudinous three-man committees which were to be found in every neighborhood, every school, factory, university, in every form of organization whatever, had on it a representative of the military. In every one of the totalitarian orders of the twentieth century, the leaders have been meticulously careful, especially in the early years of the regime, to be seen in nothing but military dress in public. Far more important than actual war in mobilizing a population is war-society, irrespective of outbreaks of war. In Russia, Italy, Germany, and all subsequent totalitarian societies, military regimen is deemed vital.

There is much reason for this. I have suggested that the heart of the totalitarian process is the relentless politicization of culture and society, the conversion, so far as possible, of social roles and relationships into ones of political significance. But in the history of mankind, the military precedes the political in the strict sense of the latter. In the ancient world, the greatest of institutional conflicts was that between the *patria potestas,* the authority endowed by tradition in kinship, and the *imperium,* the power that automatically went to the warrior-chief whenever war broke out between tribes or communities. In Rome, as Sir Henry Maine points out in *Ancient Law,* the *patria potestas* was absolute over sons as well as daughters until the son was called up for militia duty; then this most ancient of authorities was superseded by the equally absolute power of the military leader. We can go far in the tracing of the history of human society, in all parts of the world, by the greater and less ascendancy of each of the two powers, the kinship and the military. A great deal of what society presents to our contemplation is the result or surrogate of either the kinship or the military theme.

The totalitarian state of the twentieth century is the ultimate in the militarization of the social order, its values and symbols. Early in Nazism there was considerable empty rhetoric in Germany and an equal amount of credulity in Western liberal circles about renewed emphasis on family, neighborhood, local community, church, and the like, with the true place of Nazi woman being in the home or church. As events quickly proved, all of this was nonsense. By 1934, the true Nazi family was, as underground wit had it, that in which the father was of the SS, the mother in the Nazi Womens Auxiliary, and the children in some appropriate Nazi youth organization, the family reuniting each year at a Nuremberg Party Congress. For Nazi, read Soviet and even Italian Fascist, though the presence of the Vatican and the depth of the Roman Catholic tie in Italy prevented it from ever reaching the extremes of totalitarianism that are found in the Soviet Union, Nazi Germany, China, Albania, North Vietnam, Cuba, and Cambodia. Nothing comparable to the power of the Vatican existed in these countries as countervailing force or check on the twin processes of militarization and politicization.

Burke saw the revolutionary government of France proceeding rapidly in the militarization of the people. The government deals with its citizens, he observes, precisely as an army of occupation does its victims. The democratization of the army proceeds *pari passu* with the militarization, under revolutionary slogan, of the traditional social order. The link was seen early, Burke suggests, between military and revolutionary zeal, the one feeding upon the other. Had there been no threat of foreign war whatever, there is every reason to believe that under the spur of functional necessity, the *levée en masse,* the first mass conscription in world history, would have been instituted. "If the soldiers once come to mix for any time in the municipal clubs, cabals, and confederacies, an elective attraction will draw them to the lowest and most desperate part"[29]—a truth as well illustrated throughout the French Revolution as it would be in the successive steps that brought Lenin and Trotsky to power in Russia, Mussolini in Italy, and Hitler through the 1920s and early 1930s in Germany. As to the official ideals of utopian ventures, "You lay down metaphysical propositions which infer universal consequences, and then you attempt to limit logic by despotism." And "Everything depends upon the army in such a government as yours; for you have industriously destroyed all the opinions and prejudices, and, as far as in you lay, all the instincts which support government."[30]

Throughout the nineteenth and twentieth centuries, conservative thought as found in Bonald, Hegel, Tocqueville, Taine, Burckhardt, warned against the twin menaces of centralization and militarization. Tocqueville spoke for them all when he wrote: "Men of centralizing genius are fond of war, and men of military genius are fond of centralization in government." Burckhardt saw the fusion of bureaucratic power and the pullulating masses in his Europe as bound to produce in time a "military republic" and "booted commandos" as leaders. The genius of totalitarianism lies in the rigid fusion of the masses with a military power that destroys the traditional ties of cohesion even as it fashions new ones drawn from battle and garrison. In Orwell's classic, the incessant wars—or fictitious wars —engaged in by Oceania in all parts of the world were vital to the revolutionary objectives of the ruling class. As O'Brien explains, foreign war serves at one and the same time to activate revolutionary enthusiasms at home and to give all dissident thought the flavor of traitorous heresy. Long before Orwell, though, Burke paid his hostile respects to French "military democracy which . . . wherever it exists must be the true constitution of the state, by whatever formal appellation it may pass."[31] In our own day the existence of the Soviet colossus on earth mandates a considerable degree of "military democracy" of our own, but we should not compound necessary evil by labeling it liberal or humane. For us, as for Burke's French revolutionaries and Orwell's Oceanians, war and revolution are but two sides of the same coin.

PART III

HISTORY

Richard Lowenthal

13 Beyond Totalitarianism?

George Orwell's *1984* is generally recognized as one of the classics among the "negative utopias" of our time, and frequently compared in this respect with such earlier works as Aldous Huxley's *Brave New World.* This is fair enough as far as it goes, but it refers to only one aspect of this unique work. The other aspect, on which I am going to concentrate in this essay, is that Orwell's nightmare vision of the future was based on his, and his generation's, intense experience of the totalitarian regimes of our time—as Huxley's was not. Orwell did *not* believe, as critics like Herbert Marcuse or Erich Fromm later suggested, that the social conformity of advanced capitalist democracies, with full freedom of political choice, but with largely uniform (and uniformly changing) habits of consumption, was essentially similar to totalitarian party dictatorship. The tyranny with which he was concerned was not the "tyranny of customs," which has existed in vastly different political and social systems from time immemorial, but the tyranny of ruthless single-party dictatorships, which was new.

In this respect, Orwell's *1984* is less similar to Huxley's *Brave*

Author's note: This essay, except for the prologue, constitutes a shortened and revised version of a lecture delivered by the author at the colloquium on "Totalitarian Democracy and After," organized in June 1982 by the Israel Academy of Sciences and the Hebrew University of Jerusalem. The title of the lecture was "Totalitarianism and After in Communist Party Regimes."

An earlier version of section II, only more detailed and fully documented, appeared under the title "Development versus Utopia in Communist Policy" in Chalmers Johnson, ed., *Change in Communist Systems,* Stanford, Calif.: Stanford University Press, 1970.

New World than to a number of books inspired by different aspects of the same experience before and after him—starting with the Russian Zamyatin's *We,* on through Ignazio Silone's *Bread and Wine,* Ernst Jünger's *Unter Marmorklippen,* Albert Camus's *La Peste,* to Czeslaw Milosz's *The Captive Mind.* But whereas all those are either descriptive or recognizable metaphorical treatments of particular experiences of the new horror, written by people whose country was in its grip, Orwell, writing in a free country, undertook to present a general vision of a potentially worldwide phenomenon. He envisaged that, by 1984, our world might be dominated by three totalitarian empires ensuring their joint survival—and the poverty of their subjects—through permanent limited war.

Orwell was thus most explicit in describing what looked, and was intended to look, like a possible blind alley in the history of mankind. His picture of totalitarianism was in this respect similar to the original analysis of Hannah Arendt who, once important changes occurred in Russia after Stalin's death, chose to proclaim that Soviet totalitarianism had begun and ended with Stalin. But Orwell, whose Big Brother was anonymous and presumably exchangeable, had left himself no such loophole: it was the institutional system, not just the person of the dictator, which seemed to him to assure its permanence.

Of course, Orwell never intended to *predict* such a worldwide end of history; he meant to issue a powerful *warning* against existing tendencies. It might thus appear superfluous and pedantic to inquire why the "prophecy" has not come true. But at a time when ruthless party dictatorships still wield great power, and when other forms of pessimism about the future of humanity are increasingly widespread, there is still a lesson to be learned from inquiring why the worldwide and unchanging rule of totalitarianism has not happened and is not likely to happen.

We know that there are catastrophes in history. Great civilizations have declined and decayed, and there is no assurance that ours will be immune from such a fate. But there is no final blind alley for mankind as a whole. We may still perish, but we will not be frozen into a permanent nightmare state. The reason lies in a key factor that was missing from Orwell's vision: the dynamic nature of actual totalitarianism which, devoted to unending, totally planned change, ultimately falls victim to unplanned change.

This essay, then, is devoted to sketching the *dynamic* nature of totalitarianism, particularly of the Communist kind, and its likely long-term consequences for the surviving party dictatorships and, beyond that, the future of the whole phenomenon.

I

The Unique Nature and "Contradictions"
of Totalitarianism

The revolutionary single-party dictatorships of our century, which came to be described as "totalitarian" at an early stage, differ from all earlier forms of tyranny not merely or even primarily by their modern techniques of total power. What decisively distinguishes them is their ideological impulse for total and, ultimately, worldwide transformation of the structure of society. Their characteristic goals are "utopian" in the full, original meaning of the term: they aim at types of society literally impossible to achieve among human beings on this earth. Fully developed regimes of the fascist or National Socialist type aim at a perfect and, again ultimately, worldwide hierarchy of "elites," whether the latter is defined by racial criteria, or more or less arbitrarily by the holders of power; the point is that, once everybody has been assigned his "proper" place, all *legitimate* conflict is supposed to be impossible. Communist regimes, by contrast, announce as their aim a perfect and, ultimately, worldwide state of social equality; once it has been achieved, *all* social conflict will become impossible.

The typical structure of the regime needed in order to implement this utopian program is based on the extreme centralization of the ruling party and on its three basic monopolies: the monopolies of political decision, social organization, and all forms of information. The typical means to achieve this end is the revolutionary destruction of entire social groups not only for opposing the regime, but for not fitting into its plans by their very existence. Because of the utopian nature of the goals, this policy of annihilation can never achieve its purpose in the course of the original, revolutionary seizure of power, but requires repeated "revolutions from above" not foreseen in the original program. In the Nazi regime, the inevitable persistence of racial "impurities" led to ever new decisions to annihilate smaller or greater "racially inferior" groups—from those who presumably suffered from hereditary defects to the entire Jewish population, and to the entire intellectual and social elites of some of the conquered nations. In Communist regimes, the initial revolutionary destruction of the former ruling class is typically followed by further "revolutions from above," as new social differentiations arise among the peasantry or among bureaucratic and intellectual elites of both pre- and post-revolutionary generations. In either case, totalitarianism becomes a regime of *institutionalized revolution.*

Yet, because of the utopian nature of their goals, both types of totalitarian regimes suffer from inherent "contradictions" that limit their life span. The Nazi and fascist attempts to establish themselves as the ruling elites of what would be a worldwide order finally ended in self-destruction through war. The Communist regimes—the only ones to survive for long periods—have suffered from two different contradictions which have ended not in their destruction from the outside, but, rather, in severe internal crises. By depriving them of their original utopian impulse, these crises have also deprived them of the specific totalitarian dynamics of recurrent "revolutions from above," and thus changed their basic character.

The first of these contradictions is based on the fact that true Communist revolutions, as distinct from Communist seizures of power imposed from outside, have only taken place in underdeveloped countries; hence, all the "authentic" Communist regimes have in fact been compelled to pursue dual goals—the achievement of the Communist utopia on the one side, and of modernization on the other. While harmonizing the two goals proved possible initially with regard to some measures, such as the expropriation of pre-modern landowners, recurring revolutionary upheavals became increasingly "counterproductive," first in Russia and later in China, as economic development advanced, resulting finally in a running down of the institutionalized revolution and bitter conflicts among the leadership.

The second contradiction is based on the absence, in Communist ideology and tradition, of unambiguous procedural rules for decision making and leadership succession. Whereas totalitarian regimes of the Nazi-fascist types were based on a completely unambiguous "*Fuehrer* principle," and did not live to experience the problem of succession, the Communist doctrine of "democratic centralism" is obviously, indeed deliberately, ambiguous. As originally conceived, it was meant to legitimate Lenin's leadership of a leftist party by disguising it as democratic. This worked in Russia so long as Lenin ruled with unique personal authority, and in China so long as Mao's authority remained uncontested and undamaged by a number of major political mistakes. But in the succession of Lenin, and in the later years of Mao, the absence of either an uncontested leader or binding democratic rules led to bitter factional struggles. As a consequence, Stalin's leadership developed into a form of personal despotism that largely paralyzed the Soviet Communist Party for a long period. And Mao's late and incomplete attempt to establish his own form of personal despotism not only paralyzed the Chinese Communist Party but temporarily provoked a near-anarchic state of affairs. It is most remarkable that, in both cases, the primacy of Communist Party rule has been restored after the death of the despot—but it is a different kind of party rule.

What indeed developed in Russia, not yet under Stalin's immediate successors but very clearly in the Brezhnev era, was the creation of a kind of quasi-democratic decision-making process within the ruling party oligarchy; and something similar appears to be developing within the Chinese Communist Party. In both cases, this new type of oligarchy has become possible only after the running down of the institutionalized revolution and the decisive victory of developmental over utopian goals. But for both reasons, it should, in my opinion, definitely be recognized as a "post-totalitarian" regime.

In what follows, I shall try to support this thesis by sketching my interpretation of the process by which the change from a "totalitarian" to a "post-totalitarian" party regime has come about in Russia and China.

II

The Institutionalized Revolution and Its Running Down

Some Principal Stages

In the early years of the major Communist dictatorships, their leaders were forced by the struggle for power to go faster in transforming the social structure than they had originally intended. Lenin had authorized the distribution of the landed estates to the peasants immediately. But he did not intend to go at once beyond the introduction of "workers' control" in capitalist industry. The growing friction between workers and owners in the course of the civil war caused him to speed up the nationalization of industry despite the obvious difficulty of replacing many of the dispossessed owners as managers. In more backward China, where the scarcity of qualified managerial and technical personnel was even more obvious, Mao at first gave a solemn promise that all factory owners not directly tied to the former Guomindang regime would be tolerated for an extended period of time. Yet the strains of the Korean War soon caused the Communist rulers to "squeeze" the remaining capitalists;

and by the end of the "rehabilitation period" in 1952, a policy of transforming all private enterprises into "joint enterprises" under state direction was announced, though most of the owners could still remain as managers.

The conflict between the Communist regimes' interest in total control and their interest in steady economic development appeared most strikingly with regard to the issue of agricultural collectivization. After ending the "War Communist" policy of requisitioning most of the harvest, which had alienated the peasants and produced the famine of 1921, Lenin introduced the "New Economic Policy" through which the peasants were to receive the freedom to sell their produce along with secure possession of their land. At the end of his life Lenin envisaged the "cooperativization" of the countryside as a long-term aim, to be achieved by persuasion and the incentive of common use of agricultural machinery, which would by then be available in the quantities and quality required. But, as agriculture recovered and part of the peasantry became more prosperous, a growing number of Bolshevik leaders became alarmed at what they saw as a triple threat. Social differentiation among the peasants posed a threat to the future of a classless society; party control was jeopardized in the villages where the "kulaks" tended to become the natural leaders; and the willingness of the peasants to sell their produce at low state-fixed prices was less than enthusiastic. By the winter of 1927–28, the urgency of the last factor convinced Stalin of the need for a harsh "anti-kulak policy," which began with a partial return to requisitioning and culminated in massive forced collectivization—and in the famine of 1932–33. This new "revolution from above," described as such by Stalin himself in 1938, was carried out at a terrible cost in human suffering and a lasting, heavy cost to the productivity of Soviet agriculture and the number of livestock. Experience had shown that the uninhibited development of society created increasing obstacles both to the long-term, utopian goals of the regime and to the present control of the party.

Fully aware of the horrors of Soviet forced collectivization, the Chinese Communists originally intended to spread their own collectivization over three five-year plans. But a crisis in the state-controlled grain market during the winter and spring of 1954–55 led Mao to speed up collectivization dramatically, until it was more or less completed by the end of 1956. Though the Chinese Communists apparently succeeded in carrying out collectivization by less disastrous methods than the Russians, the very difference in methods and results underlines the common logic of Communist Party regimes: the commitment to utopian goals and to total control collides again and again with the tendency of a developing society to produce social differentiation, and results in a process of institutionalized revolution.

A no less typical conflict between utopian commitment and the requirements of modernization arose in both countries over the recruitment of managerial and technical elites. Stalin wavered for some time between concessions to the scarce bourgeois "specialists" in industry, and intimidating them when they were reluctant to endorse the unrealistic targets of his first five-year plan. But, as the initial results of high-speed training of working-class activists proved poor, he gradually raised the training requirements while relaxing the insistence on working-class origin; and by 1934–35 he proclaimed the need for reconciliation with the "non-party intelligentsia" regardless of origin. This tended to create a dangerous dualism between a party elite with revolutionary and ideological commitment but limited technical and economic knowledge, and a post-revolutionary technical and managerial elite without ideological traditions and with no more than tenuous links to the party. That dualism was overcome in another "revolution from above"—to wit, Stalin's bloody purge of the late thirties, which combined the liquidation of "old Bolsheviks" in general and the early "red directors" and many young managerial volunteers from the party ranks in particular. Of course, Stalin's great purge was not conceived only or even mainly as a way to solve that specific problem. But it was also deliberately used for that purpose. When it was over, the 18th Party Congress of 1939 changed the party statutes so as to throw the doors wide open to young, Soviet-trained managers and engineers regardless of origin. The ruling party, from which the bulk of the utopian-oriented revolutionary veterans had been removed, now became the organ of a post-revolutionary, ideologically conformist, and, in the main, modernization-oriented bureaucracy.

In China, economic planning started in 1952 in the shadow of Stalin's example but with a party formed by decades of war and civil war. The first five-year plan provided for absolute one-man authority of managers responsible to their bureaucratic superiors, even though very few managers were Communists. Not until the first session of the 8th Party Congress in 1956 was the party opened to "intellectuals"—meaning all the literate strata—regardless of class origin. The same congress, under the impact of Soviet de-Stalinization, reduced the control of the central planning authorities in favor of "managerial responsibility under the leadership of the [regional or local] party committee." In the following year, when the wave of intellectual criticism let loose by the "Hundred Flowers Campaign" convinced Mao that his trust in this stratum had been, at the least, premature, an "anti-rightist campaign" to intimidate the non-party intellectuals followed. In this context, the congress directive came to be interpreted as requiring strict subordination of the managers to the party committees on any issues transcending the barest routine. With a party that had not gone through a bloody Stalinist purge, and was still much closer to its revolutionary origins than the CPSU, this was bound to make the dualism between party veterans and post-revolutionary managers and technicians much sharper than it had been allowed to become in Russia—with the party veterans holding vastly superior power while possessing equal economic incompetence.

This is part of the background for the "Great Leap Forward" of 1958, which combined a new "revolution from above," introducing the "People's Communes" in agriculture (and carried out with many illusions, much violence, and corresponding damage), and an equally improvised campaign for a competitive raising of industrial targets by local and regional party committees over the heads of the managers. Some of the most damaging errors were corrected in the following years, but an overall admission of the wrongness of the utopian "general line" was avoided in order to preserve Mao's personal authority. The sixties thus began in China with an unresolved split among the country's elites, in which a few of the old leaders and many younger party officials seem to have sided with the managers' demand for rational modernization, while the utopian side was taken by the aging Mao and a number of faithful veterans in the party and the army. It was in that constellation that the shaken leader launched his last "revolution from above"—the Cultural Revolution of 1966.

The question of the relative importance of ideological propaganda, coercion, and varying material incentives in assuring labor performance is also bound to find different answers in Communist Party regimes, according to the priority assigned to utopian goals or to modernization. But the resolution of this issue has been radically different in Russia and in China. In Russia, a firmly anti-utopian decision on labor incentives was taken by Stalin as early as 1931 and, though repeatedly revised in detail, was never abandoned in principle; in this field Russia has never known a "revolution from above." In China, Mao, in his later years, became increasingly committed to a utopian reliance on ideological rather than material labor incentives, and this became a major factor in the conflicts over the "Great Leap Forward" and the "Cultural Revolution."

The only attempt at a radical leveling of wages in the history of revolutionary Russia occurred during the initial stages of "War Communism." It did not originate in utopian dreams; extreme shortages forced rationing of food and other basic needs that left little room for differentiation. But after the end of the civil war, Lenin quickly understood that such incentives could no longer be replaced by either ideological enthusiasm or requisitioning of labor under military discipline. With the abolition of rationing and of military control over the trade unions under the New Economic Policy, the scarcity of skilled labor for the newly developing industries forced a steady rise in wage differentials between 1922 and 1926. They then declined somewhat under trade union pressure to raise the level of the lowest wages, and rather more drastically in the early years of the first five-year plan, with a return to food rationing under the impact of forced collectivization and with Stalin destroying the relative autonomy of the trade unions.

The crucial turn came with Stalin's attack on "petty bourgeois egalitarianism" in mid-1931, when he, too, recognized the limits of forced enthusiasm. He now relied on a combination of coercive sanctions (such as the "labor book" and the "comradely tribunals," backed by the threat of deportation to labor camps) with wide differentiation of wages and even of rations. When rationing ended and life was supposed to become happier after the completion of collectivization, rising food prices and the raising of piece-rate "norms" by way of the Stakhanovite campaign made wage differentials even more effective.

Only after Stalin's death did his successors realize that, given the level of industrialization, not only camp labor but excessively low wages for unskilled workers were harming responsibility and diligence at the work place. In the Khrushchev era, the disappearance of camp labor as a major sector of the economy, the raising of minimum wages, and a limited reduction of wage differentials in favor of the lowest-paid groups as well as the introduction of basic social security measures marked the end of the period of "primitive accumulation." But the general character of a system of differentiated material incentives based on a frankly non-utopian orientation has been maintained.

Chinese Communist wage policy started with a Stalinist rejection of "egalitarianism" in favor of a combination of material incentives and coercion, including subjection of the trade unions to compulsory arbitration and a ban on strikes. The whole catalogue of "emulation campaigns" for steadily raising "norms," of "comradely tribunals," and the "labor book" was imitated. In spite of rising productivity, real wages even declined somewhat in 1954–55. Yet by 1956 it was becoming obvious that excessive reliance on coercion, combined with poor material incentives, was counterproductive. The party congress of that year raised the general wage level by a nominal 14.5 percent while broadening the range of differential incentives and limiting the role of piecework paid according to set norms. Bonuses for innovation as well as overtime and hardship pay were introduced in 1957. But this more rational incentive system, explicitly based on "the Socialist principle of pay according to work," proved so attractive to a growing rural surplus population that it migrated to the towns in much larger numbers than could be absorbed by industrial growth. As a result, emergency measures were introduced to lower wages for new, untrained workers along with longer apprenticeships.

However, a sharp turn away from realistic reliance on material incentives to utopian reliance on mass ideological indoctrination came with the "Great Leap Forward." At the second session of the 8th Party Congress in May 1958, the idea of weaning the working people from their "bourgeois" concern with material needs was proclaimed from the rostrum. Quickly, work norms were raised to such heights that the piece-rate system became unworkable. Time rates soon became an official part of the labor program of the "Great Leap," along with such "moral incentives" as honors for "model workers" and banners for successful factories. Of course, the turn away from differentiated material incentives was far more thorough in the new rural communes, whose members now received most of their income in kind—at first, some 70 percent—in the form of equal rations under the "free supply system."

The results were such that, by 1961, a plenum of the Central Committee once more recognized the need to offer more pay for more work during the entire period preceding the achievement of full communism, thus relegating utopia to a distant future. Private plots and rural markets were restored for the peasants, "free supplies" to commune members were restricted to 30 percent of their income, and piece rates were once more permitted, though not everywhere, in industry. But, by 1964, this return to material incentives was attacked in Mao's "Socialist Education Campaign" and finally reversed during his Cultural Revolution of 1966. In the context of his bitter conflict with the Soviet leaders and his attack on the alleged "capitalist degeneration" of their system, the Chinese leader had convinced himself that this was rooted in the Soviet decision to rely on the motivations of "economic man"—thus perpetuating what he saw as a capitalist mentality in Russia. His own alternative for China depended on changing the basic motivations away from selfish materialism toward selfless service for the community. That radical change in the consciousness of the masses could no longer be expected to follow the achievement of the classless society: it was now seen as a *precondition* of its arrival.

If we ignore passing ups and downs, the whole period of the Cultural Revolution until Mao's death and the eventual defeat of his most fanatic supporters thus appears, in one of its main aspects, as a vast effort to change the working motivation of the Chinese people by changing their consciousness through one more "revolution from above."

The "Running Down" in Russia

We have seen that Stalin, after carrying out the forced collectivization of the peasantry and then the purge of administrative elites by ruthless "revolutions from above," decided two issues —the future composition of the elites and the nature of labor incentives—by giving a clear priority to developmental over utopian considerations. Yet it would be quite wrong to conclude from that, as many observers have done, that Stalin by 1939 had generally decided to turn away from revolutionary utopianism in favor of a policy of steady modernization by non-revolutionary, not to say conservative, methods. During the subsequent war years a number of ideological concessions to patriotic and religious traditions, and economic concessions to the collectivized peasants were made; but these were forced on him by dire necessity.

Yet, even during the war, he used his characteristically totalitarian methods of annihilation, or at least mass deportation, against entire "unreliable" nationalities. Directly after the war, there was the mass deportation of returned prisoners of war to labor camps. More importantly, in the early postwar years Stalin not only expanded the revolutionary process to the territories of eastern Europe and North Korea, he also withdrew the wartime concessions at home by tightening both ideological and economic controls. Above all, from 1950 through the last years of his life, Stalin pressed for a further revolutionary transformation of Soviet agriculture. However, he did not live to see the execution of his final program; his heirs abandoned it in favor of alternatives that required less violence and were less likely to damage economic development; and even these alternatives, as proposed by Khrushchev in particular, finally had to be renounced as experience showed their heavy economic cost. In short, the running down of the revolutionary process had indeed begun in Stalin's lifetime. It ended, eight years after his death, in formal abandonment of further revolutionary transformation with the adoption of Khrushchev's new party program in 1961.

The late Stalinist drive for the further transformation of Soviet agriculture began at the turn of 1949–50, directly after Khrushchev had assumed responsibility for this field in Stalin's Politburo and Secretariat. It was signaled by rejection of a proposal made by Khrushchev's predecessor in this post, Andreyev, to assign permanent plots in the collective farms to small teams of workers in order to raise their sense of responsibility. This rejection reflected the fear that such a reform might strengthen tendencies to break up the kolkhozy (farm collectives). It was quickly followed by Khrushchev's proposal to "consolidate" the collectives into much larger units that would make better use of machinery. The effective reduction of the number of collectives by almost two thirds in less than three years did not bring the expected economic progress. What it did improve was party control by decisively raising the proportion of farms that had basic party units of their own.

The reduction also formed the basis for Khrushchev's more far-reaching proposal, launched a year later in January 1951, for resettling the peasants in new "agrotowns" in the center of the enlarged units—offering them better cultural amenities but separating them from what had been their private garden plots, forcing them to accept smaller ones on the outskirts of the new settlements. This move, however, encountered powerful opposition within the party leadership, which feared that the blow against the private plots might undermine the peasants' loyalty and productivity, and that the building materials for such a gigantic operation were beyond the country's means. In the end, the project was rejected in a secret circular of the Central Committee.

Stalin now developed an even more far-reaching project for a new social transformation of the countryside. He worked on this throughout 1952 until it was published, on the eve of the 19th Party Congress, in his last pamphlet, *Economic Problems of Socialism in the U.S.S.R.* Based on the fear that any form of market relations between the collective farms and the state sector eventually "must lead to the rebirth of capitalism," because it rested on the farms owning their produce, he proclaimed that, in order to reach the "higher stage of Communism," those market relations would have to be replaced by a form of centrally organized barter. In the pamphlet's last section, written in late September, Stalin even called for immediate, if "gradual," measures in that direction.

Clearly, the idea of replacing all market exchanges between city and country was economic utopianism, reaching an extreme of irrationality. It could only have maximized the notorious difficulty of calculating and comparing the production costs and incomes of the collective farms, facilitated their exploitation by the state, and thus critically reduced the peasants' already low incentives to work. One wonders whether objections to this new turn of the revolutionary screw arose within the Politburo. As it happens, the Congress did not deal with the proposal. But, at its end, the Politburo was replaced by a much larger "Presidium" with many new members. Khrushchev later claimed, in his 1956 secret speech, that Stalin had been preparing another violent purge of top leaders toward the end of his life. It is conceivable that the despot was approaching the political limits of his despotism as he was trying to overstep the economic limits of institutionalized revolution.

During the years of struggle over Stalin's succession, and for the restoration of the party's primacy over other centers of power that Stalin had used against it—both of which were won by Khrushchev as first secretary—the contenders vied in proposing popular reforms rather than in coming forward with ideas for further, utopian-inspired revolutionary changes. After Khrushchev's victory was completed in 1957, he first concentrated on improving the peasants' lot and on unifying uneven price scales for the sale of their produce to the government. In contrast to Stalin, he understood that the first condition for improving agricultural productivity was to make its costs and income comparable in terms of the "yardstick of the ruble." But, by the time of the 21st Congress of February 1959, when he wished to prove that Russia was ahead of China on the road to the "higher stage of Communism," he started a campaign to persuade the peasants to sell their private livestock to collective stables where the animals could be better looked after. He had already won over the Central Committee so that it revoked its earlier condemnation of the idea.

This late attempt at a new turn of the institutionalized revolutionary screw was less absurd in content than Stalin's last project and less dependent on violence than his previous efforts. Khrushchev apparently really believed his program could be carried out by persuasion; but it was no less unrealistic in its miscalculation of financial and psychological conditions. Press reports of successful sales of livestock were soon followed by disclosures that the peasants were increasingly choosing to slaughter their livestock. Though Khrushchev first attempted to explain the setbacks by blaming his subordinates for having applied intimidation instead of persuasion, it swiftly became obvious that progress toward utopia could not be achieved by persuasion—only by using coercion and paying its economic price.

By the time the draft for Khrushchev's new party program was published in 1961 in preparation for the 22nd Congress, it showed that a choice between utopianism and modernization had finally been made—in favor of the latter. The prospects of eventually merging collective and state ownership and eliminating all significant differences between town and country, along with voluntary reduction of private plots and herds and the creation of "agrotowns" in this evolution, were still mentioned. But they were no longer presented as operative tasks for the party, merely forecast as inevitable by-products of a steady rise in productivity. Hence the proclamation of the new program by the congress meant nothing less than a programmatic renunciation of the idea of further "revolutions from above." Under Stalin, the use of state power to transform society was the operative reality, and an improvement in the standard of living presented as a promise of future achievement. By 1961, only increased productivity and a higher standard of living were tasks for action: the further transformation of society had been transmuted into a mere vision of an indefinite future. After the failure of three successive postwar attempts to keep the wheels of institutionalized revolution going—Khrushchev's in 1951, Stalin's in 1952, and Khrushchev's in 1959—the oldest and most powerful ruling Communist Party had recognized that, at the stage of industrial development reached in Russia, it could no longer afford the active pursuit of utopian goals. But it had also understood that at this stage such a pursuit was no longer needed to prevent a restoration of capitalism; that particular bogey disappeared from official Soviet documents.

It was indeed a logical consequence of the extinction of the institutionalized revolution that the new party program also claimed that the Soviet Union was no longer a "dictatorship of the proletariat" but a "state of all the people." Whereas Stalin had justified his ruthless purges by talking absurdly of a "sharpening of the class struggle" just when his own constitution

stressed the disappearance of all classes, Khrushchev now had
to deny the actual class character of the new bureaucracy. But
by accepting the end of the revolutionary function of the party
dictatorship, he inevitably raised the question of the legitimacy
of its continued rule. Not content to base this legitimacy solely
on the function of preserving internal unity in the face of a
hostile outer world, he tried to solve this problem by his 1962
reform of the party organization. He divided it into separate
industrial and agricultural sectors, making the party rather
than the state administration appear as the driving force of
economic growth and improvement. Unfortunately, the operation proved economically ineffective and politically offensive to
the economic administrators as well as burdensome to the party
secretaries. All this contributed substantially to the growing
bureaucratic discontent with Khrushchev's "harebrained
schemes," which led to his overthrow by the Central Committee in October 1964. It may be said that this event, unique in
the history of ruling Communist parties up to that time, marked
the definite adjustment of the Soviet political system to the
ending of the institutionalized revolution.

The Attempt at "Uninterrupted Revolution" in China

In Russia, World War II had imposed a major interval between Stalin's great purge and the merging of the collective
farms into larger units, followed by Stalin's and Khrushchev's
abortive attempts at further social transformation of the countryside. In China, however, Mao's anti-rightist campaign of
1957 against non-party intellectuals, which had left the party's
core of revolutionary veterans intact, was promptly followed by
an intensified effort to transform China's social structure under
extreme pressure: the creation of rural "people's communes" as
part of the Great Leap Forward of 1958.

The decision to merge all the collective farms of a rural
district into a single multifunctional unit seems to have arisen
from the need to stop peasant migration to the cities, where

industry lacked the capital for employing them. The idea was to put rural surplus labor to work in low-capital industries on the spot, as well as to draft it for public works in transport and water control. The concept of using over-population in agriculture for the creation of light industry based on "intermediate technologies" was ingenious. But in creating these communes, an attempt was also made to mobilize rural manpower beyond these purposes. They were to be used as well to build primitive steel furnaces, for intense military training, and for time-consuming ideological indoctrination. That overreaching effort did, in fact, require the militarization of rural labor under district-wide commands. It soon led to a massive breakup of family households through mobilizing woman-power, to a liquidation of the peasants' private plots as causing harmful dispersal of labor, and to the replacement of the main part of the family's cash income by equal rations in kind.

That orgy of egalitarian military communism was based in part on the Chinese Communists' memory of the way they had assured collective survival in their rural fastnesses during the civil war and the war against Japan. Now forcibly imposed on the entire peasant population at this time, it was justified as a shortcut to the higher stage of full communism under a new doctrine of "uninterrupted revolution." That doctrine, first publicly expounded at the 8th Party Congress in May, and formally embodied in a Central Committee resolution in December 1958, was later attributed to Mao himself, probably with reason. It decreed that there could be no hiatus between the building of socialism and the transition to communism, just as there had been none between the seizure of power in Mao's "New Democratic Revolution" and the transition to a Socialist revolution; in other words, the revolutionary transformation of society in a Communist direction must be an uninterrupted process. The new forms of communal life and work came to be interpreted as a step accelerating that transition. For a time, even the tight rationing system was hailed as an expression of the Communist principle, "To each according to his need."

The high tide of this utopian intoxication occurred between the party congress in May, when the communes were being prepared but not yet announced, and the December meeting of the Central Committee, when they were officially sanctioned. By then, it was admitted that fully equal distribution might only be possible after fifteen or twenty years, and that full communism was even further off. In the following years, the communes' tasks, organization, and wage system were all modified under the impact of economic setbacks, peasant discontent, and Soviet criticism. But the principle that they constituted an important step on the road to communism was never renounced. By 1960 some "urban communes" were introduced as well, though not for the main tasks of industrial production. In time, the growing gulf between increasingly pragmatic measures toward economic recovery and a basically unrevised utopian ideology reflected a deadlock in the leadership between the unrepentant utopianism of Mao and the developmental orientation of other leaders.

In 1964, after the open break with the Soviets, Mao introduced what amounted to a final version of his theory. He had now come to recognize that achievement of full communism in China might take "five to ten generations or one or several centuries"; but he also concluded from Soviet experience that the danger of capitalist restoration would continue throughout the period preceding the attainment of the final goal. The reason for that danger, in his view, lay in the spontaneous reemergence of capitalist tendencies out of the unregenerated mentality of part of the people—the mentality of "economic man"—as well as the "embourgeoisement" of party and state bureaucrats who tolerated such tendencies instead of fighting them. That, in Mao's view, was what had happened in Khrushchev's Russia; and the declaration in the CPSU program that the "dictatorship of the proletariat" had come to an end was an ideological expression of that process. To prevent a similar development in China, an unremitting ideological struggle against all who succumbed to a capitalist outlook was needed. This required, in particular, a struggle to educate the young, designed to train "millions of revolutionary successors," and accompanied by a struggle against all "persons in authority walking the capitalist road," as it came to be formulated in the "Cultural Revolution."

The Cultural Revolution, inaugurated by Mao in 1966, did not really end until after his death. It was seen by Mao and his followers as another phase of their "uninterrupted revolution." But it was not primarily aimed at a further transformation of China's economic structure, however much it affected the economy. It began as an effort to transform the consciousness of the young generation and was first directed at the country's educational institutions. The mobilized youth was soon incited to "bombard the headquarters"—in other words, to attack the institutions of party and government, sparing only the army and a few central ministries. Because of the resistance that had arisen against him in the leading party cadres ever since the initial failures of the Great Leap Forward, Mao had apparently come to the conclusion that an "uninterrupted revolution" in his sense was incompatible with institutional bureaucratic stability. Unlike the Soviet leaders, the approach to the limits of institutionalized revolution did not lead him to abandon continued revolution, but to turn, instead, against the institutions of party rule.

The final phases of Maoism will therefore be treated in the context of the tendency of the Chinese Communist regime toward personal despotism and of its outcome.

III

The Transformation of Totalitarian Institutions by Personal Despotism

Vulnerability to Leadership Conflict

The previous section has shown that the process of institutionalized revolution in Communist regimes typically proceeds through inner party conflicts between policies directed to en-

sure the approach to utopia and those required for successful
modernization. It is only natural that such conflicts often take
the form of clashes between rival leaders. Power conflicts between leaders occur, of course, in many ruling parties, without
necessarily leading to the paralysis of the regime. But it is
difficult to regard it as an accident that in both the most powerful and long-lasting Communist regimes such conflicts have
resulted in the attempt of a leader to raise himself to the position of a despot free to ignore the institutions of the party, thus
producing a profound and prolonged crisis.

In the case of Stalin, his effort to become a despot above the
party, carried out by ruthless police terror, succeeded for the
entire period from the beginning of his purge in 1936 to his
death in 1953. Stalinist despotism thus lasted in Russia almost
as long as the entire preceding period since the October Revolution of 1917. However, it did not destroy the ruling party, but
merely deprived it of its primacy and turned it into one of a
number of power machines at the service of the despot, who
could paralyze its leading organs and interfere with their decisions at will. As the fiction of party primacy was maintained in
order to legitimate the despotic regime, the restoration of its
autonomy and primacy after the death of the despot proved to
be possible during the "crisis of succession" that lasted up to
the fall of 1957.

In the case of Mao, his effort to become a despot above the
party, implicitly proclaimed with the announcement of the
"Great Proletarian Cultural Revolution" by an inner party
coup, was effected more through mass mobilization than police
terror. Mao never fully achieved his aim of uncontested and
unlimited despotic rule. Yet, for a time, he effectively destroyed
the institutions of party rule, while relying chiefly on the army,
first to mobilize the improvised movements of the youthful Red
Guards, and later to try to control them. All this produced a
chaotic situation that paralyzed many governmental institutions as well. Although he tried to rebuild the party from above,
he remained dependent for years on the military leaders, one of

whom was finally accused of having tried to seize power himself. In Mao's last years, decisions seem to have emerged from an unstable balance between competing leadership groups not regulated by either institutional procedures or the authority of a despot. After his death, the party again emerged as the principal legitimate institution.

In an analysis of the dynamics and the aftermath of totalitarian Communist rule, the question thus arises as to why some important Communist regimes—though not *all* Communist regimes—have produced this type of institutional crisis: a conflict in the leadership with a tendency toward personal despotism. Nothing similar is known either in totalitarian regimes of the fascist type or in modern democratic regimes with firmly established institutions. The answer appears to lie in the ill-defined procedures originally created in Communist Party regimes to confirm the legitimacy of their leadership and the method of succession—procedures in which Lenin's "democratic centralism" is inferior to either fascist dictatorship or modern Western democracy.

To understand this, we must start with the major difference between the role of the leader as conceived in fascist ideologies and that in Communist ideology. In fascist regimes, the role of the leader is a central ideological point; he is above the party from the start, and the legitimacy of the regime is based on trust in the leader, not the party. The personal despotism which we have described as a form of institutional crisis in Communist regimes is in fascist regimes the normal or, at least, the ideal state. Hitler was a despot who ruled with the party as one of his instruments, and Mussolini would have liked to be one.

This similarity has led some serious students of the problem to suggest that the very term "totalitarianism" should be reserved for regimes of the "Fuehrerist" type—those of Hitler, Mussolini, Stalin, and Mao. However, from that starting point it becomes impossible to understand why Communist regimes could successfully institutionalize revolution for long periods before developing a personal despotism; why Stalin persisted, and Mao persisted most of the time, in vesting the legitimacy of his rule in the party even after decisively reducing its real power; and why the party's rule was restored in both Russia and China after the death of the despot or would-be despot. The crises that produced Stalin's despotism and Mao's attempt at despotism could not have occurred in the fascist regimes, because they were already despotic. They might, of course, have produced a crisis of succession if they had outlasted their founders; but in both cases, regime and leader lived and died together.

A modern democratic regime has established procedures for resolving conflicts and changing leaders by majority vote. Within a particular government, a directly elected president, or a prime minister leading the majority party, may overrule his associates; but he may himself be overruled by the electorate, or, in the parliamentary system, by a majority of its representatives. Forcible resistance by a minority to government decisions backed by a majority has no legitimacy.

But the Communist doctrine of "democratic centralism" legitimates neither the absolute power of the leader nor of the majority. It merely upholds the *leadership* so long as it is in agreement. What it describes and veils at the same time is an ingenious system that combines more or less democratic forms in the election of delegates to the party congress and to membership in party organs with a de facto monopoly of initiative reserved for the top leadership, through its right to "propose" without opposition regional and local leaders who in turn "propose" the congress delegates, who then elect the new Central Committee. This kind of democracy in form and centralism in substance normally ensures the unquestioned continuation of an established leadership, unless the leaders seriously disagree among themselves. For such situations of serious disagreement, Lenin left not a single formula but two opposing solutions, developed for different periods in the party's history. This ambiguity in the Leninist tradition in effect legitimates unresolved conflicts in the leadership: it is the historic root of the danger of such institutional crises that has nurtured such institutional crises as have occurred in both Russia and China.

The first of Lenin's two opposite prescriptions was developed for the building of the "Leninist" party along its road to power. It is rooted in Lenin's conviction of the indispensable role of a "correct" strategy, founded on a correct interpretation of Marxism. It follows that a leader who is convinced that he has that correct strategy (as Lenin was), and that the fate of the party and the revolution may depend on its adoption, must in no case submit to an erring majority, even within the leadership, on vital questions. Rather, he must force the majority of the Central Committee to submit to him by threatening his resignation; or appeal to the cadres or even to the rank and file; or go so far as to split or refound the party. The history of the Bolsheviks up to their seizure of power is full of such splits and "refoundings" practiced by Lenin; and even on the eve of the October Revolution and during the early period afterward, when his authority was supreme, he repeatedly used the threat of resignation to bring an opposing majority of the Central Committee to heel.

The opposite prescription is based on the need for preserving the party's monopoly of power, once it has been achieved, by absolute unity. It was most clearly argued by Lenin at the 10th Party Congress of March 1921. This was the congress that adopted the New Economic Policy and Lenin's model for relations between the state and the trade unions. It also laid the foundations for a fully developed "totalitarian," single-party regime. Lenin viewed continued agitation against the congress decisions by the "Workers' Opposition"—on the morrow of the Kronstadt sailors' rising—as so dangerous to the preservation of the party's power that he proposed, and carried, his famous "ban on factions" which, ever since, has been regarded as one of the "Leninist norms of party life." In its original text, it referred specifically to a ban on groups engaging in continued opposition to congress decisions. Lenin even warned against extending a ban on rival group platforms to all future congress elections. But his own argument for the ban went beyond the

specific occasion. He pointed out that a ruling party forced to
make economic concessions to hostile classes must absolutely
bar them from the decision-making process. Nor was it enough
to ban all rival parties. So long as factions could be formed
freely within the ruling party, they would inevitably become
channels for pressures emanating from the class enemy. Hence
submission to majority decisions—of course, "correct" decisions sponsored by Lenin—was vital for the survival of the
proletarian dictatorship.

Those contrasting Leninist traditions were bound to become
crucial for the evolution of future conflicts within the Bolshevik
leadership—its ambiguity left minorities a choice: to submit, or
to fight on where questions of vital importance were concerned.
But, as we have seen, the inherent dilemma of an institutionalized revolution as to whether to give priority to the utopian goal
or to economic modernization was bound repeatedly to give rise
to such conflicts—at least until a stage of development had been
reached at which the utopian impulse had spent itself. For the
conduct of leadership minorities in such future conflicts, the
Leninist tradition offered not one single clear prescription but
two contradictory ones. It thus offered no foundation for a type
of legitimacy based on procedural consensus.

In such circumstances, the Communist party regimes could
avoid an institutional crisis in the course of the institutionalized
revolution on only one condition: so long as there was a leader
with uncontested or, at any rate, overwhelmingly accepted personal authority. Opponents were likely to submit to such a
leader rather than endanger the unity of the party, since that
leader, proven right on previous occasions, just *might,* after all,
be right again. Such overwhelming authority within the party
had clearly been enjoyed by Lenin from his return to Russia in
April 1917 to his incapacitation by illness, and by Mao from the
final eclipse of his last Moscow-oriented rival in the Chinese
party, Wang Ming, in 1940 to the end of 1958. It was enjoyed
by nobody in either country during the period when their most
difficult decisions had to be made on their respective roads of

revolutionary development. As a consequence, both suffered severe institutional crises leading to the prolonged suspension of party rule in favor of personal despotism or, at least, a major attempt at it.

The Rise and Impact of Stalinist Despotism

The document known as "Lenin's Testament" shows that Lenin was fully aware of the problem of succession, in other words, of the need for a recognized single leader—even though he had never publicly stressed his own role—and that he had no solution to offer. Hence the establishment of a "collective leadership" was as inevitable as was its failure to avoid a struggle for succession. Differences on major issues were bound to arise and, in view of their ideological importance, the minority was bound to appeal to the rank and file—in other words, to engage in "factional" activities. But, contrary to the early ideological conflicts in which Lenin had established his leadership, the conflicts among his heirs developed within a ruling party that could no longer tolerate a split.

The first series of those new inner party conflicts, between 1923 and 1929, was decided in Stalin's favor by two factors. From the beginning he held the key post of "General Secretary" with its power of appointments. And he understood better than his rivals that the longer the party continued in power, and the greater the share of its members recruited after its seizure of power, the more the late Leninist principle of party-unity-above-all-else was bound to appear more convincing than the early Leninist principle of duty to split for the sake of true revolutionary policy. He thus discredited his opponents as "factionalists" plotting against "the party's" policy, while skillfully using the party machine as his own faction.

This was fairly easy when first Trotsky, then Zinoviev and Kamenev advocated a change from the New Economic Policy to revive the class struggle in the countryside and increase the pace of industrial growth at the expense of the peasantry. It became more difficult when, from the turn of 1927–28, Stalin himself began to move in a similar direction, finally advocating a radical program of forced industrialization, forced collectivization, and forcible "dekulakization." Now *he* was the innovator. At first, he had no majority in the Politburo against his former supporters around Bukharin. Yet in the course of the preceding struggles he had in fact acquired sole control of appointments and dismissals in the party, the state apparatus, and the secret police, and had thereby created a large network of men dependent on him for their careers. With their help, he succeeded within two years in pushing the critics of his new "left" turn, notably Bukharin, into the role of a "right opposition." And the "unity reflex" worked in his favor.

By 1929 Stalin had thus achieved victory in the succession struggle after Lenin's death, and still achieved it by inner party methods—by use and abuse of the party apparatus. The political system inherited from Lenin had not yet changed basically, even though it was used in a different style and for different policies. The years of the first five-year plan and of forced collectivization had not only brought other important decisions, such as those on wage policy and training of experts discussed above; they also revived a climate of massive violence, in which the borders between plain failure to achieve planned results, non-compliance, and active sabotage were increasingly blurred, while any attempt at inner party opposition was driven underground and treated as a conspiracy. Even earlier, Stalin's defeated opponents had been required not only to submit to party discipline but to "disarm ideologically," in other words, to admit that their views were wrong. Such was the meaning of the new concept of the "monolithic party."

Those years of "revolution from above"—with their mass deportation of alleged kulaks, which destroyed the independent peasantry—created a whole new class of state slaves in labor camps and culminated in a severe famine. They also strengthened Stalin's position by convincing party members that only his strong arm could prevent a total collapse of the regime. All that amounted to a tendency for a transition from apparatchik rule within the party to what eventually became personal despotism above it. But, as late as 1932, the refusal of the Politburo to approve the death sentence for the anti-Stalinist "conspirator" Ryutin showed that the institutions of the party were not yet subordinated to Stalin's every whim; the despotism was not yet complete.

It became complete in the years after the collectivization drive and the end of the famine—between the 17th Party Congress of February 1934 and the full start of the blood purge in the summer of 1936. Scholars still disagree about the nature and extent of behind-the-scenes opposition at that "Congress of Victors" to Stalin's continuing in sole control, now that his brutal rule no longer seemed indispensable to protect the regime from collapse. But evidence from dissident Russian sources is still accumulating that there was a movement at that congress to reduce and control his power, and the assumption that he learned about it is the likely explanation of his determined turn to achieve full independence from the party by relying on personal control of the secret police. At any rate, Stalin moved at that time to put those who would serve him as executioners into positions of authority. Even if proof that Stalin himself arranged the assassination of his close collaborator Kirov in December 1935 through orders to the secret police rests only on indirect evidence, there is no doubt that he proceeded at once to exploit it with a vengeance. The danger of war, and the need for extreme flexibility at the top to avert it, may indeed have offered Stalin a justification for despotic power; the fact that his power within the party institutions had begun to appear insecure for the first time in years was motive enough.

The Great Terror was that seizure of despotic power. The institutions of the party were not destroyed, but effectively deprived of a life of their own; they were turned into mere propaganda organs at the disposal of the despot, parallel but not superior to other administrative organs such as the economic bureaucracy and the military. If any one branch of Stalin's government after 1936 was superior to the others, it was clearly the secret police, which for a time was able, on Stalin's orders, to arrest, torture, and execute Central Committee members, generals, and top economic administrators by the hundreds. But even the secret police remained strictly subordinate to the despot who, issuing orders through his personal secretariat, could dismiss and destroy its chiefs at will.

As we have seen, Stalin also used the blood purge as a new "revolution from above," decimating the old elite of revolutionary veterans and subsequently opening the party to a thoroughly frightened new elite of post-revolutionary bureaucrats and managers. For he had no intention of renouncing the services of the nominally still "ruling" party. After all, he derived his public legitimacy from being its General Secretary, and was fully aware of the need for a variety of institutional tools in running his empire. The same 18th Congress, held in March 1939, which changed the party's statutes to endorse its new composition brought about by Stalin's sanguinary version of the "circulation of elites," also signaled a limited revival of the party's activity by assuring the delegates that a similar mass purge would not be repeated. This assurance may have been both needed and doubted by those to whom it was addressed in view of the fate of the majority of delegates to the previous "Congress of Victors," later seen to have been instead a congress of (prospective) victims.

It was, then, as an organized body without a soul, as a machine without a will, that the CPSU survived the long final period of Stalin's rule. Thirteen years were to pass before a party congress was held again. We know from Khrushchev that the Central Committee rarely met during those years, and the Politburo mostly in subgroups called together by Stalin at his pleasure. We also know that during the war Stalin assumed personal direction of the government as well as of the party; the GKO (State Defense Committee) he formed at that time was a far more important center of decisions than the Politburo. As for the institutionalized revolution which we described as the essence of totalitarianism, the revolutionary process was suspended during the war years, and the party as the key institution was reduced to an auxiliary role. But neither was dead; both were seen by the despot as still important for *his* role after the war. We have mentioned how efforts to revive the revolutionary process were made, with partial if declining success, in Stalin's very last years. They could not have been made without some reactivation of the party. But the primacy of the party over the other power centers was not restored in Stalin's lifetime, nor was the personal security of its senior officials. Though there was no more mass bloodletting on the scale of 1936–38, the "Leningrad affair," the "Mingrelian affair," and the "Zionist plot in the Crimea" all took their toll. And, of course, there was the persecution of leading East European Communists as "Titoists." Finally, the very last months of Stalin's rule were, according to Khrushchev, devoted to preparing another major purge—of which the Slansky trial in Prague and the "plot of the Kremlin doctors" seem to have been harbingers.

During all those years, Stalin's power was greater than Lenin's had ever been; by contrast, his authority, and the spontaneous respect and trust offered him, had at first been incomparably smaller. Ultimately, it was his fundamental insecurity that caused him to seize despotic power after he had defeated all his rivals. For all the mad elements in the purge, Stalin was not clinically mad. That he was able, despite initial miscalculations, to lead the Soviet Union to victory over Hitler proves it, and thus strengthens the argument for seeing the blood purge as a piece of utterly ruthless but calculated politics by a man who had reason to feel insecure in possession of power.

But the objective situation changed after the war: because of Soviet sacrifices and Soviet victory under his leadership, Stalin enjoyed greater genuine authority than ever before. Probably, he could then have afforded to renounce his despotic measures and restore the institutional practice of a party dictatorship of

the "Leninist" type. But by that time he was no longer able to
conceive of doing so. Despotic rule had become, in his mind,
identical with his personal security and indeed his way of life.
For all we know, his rule faced no danger in his final years. The
only danger originated in his own personality, twisted and
scarred as it had become by a life spent in persecuting others.
Thus he became an obstacle to any attempt at restoring institutional Communist rule. It could be undertaken only after his
death.

The Institutional Crisis of Late Maoism

Decisions on China's development after victory in the civil
war were objectively far more difficult than in Russia. The
productive forces needed for modernization were far more
backward and qualified cadres much scarcer in China in 1949
than in Russia in 1921. Yet the early years of the Chinese
People's Republic saw far less serious conflicts in the leadership
about the road to take than the Russian twenties—partly because a leader with unchallenged authority survived in the
person of Mao, but partly also because many crucial decisions
were at first simply taken over from the Soviet model. This
applies particularly to the first Chinese five-year plan. Early
differences on the speed of agricultural collectivization did not
involve matters of principle, and did not hamper the united
implementation of Mao's decisions.

The first impact of Khrushchev's de-Stalinization in 1956
was to weaken the influence of the Soviet model but not the
authority of Mao. On the contrary, the two Chinese Politburo
decisions on the subject—in April and December 1956—clearly
expressed Mao's ideas. He underlined Khrushchev's strictures
against Stalin's "Great Power Chauvinism" in inter-Commu-
nist relations, but expressed regret at the poor Marxist quality
of Khrushchev's philippics. In attempting a more balanced,
"scientific" appreciation of the merits of the dead despot, he
appeared to be staking a claim for his independence from Sta-

lin's successor in matters of theory and, indeed, for his superior standing in that field. Hence the fact that the first session of the 8th Chinese Party Congress in that year removed the reference to the "Thought of Mao" from the party statutes, while clearly a tribute to the condemnation of the "cult of personality," should not be taken as evidence of any weakening of Mao's authority at that time.

Such a weakening must have begun, however, when the experiment in freedom of discussion started after that Congress, the "Hundred Flowers Campaign," got out of control in the following year. It had unloosed a flood of criticism of the Communist regime and showed that Mao had greatly overestimated the loyalty the intellectuals would proffer if freed from censorship. For Mao, it was a traumatic lesson in how slowly "social consciousness" adapted itself to imposed changes in social structure. For the intellectual critics, it brought an end to the experimentally granted freedoms and persecution in a new "anti-rightist campaign." At the same time, the raising of minimum wages by the Congress produced a mass influx of peasants into the towns. As previously noted, they could not be absorbed by industry. It was dramatic proof that the Soviet model of development could not be imitated in a country where the shortage of capital in relation to the rapidly growing population was much more severe. The search for an indigenous Chinese road to modernization had to be started in earnest.

It was begun in 1958 by Mao's gigantic experiment known as the "Great Leap Forward." We have earlier described its two main aspects: a new "revolution from above" imposed on agriculture by creating "People's Communes," initially with strong utopian features, and a campaign for a competitive raising of industrial targets by local and regional party committees over the heads of the managers. When the first major corrections of the Commune program were undertaken by the Central Committee in December 1958, apparently with Mao's consent, he took the occasion to resign his position as head of state and also indicated his intention to retire gradually from the daily conduct of affairs to a more detached role, while still preserving his ultimate authority. But this did not prevent the Minister of War, Peng Dehuai, from making a general attack on the concept of the Great Leap at the following Central Committee session held at Lushan in the summer of 1959. While Peng was subsequently removed from office and his demand for a reversal of Mao's line was rejected in principle, a number of further corrections were imposed in practice. From that moment on, the Chinese Communist leaders have remained deeply divided on what road of development to follow.

What it all amounted to was that the aging Mao—under the pressure of objective difficulties in Chinese modernization, and of what he saw as the ideological degeneration of the Soviet Union, with which he was increasingly in open and bitter conflict—had developed a militant preference for utopian over modernizing solutions to the basic dilemma in Communist policy. This manifested itself not only in his initial concept of "People's Communes," but in his general insistence on increasing egalitarianism rather than relying on differential material incentives, and on giving aging revolutionary veterans authority over post-revolutionary managers and technicians. Perhaps most important was his belief in the need to change people's consciousness before effectively changing their material conditions of life. But with his authority weakened by repeated failures, Mao was no longer able to push the leadership into united support of his policy through his control of the party machine. From 1958–59 to the beginning of the Cultural Revolution in 1966, the "struggle between the two lines" swayed back and forth in the Chinese Central Committee. The new President, Liu Shaoqi, presumed by many to be Mao's successor at the head of the party as well, and the party's General Secretary, Deng Xiaoping, increasingly opposed Mao, while Zhou Enlai, the head of government, remained loyal to the principle of Mao's leadership but persisted in advising Mao to moderate his policies. In fact, those policies were gradually whittled down between 1960 and 1962. Yet Mao felt less and less able to submit to what he regarded as a "revisionist" majority that was pushing China down a road which, in his view, had led Russia to bureaucratic degeneration and, indeed, to a kind of restoration of capitalism.

As the struggle dragged on, Mao came increasingly to pin his hopes on the army. There the civil war spirit of solidarity and sacrifice had been kept alive most effectively and his supporter Lin Biao had taken over command from Peng. And Mao also pinned his hopes on the education of a young generation of "revolutionary successors." Increasingly, he viewed the established hierarchies of party and state as obstacles to his concept of "uninterrupted revolution." By 1964, the same year in which he elaborated this long-term concept in his basic document on "Khrushchev's Phoney Communism," he started two propaganda campaigns designed to isolate the "revisionist" party establishment: "Learn from the Army" and "Socialist Education." Having thus prepared the ground, and finding himself still unable to force a clearcut decision in his favor in the established organs of the party, he finally decided in 1955–56 to launch the "Great Proletarian Cultural Revolution."

Without clear authority from the split Central Committee and probably against the will of its majority, Mao mobilized a mass movement of university and high school students with the logistic support of the army, which apparently had also helped to assemble at the critical moment the Maoist wing of the Central Committee to approve the decision. The character of this Cultural Revolution as a military *coup d'état* making Mao's rule formally independent from the party institutions became obvious when Mao, in his appeal to the Red Guards, declared rebellion against the constituted organs of party and state—always excepting the army—as justified.

Once established as a ruler free of institutional limitations, Mao proceeded to destroy a large part of the institutions of Communist rule. He dissolved the official Communist youth organization and the trade unions, and effectively stopped the functioning of the party organs by allowing the Red Guards to occupy their offices and granting them the same freedom with regard to most government ministries, including, for a time, the Ministry of Foreign Affairs, with the exception of a remnant around premier Zhou Enlai who miraculously kept the rudiments of administration going.

Altogether, the parallel and contrast to Stalin's establishment of his despotic rule are equally striking. The parallel lies in the crucial fact that the leader's power was made independent of the institutions of party rule. The central difference lay in Mao's relying for that operation primarily on a mass movement of youngsters backed by the army, not on the secret police—a reflection of his desire to continue rather than control the revolution.

Yet the method of mass mobilization against the political and administrative institutions had its own anarchic logic. Mao, who had first called on various army units to support the Red Guards against the "bureaucratic resistance" of some non-Maoist party and trade union units, soon had to call on them once more to restore order as various Red Guards began to fight each other or ransacked the files of the Ministry of Foreign Affairs. As a result, Mao became increasingly dependent on the army as the one apparatus of power that had remained intact and no longer faced any serious competition. It was the army, then, that from the turn of 1967–68 proceeded to liquidate the mass movement and to furnish the backbone for the new institutions that now emerged: first, the "Revolutionary Committees" in the regions and leading cities, to which some supposedly Maoist party officials and some supposedly reliable Red Guard leaders were coopted; and, finally, the party as reconstituted from above around this tripartite core.

If Mao had in fact intended to make himself a despot—and the fantastic cult of his person with the quasi-religious recitals from his *Little Red Book,* repeated several times a day in offices and factories, in trains and planes all over the country, leaves little doubt that he did—the attempt failed. He had become dependent, for a time at least, on the army as the new key institution. An outward expression of that outcome was the fact that, when the 9th Congress of the CCP was called in the spring of 1969 in order to revive the party from its coma, it incorporated into its new statutes, along with confirming Mao's leadership for life, the decision that his new deputy should also become his eventual successor: Lin Biao, the head of the armed forces.

In fact, however, the upheaval of the Cultural Revolution had no more resolved the underlying policy conflicts on China's road of development than it had created stable new institutions or resolved the question of ultimate power. The reconstituted organs of party and government could not manage their tasks without rehabilitating a considerable number of former leading cadres, who had been persecuted for opposing Mao's ideas and were now converted to them only outwardly. Next to them sat a smaller but important number of true Maoist supporters of the Cultural Revolution. The military leaders, who had backed it at first and been sobered in its course, held the balance. In view of the renewed deadlock, and the waning authority of Mao, it was hardly surprising that his designated successor should now try to seize the reins. Lin Biao apparently conceived the idea of pursuing the Maoist road of development, but not by the kind of mass mobilization that had resulted in anarchy; rather, by military authority and discipline, as a true revolution from above. Mao's great ideas, he had come to believe, could only be imposed on China by open military despotism, with himself as the despot. Whether that idea had already taken the form of a concrete plot, as was later alleged, we do not know. But it was clearly implicit in his political course. It ended by arousing the united opposition of civilian leaders in both camps, joined by many regional commanders who proceeded to crush him in Mao's name, with the result that he lost his life and was branded a traitor.

Following this failure of the second attempt at a despotic solution, the CCP had to be reorganized again at its 10th Congress in 1973. The man who now emerged as the central figure, thanks to his supreme political skill and to his earlier self-effacement, was Zhou Enlai. He was accepted as loyal by Mao, as a moderate by the anti-Maoist pragmatists, and as an indispensable symbol of order and continuity by the bulk of the military leaders. But he was a dying man. While Zhou was continuing the rehabilitation of moderates, including Deng Xiaoping, and slowly reducing the excessive numbers of military men in the central and regional party leadership (probably to the relief of most of them), the struggle between the followers and opponents of the Maoist road increasingly assumed the character of a dual succession struggle—for Zhou and for Mao.

The campaign by the Maoist hard-core faction (later named "the Gang of Four" after its ultimate failure) against "Lin Biao and Confucius" was in fact intended to discredit Zhou, with his mandarin background, as a "Confucian," that is, a conservative. This and the renewed banishment of Deng, whom Zhou had made his deputy and presumptive successor, after Zhou's death in April 1976 and a Deng-inspired mass demonstration in his memory in Peking's central square, showed the intensity of the struggle. By the time of Mao's death in September of the same year, neither the policy questions nor the institutional question had been resolved. Mao left his lifework in a state of open political and institutional crisis under a regime that, if it could be described as a political system at all, was certainly no longer totalitarian.

IV

Toward Post-Totalitarian One-Party Rule

It should be clear by now that the deaths of Stalin and Mao caused much greater changes than are commonly implied in talking about a crisis of succession. Both left their countries with an unsolved crisis of the political institutions and with unsettled problems concerning the future road of development. But the nature of the institutional crisis and of the developmental dilemmas was quite different in the two countries.

In Russia, the CPSU had continued to exist throughout the seventeen years of Stalin's autocratic rule, and the fiction that Stalin was ruling in its name had never been abandoned. But the party had never in Stalin's lifetime recovered its institutional primacy in relation to the other centers of power, leaving the leader as the sole arbiter between them. His disappearance left an open contradiction between the legitimate claim of the party to primacy and the uncertain balance among the various power machines, with no one holding sufficient authority to be recognized as the uncontested arbiter.

In China, the fiction that Mao was ruling in the party's name had been more or less abandoned in the early years of the Cultural Revolution. But its restoration had begun with the party's reconstruction in 1968–69, and been pushed more seriously after the death of Lin Biao. The 10th Party Congress of 1973 ended the period of obvious military predominance. It may even be said that by the time of Mao's death, the primacy of the Communist Party among the existing power structures had become somewhat more real as compared with the CPSU at Stalin's death. Credit for this clearly belongs to Zhou Enlai's subtle hand.

But if the CCP started the post-Mao period in a somewhat better position relative to the other power machines than had been the case in the CPSU, it had the crucial disadvantage of being far more deeply divided than the CPSU at Stalin's death. China's unsolved problems of modernization in 1976 were far more urgent than Russia's in 1953. The Soviet leaders who took over from Stalin may have differed in the firmness of their belief that another turn of the revolutionary screw would be needed in Soviet agriculture. But, governing a fairly developed industrial country with a number of acute weaknesses causing mass discontent, they were all agreed that it was more urgent to remedy those weaknesses than to transform the structure of society further. As we have seen, Khrushchev made his final bid for social transformation only years later, after he had won the succession struggle. If the end of the process of revolutionary transformation had not yet finally arrived in Russia by 1953, but was only decided by the failure of Khrushchev's last attempt in 1961, it was already close enough in 1953 to affect the climate of discussion.

The Chinese Communists, ruling a far less advanced country, were after, as before, the death of Mao profoundly divided over the respective priorities of uninterrupted revolution versus rational economic modernization. The Russian "succession crisis" took the form of struggle between the proponents of rival power machines, in which the first secretary of the party had the advantage of its traditional legitimacy. The Chinese succession crisis, in contrast, took the form of a continuing struggle between utopian revolutionaries and practical-minded modernizers, in which the utopians were now deprived of their former chief asset—the protection of Mao.

Khrushchev's Restoration of Party Primacy

The first steps toward reviving the Soviet party's initiative were the replacement of the large and unwieldy Presidium created at the CPSU 19th Congress by a small group of top leaders within two days of Stalin's death, and the decision one week later to release Malenkov from his party office. He had first been appointed both head of government and first secretary of the party, but seemed to favor the governmental role. His removal was meant to prevent the accumulation of key positions in the hands of one man. This left Khrushchev as senior party secretary, even though he received the title of "First Secretary" only later in the year, while Malenkov remained chairman of the Party Presidium.

In the meantime a far more decisive event toward restoring the party's primacy had occurred with the fall and arrest of Beria, announced in late June 1953. For Beria had resumed the combined control of the Ministries of the Interior and of State Security immediately after Stalin's death. In view of the role of the secret police and of Beria himself in Stalin's time, he was viewed by all concerned, and certainly by Khrushchev, as the greatest danger both to their individual safety and to the authority of the party. Beria had given no indication so far of wishing to use his powerful office for new purges; he had even taken the initiative in quashing the prosecution of the alleged "doctors' plot." But he had given ample reason to arouse concern by seeming to seek popularity through visible interference in various fields of domestic and foreign policy.

Among these apparently was a bold attempt, originally undertaken with Malenkov's support, to prevent West German rearmament by secret feelers to the West about reunifying Germany on terms more attractive to the West than Stalin had offered in his notes of the previous year. When the Western leaders failed to show interest, and the ensuing disorientation among the East German Communist leaders contributed to the uprising of June 17, Malenkov dropped Beria, and the Party Presidium condemned, deposed, and arrested him. He was accused of being a foreign agent who had plotted to seize power by putting the secret police above party and government. The affair ended with the execution of Beria, and a group of his associates, after a trial announced in December 1953. In the next three years, three other groups of former secret police officials close to Beria, and one investigator who had played a key role in staging the "doctors' plot," were also executed. These have remained the only political executions of senior officials in the post-Stalin Soviet Union.

What matters in our context was not the fate of Beria and his men as such, but the *capitis diminutio* of the secret police, which became the signal for a lasting reduction of its power. Its labor camp empire, a major sector of the Soviet economy in Stalin's time, was dismantled, even though camps on a more limited scale were preserved, just as the end of Stalinist mass terrorism against whole categories of citizens did not mean the end of the lawless persecution of individual critics. But for the balance among the institutions of leadership the crucial change was that the state security apparatus lost the power to intervene in inner party affairs; conversely, a number of senior posts in this apparatus were now filled by men "from outside," in other words, from a strict party career.

The next major struggles concerned the relative primacy of the party and government machines. Even after Beria's removal, Khrushchev, the senior party secretary, still ranked only as number three in the Party Presidium, apparently on the ground that the secretariat was merely an executive instrument of the policy-making Presidium—whose chairman was the head of government; and agreed decisions were announced by "the Council of Ministers and the Central Committee" in that order. This occurred at a time when there was hardly any difference between the speeches of Malenkov and Khrushchev on the need to improve the situation of the peasants, or between their outlook on the need for widening the scope of autonomy for the East European "satellites," or between their attitude on the secret preparations for an attempted reconciliation with Tito.

There may have been more real differences on the amount of diplomatic concessions to the West needed to survive the period of post-Stalin uncertainty. This is indicated by Malenkov's half-involvement in Beria's abortive feelers on the German problem, and by the contrast between his statement that a nuclear war would destroy human civilization and Khrushchev's insistence that it would only destroy capitalism. But the issue on which Khrushchev finally chose to rally a majority against Malenkov in winter of 1954–55 and force his resignation in February 1955 —the charge that he had gone too far in favoring the expansion of consumer goods at the expense of heavy industry and arms production—was little more than a pretext, calculated to appeal both to the Stalin-reared economic bureaucracy and the armed forces. Little had in fact been done in that direction. The underlying drive of Khrushchev to restore the party's primacy by playing one of the rival power machines against the other thus seems to have been more vital than any alleged policy differences.

A more substantial conflict arose, however, in 1955 between Khrushchev and Molotov on policy toward Tito's Yugoslavia. Here Khrushchev was clearly the innovator and Molotov the defender of the Stalinist tradition. Khrushchev was convinced that a more rational division of labor with the East European "satellites," which required granting them more real autonomy, must be made safe from hostile "Titoist" exploitation by a timely reconciliation with Belgrade. He believed this would enhance rather than diminish Soviet prestige. Molotov saw the danger in this: a "rehabilitation" of Tito would weaken the position of the Stalinist leaders in eastern Europe who had imprisoned or executed their rivals as "Titoists," and undermine Soviet authority in those countries as well. Khrushchev had his way and, visiting Tito together with Malenkov's successor Bulganin, achieved a limited reconciliation by blaming the anti-Titoist campaigns of the late 1940s on Beria, though Tito insisted on blaming Stalin himself. Molotov, who despite his position as Foreign Minister had been left out of the visit, vainly opposed Khrushchev's action in the Party Presidium and remained isolated when he brought it before a Central Committee plenum in July 1955. In summer 1956 he had to resign his ministry before Tito's return visit.

In isolating first Beria and then Malenkov, Khrushchev had been able to rely on the natural tendency in the post-Stalinist collective of leaders to rally against whichever of them appeared to become too strong for the comfort of the others. After the fall of Malenkov and the eclipse of Molotov, and with his own increasingly prominent role on the world stage, Khrushchev had himself moved into the exposed position of an emerging number one. Thus one major motive for his decision to use the 20th Congress in February 1956 not only to disavow the "cult of Stalin's personality" but to expose Stalin's crimes against loyal Communists and, more generally, to lay bare the harm done by Stalin's despotism to the party as an institution, must have been the wish to reassure the entire party and government elite that nothing of the kind would occur under his leadership, that *he* was going to keep to Leninist norms of party life. In fact, this reckoning with Stalin, long prepared in its content by the collection of materials but improvised in its form and originally half-concealed, was a necessary part of restoring the party institutions.

There were, of course, other motives as well. The talks with Tito must have convinced Khrushchev that it would not do to blame the blood purges on Beria alone. And he must have been aware that even the partial disavowal he had made in Belgrade was having important repercussions in the rehabilitation of purge victims in Poland and Hungary. Finally, and here de-Stalinization is directly linked with the evolution of general Soviet policy, Khrushchev had during the preceding year emerged as an innovator in many fields. That impulse for innovation had naturally encountered a great deal of resistance among bureaucrats and senior leaders reared in the Stalinist tradition, who often used the "proven value" of that tradition as a conclusive argument. Thus Khrushchev was driven to the conclusion that this resistance to innovation could only be broken if the myth of Stalin's infallibility was destroyed. Yet, while Khrushchev's de-Stalinization weakened bureaucratic resistance by depriving it of its key defense, it paradoxically reinforced resistance by increasing the personal security of the bureaucrats.

Although at the first post-Stalin party congress Khrushchev had given the major public report of the Central Committee, apart from the "secret speech," and although provincial party leaders beholden to him had for some time been speaking of "the Central Committee with Khrushchev at the helm," his personal primacy was not yet formally sanctioned. In fact, since the plenum of July 1955 which saw his victory over Molotov soon after his victory over Malenkov, the official list of members of the Party Presidium had become alphabetical, no longer indicating rank. Moreover, that list—still containing a substantial majority of government members, including Malenkov and Molotov, over the members of the party Secretariat—was confirmed without change at the 20th Congress. (The only changes in Khrushchev's favor had taken place at the levels just below these, in the election of the additional Presidium candidates and Secretariat members, and in the election of more provincial party secretaries to the Central Committee.) The heads of the government bureaucracy, by being entrenched in the Party Presidium, were still in an apparent position to more than balance the representatives of the party machine and Khrushchev as its exponent.

In this situation, the post–de-Stalinization upheavals in Poland and Hungary during the fall of 1956 were bound to bring, at the least, a temporary weakening of Khrushchev's position. Not only did they seem to confirm the warnings of Molotov (whom Khrushchev actually had to take along to his talks in Warsaw), but the sudden need to help the economies of both countries to recover from the crises upset Soviet economic plans, which had been overly ambitious anyhow. By November, Molotov was given the Ministry of State Control with considerable powers to intervene in various sectors of government. By December, a Central Committee plenum was severely criticizing planning errors and entrusting revision of the plans to a "State Economic Commission" of senior economic administrators. But by the time of the next plenum in February 1957, Khrushchev had apparently succeeded in recovering a majority by mobilizing his loyal provincial secretaries against the economic bureaucracy. This plenum not only resumed his ambitious slogan for overtaking, "in a historically short period," the most developed capitalist countries in output per capita; it severely criticized the ministerial administration of the economy as inefficient and accused it of paralyzing the initiative of managers and technicians by remote control. The plenum proposed the replacement of control branch ministries with an "operative direction by economic regions," subordinate only to "country-wide centralized planning." It also censured the methods of Molotov's state control apparatus and demanded its "radical reconstruction." The Party Presidium and the Council of Ministers were directed to submit proposals for this wholesale economic reorganization to the Supreme Soviet.

This proposed structure for breaking up the economic bu-
reaucracy, and replacing all or most of the branch ministries
with strong regional bodies that came to be called "Councils for
National Economy," caused the closest approach to a pre-
Stalin "factional struggle" in the post-Stalin "succession crisis."
When Khrushchev, at the end of March, put forward his full
reorganization plan, it was published by the Party Presidium
and the Council of Ministers not as their joint proposal to the
Supreme Soviet, but as "Comrade Khrushchev's Theses for
Discussion." During the subsequent press debate only one close
associate among the Presidium members supported him; all the
others kept silent. In the Supreme Soviet session in May, when
Khrushchev's "Draft Law" was passed, not a single member of
the Presidium spoke. In fact, a majority of the Presidium members—all holders of government positions except for candidate
Shepilov, an ideologue and former protégé of Khrushchev's—
had by then gotten together. On the apparent initiative of die-
hard Stalinists like Molotov and Kaganovich, resentful victims
of Khrushchev's rise—Malenkov, for example—were joined by
top economic administrators like Pervukhin and Saburov. They
had a common purpose: Khrushchev must be overthrown before his impulsive foreign and economic policies ruined the
country, or before he established a personal dictatorship.

The chairman of the Council of Ministers, Bulganin, and the
head of sate, Voroshilov, joined their ranks. On June 18, when
a meeting of the Presidium opened, the hour to strike had
evidently arrived. But Khrushchev and his minority of supporters outflanked them, insisting on a decision by the full Central
Committee. By the time its members, or most of them, assem-
bled in an improvised plenum on June 22nd, the "factionalists"
found themselves isolated.

It seems certain that the rapid calling in of the Central Committee members was made possible by the army, then led by
Marshal Zhukov (once victimized by Stalin and reinstated in
the course of de-Stalinization), who made planes available. The

army's attitude may also explain why Khrushchev's opponents were unable to publish a decision of the Party Presidium at once, without waiting for the June 22nd plenum. That plenum, at any rate, became a turning point. The "plotters" were on the defensive from the start, and most of them tried to make excuses for their conduct. When the plenum ended on June 29, it had voted a condemnation of Molotov, Malenkov, Kaganovich, and Shepilov, depriving them of their membership in the Central Committee and its higher organs "for factional activities." The roles of Bulganin, Voroshilov, Pervukhin, and Saburov were not disclosed at the time. Of these, only Saburov was not reelected to the Presidium.

But the Presidium was also broadened to fifteen full members and nine candidates. The new members were all clear supporters of Khrushchev—plus Marshal Zhukov. Thus from July 1957, not only was Khrushchev the uncontested head of the collective leadership, but the representatives of the party machinery had firm majority in the Presidium. Government representatives were reduced to a bare remnant of three. The primacy of the party apparatus and of its first secretary were at last clearly established.

Yet Khrushchev and his closest supporters did not feel that their position was finally secure. Twice in the process of restoring its primacy, the party had been dependent on the backing of the armed forces: at the first step toward overthrowing Beria, and at the final step of defeating the coup of what was now dubbed the "anti-party-group." From the viewpoint of single-party rule, such a situation was tolerable only if the armed forces were firmly under the party's control. But in the course of the "succession struggles," that control had been clearly weakened; and the military had been able to make its weight felt in its own perceived interest rather than as an instrument of a united party's command. While the results so far had been satisfactory for Khrushchev and his machine, the conditions under which they had arisen were not. Moreover, Marshal Zhukov appeared to have deliberately used the situation for more purposes than to rehabilitate the military victims of Stalin's purges, which seemed unobjectionable, and to enhance his own wartime reputation, which was natural though it gave rise to some controversy among his colleagues. He also moved to reduce the influence of the political administration of the armed forces which was, in fact, a department of the Central Committee, and thus increase the independence of the professional officer corps. It was this last development that Khrushchev saw as intolerable.

In late October 1957, while Zhukov was on a journey abroad, some articles appeared in the military press stressing the vital need for subordination of the armed forces to party control. On the day of his return, October 26, his replacement as Minister of War was announced. Before the end of the month a Central Committee plenum met and discussed charges that he had tried to curtail the work of party organizations in the army and had developed his own cult of personality. A number of army leaders spoke as witnesses against him, and Zhukov admitted that some of the charges were justified. The Central Committee decided to remove him from its ranks and to provide him with another job. There was no visible opposition. The last of the power machines treated as independent of the party in Stalin's time had lost that role. The control of *all* levers of power by the ruling party—the basic institutional characteristic of totalitarianism—had been fully restored.

Khrushchev, who had achieved that restoration, also meant to use it to continue the other, dynamic characteristic of totalitarianism: the revolutionary transformation of society in the direction of utopian goals, even if by less violent methods than had been used in Stalin's time. We have seen how, after consolidating party rule and carrying out a number of popular reforms in the first six years after Stalin's death, he gave a signal for structural transformations in agriculture at the 21st Congress in 1959. We have also seen how the attempt failed and how, in the party program approved by the 22nd Congress in 1961, he accepted the lesson that, at the level of economic development achieved in Russia, the revolutionary process had exhausted itself, and the "dictatorship of the proletariat" was proclaimed to have ended in the first country ruled by it. In other words, the restored institutions had survived the revolutionary process.

This was bound to create new problems of ideological legitimation for the party and of leadership style for Khrushchev himself. It was not enough for the new program to announce that the Soviet Union would surpass the United States in per capita output by 1970, and enter the age of Communist abundance by 1980. Khrushchev had also to find a credible new role for the party in this post-revolutionary age of promise. Thus, in 1962 he tried to divide the party organization from top to bottom into separate industrial and agricultural sectors, charged with the direct guidance of economic administration. The attempt proved unpopular not only with the economic administrators exposed to increased party interference in their work, but also with the regional and local party secretaries who had hitherto been Khrushchev's chief supporters; they now found themselves burdened with new responsibilities for which few of them felt competent. At the same time, discontent was increasing in the political and bureaucratic elites at his general tendency to impose improvised decisions in military and foreign policy. The Cuban missile adventure and the tactical conduct, though *not* the substance, of the conflict with Communist China were the most spectacular examples.

The point was that the man who had done most to restore the party's primacy after a longer period of despotism found it utterly uncongenial to conform with binding procedural rules. It was not that he nursed secret hopes of becoming a despot himself. He had seen too much of Stalin's methods; his horror of them, if expressed belatedly, was sincere. But he remained a dynamic leader of a bygone revolutionary age, always believing in impending great changes, always ready to improvise new initiatives to exploit what seemed to be new opportunities, often too impatient to wait for institutional authority. Again and again he would take major decisions without adequately consulting his colleagues, or seek to overcome their hesitation by appealing to "public opinion." In the end, his personality became the last obstacle to completing the post-revolutionary institutionalization of the Soviet system he had done so much to make possible—and the system he had created rejected him. First, the Party Presidium, which he had packed with his trusted supporters after the rebellion of 1957, and then the Central Committee plenum, which had backed him against that rebellion, voted in October 1964 to depose him in order to assure procedural regularity and to protect the party and the country from his "harebrained schemes."

Brezhnev's Stabilization of Post-Revolutionary Institutions

There was no "succession crisis," indeed no institutional crisis at all, after the overthrow of Khrushchev. On the contrary, the unprecedented change of leadership by a vote of the Central Committee was the prelude to a new period of unprecedented institutional stability. The new Politburo, with Brezhnev as General Secretary and Kosygin as chairman of the Council of Ministers, both of whom Khrushchev himself had selected as his right-hand men, was to rule continuously for the next eighteen years, to the death of both. Occasional individual changes in its composition did occur, many of them forced by biological necessity and a few by substantial disagreements, but without a single political crisis caused by anything approaching factional groupings. The accepted end of the revolutionary process had left the members of the party elite without ideological motives for defying the majority; and the coherent institutions left by Khrushchev made it easy for them to add the one thing to which he had been an obstacle: clearly established procedures of decision making. In advanced industrial countries these constitute one essential condition, though not by themselves a sufficient condition, for the legitimacy of a regime.

The resulting post-totalitarian system may be described as an

authoritarian bureaucratic oligarchy—not in the sense that
there is no clearly recognizable leader, but that his powers over
the other members of the Politburo are not markedly greater
than those of a Western prime minister over the members of his
cabinet. Its essential difference from a Western democratic system lies in the relations between the ruling group as a whole
and the people who have no means to remove it. Against the
background of the factional struggles after Lenin, of Stalin's
despotism, and of the institutional rivalries after Stalin, the
advantages of such a system of oligarchic stability appear
considerable. But there is a price which the people of the Soviet
Union, and of the whole Soviet empire, have had to pay and are
still paying: excessive bureaucratic conservatism, a stupendous
lack of innovation and initiative (except in the military field),
and increasingly absurd over-aging of leading and middle
cadres. Those features appear today as the ironic nemesis of the
final overcoming of decades of institutionalized revolution. But
they do not detract from the basic lesson of the Brezhnev
regime: proof that post-totalitarian one-party rule can work.

A "Premature" End of the Chinese Revolution?

In China after Mao's death in September 1976, the most
urgent problem was not the primacy of the party as such, as in
Russia after Stalin. The secret police had not been the decisive
factor during the Cultural Revolution; the army had lost its
taste for playing an independent political role after the fall of
Lin Biao; and the reorganized party, however deeply divided in
itself, was the only institution that had recovered a minimum
of legitimacy. The critical problem was precisely the deep "factional" conflict still dividing the party between the self-declared
heirs of the utopian revolutionary policies of Mao, headed by
his widow Jiang Qing and the Shanghai party leaders, and the
modernizing followers of the late Zhou, now headed by Deng
Xiaoping—a conflict closer in its bitterness to latent, and not
always latent, civil war than to ordinary factionalism.

The first crucial move was made by a man who seemed to be an unoriginal but skillful operator in a balancing position: Hua Guofeng, a former security chief who had always been loyal to Mao and had become head of government after Zhou's death, but who had never played a major ideological role in the Cultural Revolution. He now announced that Mao had designated him as his successor and that he had, with the approval of the Politburo (and with the visible support of Mao's personal bodyguard), arrested Jiang Qing and her Shanghai friends, "the Gang of Four," for plotting to seize power. Despite a later show trial, we have little direct evidence as to whether such a "plot" existed. But there is ample political evidence that this group was aggressively out for power, and that its victory would have meant a full-scale resumption of the Cultural Revolution with all its horrors.

At the same time, Hua, with little authority of his own beyond his alleged designation by Mao, was eager to present himself as the most faithful of Maoists, while wary of endangering his new position by actually restarting a revolutionary upheaval. Thus he propagated the doctrine that all Mao's policies and instructions must be accepted as valid forever. For the first two years after Mao's death he prevented any fundamental criticism of Mao's policies during the Cultural Revolution, as distinct from particular excesses and crimes attributed to the "Gang of Four." Hua also tried to oppose the second rehabilitation of Deng Xiaoping, which nevertheless was decided on by a Central Committee plenum in July 1977. Addressing the 11th Party Congress in August, with Deng already present, he still repeated Maoist slogans of "continuing the revolution under the dictatorship of the proletariat" and "grasping class struggle as the key link."

The ruling party of a great country could not stagnate in this kind of political and ideological limbo for long. As a result of the official campaign against the real Maoists, "the Gang of Four," and of Deng's return, Hua's balancing act became increasingly difficult. Deng soon started opposing Hua's dictum on the infallibility of Mao with a campaign for "seeking truth from facts." By the time of the Central Committee plenum of December 1978, now officially regarded as a more important turning point than the downfall of "the Gang of Four," "grasping class struggle as the key link" was rejected as an absurd slogan in the absence of hostile classes, and replaced by recognizing the country's modernization as the primary task. At the same time, the slogan of "seeking truth from facts" was officially endorsed, giving the signal for an increasingly open criticism of the policies of the late Mao as pursued during the Cultural Revolution and, in part, the Great Leap Forward.

From now on, Deng, recognized as the spiritual heir of the late Zhou Enlai, came increasingly to the fore as the effective political leader of the party, without aspiring (partly because of his age) to become its nominal leader. Thinly hidden in second-rank positions in party, army, and government, he gradually moved a number of somewhat younger cadres into leading positions, culminating in the replacement of Hua Guofeng first as head of government and then, in June 1981, as party chairman by nominees of Deng.

The Central Committee plenum of June 1981 which replaced Hua Guofeng with Hu Yaobang, while allowing him to remain one of the party's "deputy chairmen" (the last on the list), was, however, still more remarkable for another decision. It adopted a long, and long in preparation, critical resolution on the history of the Chinese Communist Party since the founding of the Chinese People's Republic—a carefully balanced document of partial "de-Maoization." The document fully recognized Mao's earlier merits in theory and practice as decisive both for the Communist road to power and for the building of the foundations of a socialist order. But it criticized some of his policies during the Great Leap Forward as mistaken, and rejected the Cultural Revolution as having been altogether wrong, with grave damage to the country and to the Communist cause. Mao was held fully responsible for this overall policy, as distinct from the individual crimes of Lin Biao and the Gang of Four for which only they (and not Mao) were accountable.

If those decisions can be regarded as the final results of a long and bitter struggle—and that is suggested both by the striking degree of ideological exhaustion noticeable in both the country and in the party, and by the balance and maturity of the key document of 1981 (the intellectual level of which considerably surpasses anything produced by official Soviet "de-Stalinization" at the time)—it would appear that the Chinese Communist regime has abandoned the attempt at a revolutionary transformation of society in favor of a clear priority for modernization. After more profound chaos than the Soviet Union ever experienced in Stalin's times, China seems to have combined the restoration of the party's primacy with the abandonment of its utopian goals more quickly, and at a much lower stage of economic development, than Russia did. In effect, it has created another major post-totalitarian Communist party regime on a more modest economic level. But the fact that this radical change has occurred at a stage when the problems of Chinese modernization are still far from solved forces the observer to qualify his conclusions with a question mark of uncertainty.

Indeed, the tremendous difficulties of modernizing a vast country with China's enormous population are obvious on general grounds and visible in the early setbacks of an overoptimistic modernization policy. To this must be added such other problems as a massive generational change in a partly demoralized party with an overaged leadership, widespread skepticism in the population due to the experience of the last fifteen years, and China's serious shortage of capital and of qualified technical, scientific, and managerial cadres. Given all those obstacles, the present attempt at solving China's problems appears to this observer as courageous and remarkably rational if inevitably tentative in many fields. Whether postrevolutionary, post-totalitarian China will succeed where Mao's revolutionary China was shipwrecked, he cannot venture to forecast.

V

Beyond Totalitarianism?

The signs of the running down of totalitarian revolutions, and of the disappearance of personal despotisms developed in their course, have been hailed by some Western observers as indicating not only the prospect of a new era of stability for the long-suffering countries concerned (which has proved true for Russia and may prove true for China), but also the prospect of some kind of gradual "liberalization." That seems to me a somewhat too hopeful description of the kind of change that has taken place. If the policies of massive annihilation of entire social or national groups have been abandoned along with the utopian hopes that inspired them, the policies of enforced (and dull) uniformity have been largely preserved. If the "Gulag Archipelago" has ceased to cover a major part of the Russian landscape, the suppression of dissenting groups by imprisonment, forced labor, or "psychiatric" torture continues. Some of the boldest contributors to the Peking "wall of democracy" during a brief transitional period have also suffered long prison sentences. Those countries have not gone from tyranny to freedom, but from massive horror to a rule of meanness, ensuring stability at the risk of stagnation.

George Orwell had an early vision of the meanness and shabbiness in which it all might end. But, in that vision, this was to happen *after* the worldwide expansion of the totalitarian regimes. In fact, such expansion is difficult to conceive once the revolutionary impulse has become extinct and meanness and stagnation reign. In the world as it now is, the stabilization of post-totalitarian and post-revolutionary institutions of Communist one-party rule in Russia, and the serious effort at stabilizing comparable institutions in China, thus raises the question of the future of totalitarianism as defined in this essay, at any rate in its Communist form.

Most of the Communist Party regimes in East Central Europe have long since ended the process of institutionalized revolution. Its conceivable continuation for some time in Vietnam or Albania, or even in Cuba, would hardly be a major political phenomenon by itself. Totalitarian regimes of the fascist or National Socialist type have not arisen since the collapse of National Socialist Germany and fascist Italy as a result of World War II. The future of totalitarianism as a major feature of contemporary political history would thus seem to depend on whether new totalitarian movements can arise and come to power. I believe this to be unlikely, at any rate for totalitarian movements with a Communist ideology.

This skeptical view is not based on a new version of the notion current in the late 1950s that we were experiencing an "end of ideology"—a view I did not share at the time. Now, as then, I am acutely aware that radical dissent from the values and institutions of the Western democracies is by no means approaching an end, either in their own countries or in the non-Western world. Such dissent is an expression of the growing difficulty of passing on the basic values of Western civilization either to the young generations of the West, or to those of the non-Western countries whose native civilizations have been disrupted by the Western impact. Indeed, I am inclined to view that difficulty as a long-range historical phenomenon. But it seems to me that this radical dissent is tending to take, in this final quarter of the twentieth century, quite different directions from those it took in the second and third quarters, which saw the high tide of the totalitarian phenomenon.

In its Communist form, that high tide was based on the ideas of "totalitarian democracy" (as defined by Jacob Talmon), derived from the radical wing of the Enlightenment, and developed into a full-blown secular religion, complete with its own sacred history, by Karl Marx. When that secular religion was transformed into the ideology of a totalitarian party, and finally into a totalitarian regime by Lenin, and spread to his followers in other countries, it retained the limitless utopian optimism that salvation on earth was possible in our time. In contrast, the present post-Marxian and, indeed, post-enlightened dissent in the West develops in an ideological climate of profound pessimism, of apocalyptic visions of mankind's impending destruction by nuclear war, by irremediable poisoning of the environment, or by hunger due to the unmanageable explosion of the world's population. More generally, under the impact of two world wars, of the horrors of totalitarian and despotic dictatorships, of the limits of economic growth, and of the nuclear arms race, enlightened belief in the unlimited possibilities of human reason has given way in many Western minds to a mood reflecting despair about the rational faculties of man.

At this point, it might be objected that the nationalist and fascist forms of pre-totalitarian ideas and totalitarian movements were also based on a rejection of the heritage of the Enlightenment. But the mood we observe in an important part of today's young generation in the West appears to be equally far from a belief in power as from a belief in reason. Rather, it tends to express itself either in a return to religious, or frequently pseudo-religious, beliefs in transcendental sources of salvation, or in desperate attempts at a flight from society and its uncontrollable dangers, or in anarchic forms of more or less violent protest. For where there is no vision of a better social order, there is also no basis for any type of secular messianism directed at total power. In its place we observe religious or secular ways of withdrawal from a hopeless world, or peaceful or violent forms of an apolitical Great Refusal.

It seems impossible at the present time to predict whether that mood will last in our Western societies. Much will depend on the success of rational efforts to control the very real worldwide dangers which have created that climate. But, assuming its continuation for argument's sake, such a climate seems unlikely to give rise to new fanatical movements aiming at totalitarian power. Rather, it would be liable to produce anarchic forms of political decay, leading eventually to the naked rule of military force without any legitimation beyond the maintenance of "order"—as in the praetorian forms of Caesarism in late antiquity.

Since such a development would appear like a fulfillment of a Spenglerian "Decline of the West," and since the Communist world appears to have arrived at a somewhat different but hardly less marked state of ideological exhaustion, the future of totalitarianism would seem to depend on the Third World. There, a number of the new states have in their first or second generation produced nationalist single-party regimes with more or less "Socialist" elements in their official ideology, though in most cases neither the regimes nor the ideology appear coherent and dynamic enough to deserve the label of "totalitarianism." In particular, most of the regimes that for a time took a pro-Soviet stand have been unable, if not unwilling, to follow the model of Soviet-style communism, while some of the more recently created pro-Soviet regimes owe their orientation to military rather than ideological ties. What real kinship there is arose from the desire of the new elites in those countries to achieve quick modernization without a serious effort to assimilate Western values, with the Soviets appearing as a ready-made model for this kind of watered-down Enlightenment. But, in the course of time, faith in a Soviet version of Western utopian visions appears to have declined in the Third World as well. Some of this can be attributed to the diminishing attraction of both the Soviet and Chinese models, and some to the often intractable local difficulties of modernization.

The types of movement that really may acquire increasing importance in underdeveloped countries facing such difficulties are those that are anti-Western without being pro-Communist: they embody cultural resistance against the Westernizing aspects of modernization, reinforced by the initial failures of attempts to impose such modernization from above. It can be argued that the Chinese Cultural Revolution, regardless of Mao's ideological intent, drew much of the destructive energy of its early, spontaneous phase from this kind of cultural anti-Westernism. Pol Pot's Red Khmer forces in Kampuchea, supported by China in their seizure of power in the seventies, showed a similarly profound anti-modernist spirit in their deliberate expulsion, and in part annihilation, of the town population. Evidently such movements, although they may use the Marxist–Leninist label, have less in common with the heritage of Marx, even in its totalitarian Leninist version, than with the extreme manifestations of the Islamic fundamentalist revival—such as Khomeini's anti-modernist revolution and his terrorist regime in Iran, or Qaddafi's Libyan regime with its deliberate promotion of international terrorism as a means of weakening the West.

The future of such movements and regimes may well depend on whether, once in power, they remain as consistent in their anti-modernism as in their anti-Westernism. Clearly, they do not hesitate to acquire modern weapons. Since the modernization of military organization has generally proved the easiest first step in underdeveloped countries, they may eventually be ready to extend it to other fields, dragging their traditionalist followers along by their common hatred of the West. There are parallels here even to the evolution of Hitler's "National Socialism," which in its early propaganda included such features as the glorification not only of traditional customs but of small-scale enterprise and "blood and soil"; yet on its road to power and afterward, it was in no way inhibited in its cooperation with modern large-scale industry. In that sense, it is conceivable that a variant of fascism linked with religious traditionalism may still have more of a future in parts of the underdeveloped world than other forms of totalitarianism seem to have anywhere. But this is rather far from Orwell's vision.

On the whole, then, it would appear that the basic ideological trends of the final part of our century are no longer linked with self-generated perversions of the Western tradition. They are, rather, due to a growing failure of Western civilization to transmit its basic values, which have created the modern world, either to its own young or to non-Western countries. For that reason, the new movements, within the West and among its enemies, lead us beyond totalitarianism. They belong to a new chapter of history.

Notes

2. The Fate of *1984*

1. Brander, *George Orwell* (New York: Longmans, Green & Co., Inc., 1954), p. 184.
2. *Collected Essays, Journalism and Letters of George Orwell* (New York: Harcourt, Brace & World, 1968), vol. 2, p. 9.
3. Freud, *Totem and Taboo* (New York: W. W. Norton, 1950), pp. 85ff.
4. Orwell, *The Road to Wigan Pier* (London, 1937), p. 18.
5. Freud, *Civilization and Its Discontents* (New York: W. W. Norton, 1961), pp. 11, 12.
6. *Collected Essays*, op. cit., p. 15.
7. Orwell, *Down and Out in Paris and London* (New York: Harcourt, Brace & World, 1961), pp. 14–15.
8. *Collected Essays*, op. cit., p. 15.
9. Orwell, *Animal Farm* (New York: Harcourt, Brace, 1946), p. 128.

3. "The Golden Country": Sex and Love in *1984*

1. Crick, *George Orwell: A Life* (Boston: Little, Brown, 1980), p. 200.
2. Reich, *The Mass Psychology of Fascism,* trans. Vincent R. Carfagno (Farrar, Straus & Giroux, 1970), p. 168.
3. "Looking Backward from *A Clockwork Orange,*" in *The Psychoanalytic Study of the Child,* vol. 31, p. 535. We might add that a work such as *Brave New World,* where sex is dispensed like a non-prescription drug, or Zamyatin's *We,* in which coupons are issued for multiple sex partners, represents the period between latency and adolescence, when there is often regression to a pre-Oedipal stage in the attempt to deal with instinctual drives.
4. Eugen Weber, "The Anti-Utopia of the Twentieth Century," *The South Atlantic Quarterly,* LVIII (Summer, 1959), p. 446.
5. I-330 is referred to as E-330 and the hero, D-503, as Z-503 in the Bernard Guerney translation (London: Jonathan Cape, 1970), which has supplanted the Zilberg translation. However, I'm using the old letters since so many of the critics do.

6. "Make Way for Winged Eros: A Letter to Working Youth," in *Selected Writings of Alexandra Kollontai,* trans. Alix Holt (New York: W. W. Norton, 1977), p. 290.

7. See, for example, Daphne Patai, "Gamesmanship and Androcentrism in Orwell's *1984,*" *PLMA* 97 (1982): 856–870; and Erika Munk, "Love Is Hate: Women and Sex in 1984," *The Village Voice,* Feb. 1, 1983.

8. Freud, *Group Psychology and the Ego,* SE XVIII, p. 140.

9. Cf. my article, "Dystopia Now," *Alternative Futures: The Journal of Utopian Studies* (Summer 1979), pp. 55–67.

4. Orwell and the English Language

1. Irving Howe, editor, *Orwell's 1984: Text, Sources, Criticism* (New York: Harcourt, Brace, Jovanovich, 1982, cited hereafter as *1984: HBJ*), p. 133.

2. *1984: HBJ,* p. 89.

3. Ibid., p. 84.

4. "The Principles of Newspeak," *1984: HBJ,* p. 201.

5. "Shooting an Elephant," *The Collected Essays, Journalism and Letters* (London: Secker & Warburg, 1968; Penguin edition, 1971, cited hereafter as *Essays*), vol. 1, p. 269.

6. "Rudyard Kipling," *Essays,* vol. 2, p. 215.

7. *1984: HBJ,* p. 117.

8. Ibid., p. 115.

9. "On Liberty," in *Utilitarianism, Liberty, and Representative Government* (London: Everyman Library, J. M. Dent, 1910), p. 73.

10. "The Lion and the Unicorn," *Essays,* vol. 2, p. 79.

11. "Rudyard Kipling," ibid., p. 218.

12. "The English People," ibid., p. 42.

13. "The Lion and the Unicorn," ibid., p. 77.

14. "The English People," ibid., p. 42.

15. "Politics and the English Language," *Essays,* vol. 4, p. 170.

16. "Writers and Leviathan," ibid., p. 467.

17. "Politics and the English Language," ibid., p. 157.

18. "In Front of Your Nose," ibid., p. 154.

19. "What Is Science?" ibid., p. 29.

20. "Politics and the English Language," ibid., p. 157.

21. "In Front of Your Nose," ibid., p. 154.

22. "Literature and Totalitarianism," *Essays,* vol. 2, p. 163.

23. *1984: HBJ,* p. 36.

24. "Politics and the English Language," op. cit., p. 169.

25. "Maggot of the Month," *1984: HBJ,* p. 299.

26. "Charles Dickens," *Essays,* vol. 1, p. 464.

27. *1984: HBJ,* p. 137.

28. Ibid., p. 3.

29. Ibid., p. 11.

30. *Technology Review* (June–July 1979), 74.
31. "The English People," op. cit., p. 54.
32. *Newsweek,* Oct. 4, 1982, p. 38.
33. *Boston Globe,* Nov. 28, 1982, p. A1.
34. Singer, *Quantitative International Politics* (New York: Free Press, 1968), p. 3.

5. *1984* on Staten Island

1. G. D. H. Cole, *Essays in Social Theory* (London: Macmillan, 1950), p. 94.
2. Fidelio alludes to a dream of Winston's that is one of O'Brien's first steps toward trapping Winston in thoughtcrime. A voice in a pitch-dark room says to him, "We will meet in the place where there is no darkness." See George Orwell, *1984* (New York: New American Library/Signet, 1950), pp. 24, 201.
3. Andrew Levison, *The Working-Class Majority* (New York: Penguin, 1975).

6. Does Big Brother Really Exist?

1. Hannah Arendt, *The Origins of Totalitarianism* (New York: Harcourt, Brace, 1951), p. 391.
2. Emil Lederer, *State of the Masses* (New York: W. W. Norton, 1940).
3. Sigmund Neumann, *Permanent Revolution* (New York: Harper & Brothers, 1942).
4. *The Origins of Totalitarianism,* p. 432.
5. Carl J. Friedrich and Zbigniew K. Brzezinski, *Totalitarian Dictatorship and Autocracy* (New York: Frederick A. Praeger, 1956), part VI.
6. *The Origins of Totalitarianism,* p. 245.
7. Franz Neumann, *Behemoth* (New York: Oxford University Press, 1942), pp. 372–373.
8. *The Origins of Totalitarianism,* pp. 315, 335.
9. Merle Fainsod, *How Russia Is Ruled* (Cambridge, Mass.: Harvard University Press, 1953), p. 354.
10. Friedrich and Brzezinski, *Totalitarian Dictatorship and Autocracy,* p. 132.
11. Zbigniew K. Brzezinski, *The Permanent Purge* (Cambridge, Mass.: Harvard University Press, 1956), p. 30.
12. *The Origins of Totalitarianism,* p. 374. In the introduction to the new edition of *The Origins* published in 1966, Arendt took account of recent historical evidence and publications pointing to the need for a view of totalitarianism that would ascribe a key motivating role to the totalitarian leader. For an insightful general interpretation and critique of her thought on totalitarianism, see Stephen J. Whitfield, *Into the Dark: Hannah Arendt and Totalitarianism* (Philadelphia: Temple University Press, 1980).
13. George Orwell, *My Country Right or Left. 1940–1953.* edited by Sonia

Orwell and Ian Angus, vol. II (New York: Harcourt, Brace, 1968), p. 135.

14. Isaac Deutscher, "1984—The Mysticism of Cruelty," *Heretics and Renegades* (London: Jonathan Cape, 1955), p. 36.

15. Roger Garside, *Coming Alive: China After Mao* (New York: McGraw-Hill, 1981), pp. 46, 47, 48, 49, 50.

16. *The New York Times,* December 6, 1981, p. E7.

17. Leon Trotsky, *The Revolution Betrayed* (New York: Pathfinder, 1972), p. 277.

18. Neumann, *Behemoth,* pp. 366, 469.

7. On "Failed Totalitarianism"

1. *1984* (New York: Signet, 1950), p. 156.

2. J. L. Talmon, *The Origins of Totalitarian Democracy* (New York: Frederick A. Praeger, 1960), p. 6.

3. See especially Jeane J. Kirkpatrick, *Dictatorship and Double Standards* (New York and Washington, D.C.: American Enterprise Institute and Simon & Schuster, 1982), pp. 23–52.

4. Talmon, *Totalitarian Democracy,* "Introduction."

5. The best description is still Franz Neumann, *Behemoth: The Structure and Practice of National Socialism* (New York: Oxford University Press, 1942).

6. *1984,* p. 161.

7. Arendt, *The Origins of Totalitarianism* (New York: Harcourt, Brace, & World, 1966), pp. 437ff.

8. *1984,* p. 156.

9. Kirkpatrick, *Double Standards,* loc. cit.

10. Eugene Victor Walter, *Terror and Resistance: A Study of Political Violence* (New York: Oxford University Press, 1969).

11. Lord Byron, *The Bride of Abydos,* I:20.

12. *The Politics,* 1313a–1314a.

13. *1984,* p. 22.

14. *New York Times,* Sept. 16, 1982, p. A2.

15. See Tucker, "Does Big Brother Really Exist?" in this book.

16. *1984,* p. 227.

17. Saint-Just, *L'Esprit de la Revolution* (Paris, 1963), p. 148.

18. Milovan Djilas, *The New Class: An Analysis of the Communist System* (New York: Frederick A. Praeger, 1957).

19. *1984,* p. 199.

10. *1984*: Decade of the Experts?

1. George Orwell, *1984* (New York: Harcourt Brace, 1949), p. 74.

2. Helmut Schmidt, in Horst Ehmke, ed., *Perspectiven sozialdemocratischer Politik im Übergang zu den 70er Jahren* (Reinbek, 1969), p. 37.

3. Karl Steinbuch, *Falsch programmiert* (Stuttgart, 1968), p. 144.
4. Oswald Spengler, *Man and Technics* (New York: Alfred A. Knopf, 1932), pp. 90–91.
5. Press release of the DKP, No. 30/77 (Düsseldorf, Jan. 4, 1977).
6. Taken from the party program of the Communist Party of the Soviet Union, 1961.
7. Ernst Bloch, *Das Prinzip Hoffnung* (Frankfurt, 1959), vol. 2, p. 184.
8. Friedrich Engels, *Von der Autorität*, in *Marx-Engels Werke*, vol. 18, p. 306.
9. Karl Marx, *Das Kapital*, vol. 3, in *Marx-Engels Werke*, vol. 25, p. 828.
10. Cf. Herman Kahn and Anthony J. Wiener, *The Year 2000* (New York: Macmillan, 1967).
11. Lewis Mumford, *The Myth of the Machine* (New York: Harcourt, Brace & World, 1967).

11. *1984*—The Ingredients of Totalitarianism

1. Lee David Goodman, "Countdown to 1984," *The Futurist* (December 1978).
2. David Flaherty, *Privacy in Colonial New England* (Charlottesville, Va.: University of Virginia Press, 1972).
3. James Rule, Douglas McAdam, Linda Stearns, and David Uglow, *The Politics of Privacy* (New York: Elsevier, 1980).
4. The most noted proponent of this view is the French sociologist Jacques Ellul.
5. Daniel Bell, "Communications Technology—For Better or for Worse," *Harvard Business Review* (May–June 1979), 36.
6. This argument is developed in much more detail in Rule, McAdam, Stearns, and Uglow, *The Politics of Privacy*, part III.

12. *1984* and the Conservative Imagination

1. Burke, *Reflections on the Revolution in France* (1790), edited by William B. Todd (New York: Holt, Rinehart & Winston, 3rd printing, 1965), pp. 191–192.
2. Tocqueville, *The Old Regime and the French Revolution* (1856), trans. Stuart Gilbert (Garden City, N.Y.: Doubleday Anchor Books, 1955), p. 12.
3. Rousseau, *The Social Contract and Discourses*, translated and edited by G. D. H. Cole (New York: Everyman's Library, E. P. Dutton, 1950), p. 139. I have dealt at length with Rousseau's and the French Revolution's totalitarian cast in my *Social Group and French Thought* (University of California Library, 1940; New York: Arno Press, 1980) and also in *The Quest for Community* (New York: Oxford University Press, 1953). The most complete study of the totalitarian character of the French Revolution is J. L. Talmon's *The Origins of Totalitarian Democracy* (Boston: Beacon Press, 1952).

4. Cited by George Rudé, ed., *Robespierre* (Englewood Cliffs, N.J.: Prentice-Hall, 1967), pp. 69–73 *passim*.

5. Hannah Arendt, *On Revolution* (New York: Viking Press, 1963), pp. 94–95.

6. Burke, *Reflections on the Revolution*, p. 226.

7. Ortega y Gasset, *The Revolt of the Masses* (New York: W. W. Norton, 1932), p. 131.

8. Ibid., p. 134.

9. Christopher Dawson, "Religion and the Totalitarian State," *Criterion* (October 1934), reprinted in Russell Kirk, *The Portable Conservative Reader* (New York: Viking Press, 1982).

10. Tocqueville, *The Old Regime*, p. 20.

11. Jeane J. Kirkpatrick, *Dictatorships and Double Standards* (New York and Washington, D.C.: American Enterprise Institute and Simon & Schuster, 1982).

12. See *The Quest for Community*, p. 205: "In the totalitarian order the political tie becomes the all-in-all. It needs the masses as the masses need it. It integrates even where it dissolves, unifies where it separates, inspires where it suffocates. The rules of the total community devise their own symbolism to replace the symbolism that has been destroyed in the creation of the masses"—p. 206.

12a. Rousseau, *The Social Contract*, p. 38.

13. George Orwell, *1984* (New York: New American Library, 1981), p. 222.

14. Rousseau, *Discourse on Political Economy*, ed. G. D. H. Cole, op. cit., pp. 297–298.

15. Cited by John Morley, *Rousseau*, vol. 2, p. 152.

16. *Democracy in America*, trans. Phillips Bradley (New York: Alfred A. Knopf, 1944), vol. 2, pp. 318–319.

17. Ibid.

18. Burke, *Reflections on the Revolution*, pp. 118, 226.

19. Peter Drucker, *The End of Economic Man* (New York: John Day Co., 1939), p. 67.

20. Hannah Arendt, *The Origins of Totalitarianism* (New York: Harcourt, Brace, 1951), p. 305.

21. Orwell, *1984*, pp. 169, 177, 60.

22. Burke, *Reflections on the Revolution*, pp. 134–137 *passim*.

23. Tocqueville, *The Old Regime*, pp. 140–144 *passim*.

24. Rousseau, *Social Contract*, p. 38.

25. Robert R. Palmer, *The Age of Democratic Revolution* (Princeton, N.J.: Princeton University Press, 1959), p. 114.

26. Rousseau, *Social Contract*, p. 18.

27. Cited by Palmer, op. cit., p. 35.

28. Ibid.

29. Burke, *Reflections on the Revolution*, p. 269.

30. Ibid., p. 275.

31. Burke, *Reflections*, pp. 262–263.

About the Contributors

BERNARD AVISHAI teaches in the Writing Program at the Massachusetts Instiutute of Techonology and writes regularly on politics for the *New York Review of Books*. He is the author of *The Tragedy of Zionism*.

ELAINE HOFFMAN BARUCH is Associate Professor of English at York College of the City University of New York and is co-editor of the forthcoming book *Women in Search of Utopia* to be published by Schocken Books.

LUTHER P. CARPENTER wrote *G. D. H. Cole: An Intellectual Biography* and is now writing a book on the functioning of the French welfare state since 1945.

MILOVAN DJILAS, the noted Yugoslav writer and dissident, is the author of the classic study *The New Class: An Analysis of the Communist System* and other books.

IRVING HOWE, Distinguished Professor of English at the City University of New York, is co-editor of *Dissent* and author of *World of Our Fathers* and *A Margin of Hope: An Intellectual Autobioraphy,* among other books.

LESZEK KOLAKOWSKI, whose books include the three-volume *Main Currents of Marxism* and *Religion,* was formerly Professor of the History of Philosophy at the University of Warsaw and currently teaches at All Souls College, Oxford, and the University of Chicago.

RICHARD LOWENTHAL, Emeritus Professor of the Free University, West Berlin, has been a lifelong student of totalitarian movements and systems, on which he has taught and published in the United States, Britain, Germany, and Italy.

MARK CRISPIN MILLER teaches in the Department of Writing Seminars at the Johns Hopkins University.

ROBERT NISBET, Albert Schweitzer Professor Emeritus of Columbia University, is a fellow of both the American Philosophical Society of Philadelphia and the American Academy of Arts and Sciences. His most recent books are *History of the Idea of Progress* and *Prejudices: A Philosophical Dictionary.*

JAMES B. RULE is Professor of Sociology at the State University of New York at Stony Brook and has written and consulted widely on issues in technology and society.

JOHANNO STRASSER is a writer and editor who teaches at the Free University in West Berlin.

ROBERT C. TUCKER is Professor of Politics at Princeton University. His most recent book is *Politics as Leadership;* his *Stalin and Soviet Russia: A Revolution from Above 1929–1939* is forthcoming.

MICHAEL WALZER is a Professor of Social Science at the Institute for Advanced Study, in New York City, and the author, most recently, of *Spheres of Justice: A Defense of Pluralism and Equality.*